THE PAST RECAPTURED

The Past Recaptured

*Great Historians and the
History of History*

M. A. FITZSIMONS

UNIVERSITY OF NOTRE DAME PRESS
NOTRE DAME   LONDON

Library of Congress Cataloging in Publication Data

Fitzsimons, M. A. (Matthew Anthony), 1912-
The past recaptured.

Bibliography: p.
Includes index.
1. Historians—Europe.   2. Historiography—History.
I. Title.
D14.F57   1983   907.2   83-1168
ISBN 0-268-01550-3

Manufactured in the United States of America

095294

To the memory
of two teachers,

Father John Monaghan,
Cathedral College, New York City,

and

Professor Harry J. Carman,
Columbia College

Contents

Preface   ix

1. Introduction   1

2. Herodotus: History and Inquiry   6

3. Thucydides: History, Science, and Power   27

4. Tacitus: The Mind of the Moralist Historian   50

5. Bede: Monastic Historian in a Barbarian World   72

6. William Camden: The English Renaissance and the Modern State   89

7. Voltaire: History Unexemplary and en Philosophe   106

8. Edward Gibbon: History as Art   128

9. Ranke: History as Worship   148

10. Burckhardt: History as a Humanity   171

11. Acton: History and Conscience   188

Notes   207

Index   225

Preface

MY FIRST EFFORTS to compose this book were made in 1973 at the Villa Serbelloni, Bellagio, where for one month my wife and I enjoyed the hospitality of the Fondazione Culturale Rockefeller and faced the challenge of no remaining problem except myself. Versions of three chapters, those on Thucydides, Tacitus, and Voltaire, and the chapter on Ranke appeared in *The Review of Politics*. Professor Bruno Schlesinger encouraged me by yearly invitations to lecture on Bede and Toynbee to the students in the Program of Humanistic Studies at St. Mary's College. Early in 1981 an invitation to lecture on Gibbon, Burckhardt, and Acton to students and colleagues at the University of Notre Dame added impetus to the drive to complete the book. I am grateful to the audience and especially to Father Thomas Blantz, C.S.C., head of the History Department, who tempts people to take his courtesies for granted. Frances, my wife, labored patiently and impatiently to type piles of scrawled manuscript which with my uneconomic notes might form one level of a city in an archaeologist's dig.

1. Introduction

THIS WORK PRESENTS an account of historical writing as an introduction to history. I have written essays on ten historians from Herodotus to Lord Acton. My subjects were chosen, with allowance entreated for the limitations of my knowledge, to reveal the intellectual history of historical writing, the achievements of some great historians, and persisting and changing views of the nature and value of history.

I undertook this work in 1973 in place of a general history of historical writing. The latter makes scholarly demands disproportionate to the rewards it may allow: a general historiography, however useful, is likely to become a hive of names, a directory, a reference book, at best a textbook.

This book, then, is written not in place of a better one but to avoid a worse one. It is written in the conviction that the best introduction to history is historical — that is, a history of history. This is to reject a fallacy, more tendency than formulated principle among scholars, that regards only the most recent historical scholarship as history. Earlier work is regarded as out of date and under a kind of proscription, as though several years and a few revisions had reduced it from history to the ranks as a source and the reading fare of the history buff, an amateur rather than a professional "player" of history.

Because it is a tendency, happily it does not prevail as an uncontested faith, but it is common enough. This fallacy of historians is analogous to the view that to read the works of early scientists, even Newton's *Principia*, is antiquarian pedantry, delving in theories that have been superseded, and a waste of time. In this matter, there is less excuse for the erring general historian than for the historian of science, who may be misled by pretensions to certainty that the historian should have forsworn in early studies. The growth of knowledge in science and history is not cumulative bookkeeping but a rewarding humanistic study that may reveal more about the human mind and our approximate knowledge of human affairs than even a first reading of a philosophical masterpiece on human understanding.

The works of Herodotus, Bede, Gibbon, and Burckhardt are genuine works of history that the student of history should read. Lest the injunction appear to be another reckless call for more reading in our limited (though lengthening) life spans, I hasten to emphasize the necessity of priorities and selections, the unrelenting guides of historical research which, if not examined carefully, may predetermine the results of inquiry. And priorities and selection that exclude the study of historical works of art and acquaintance with great minds and spirits are likely to be the issue of cynicism or sloth about the goals of education or of the solipsism of the individual historian who declares that whatever he does is history and presumably good.

To read the history of history and the great historians is to be challenged about the value of historical study. Have modern historians been too sweeping in rejecting the moral value of history? Is history a study from which prudence may be acquired? And how does one distinguish prudence from cunning or expediency or wisdom? Are truth and factual accuracy the same? If historians differ so much, what strength do historical examples, that may have been or may be revised, add to an argument? The central value of studying the history of history is a form of tolerance based on the painful recognition of how difficult it is to reach more than approximate truth about human affairs in *more* than simple societies. Even a modest acquaintance with civilizations or centuries reveals how many unexpected ways there are of looking at things, and how quickly the conscience of a society may change on some matters.

It is, I believe, vital that to be aware of the incompleteness of our knowledge, of its need to be revised or superseded, is not the prelude to systematic relativism, which must be as frustrating to pursue as it is likely to be disastrous. The truth, that which presents a matter as it is and as touched with some ultimate significance, must be our goal so that it may be our guide. With all its inadequacy, as we possess it at any moment, it is all that we can have.

We must therefore use our knowledge of inadequacy, not to despair or surrender, but to inculcate the tolerance that encourages discussion, the reduction of error, and the growth of knowledge by reciprocal criticism and self-correction so that our limited knowledge approaches the best it can be. What I have in mind is the opposite of the prayer of the intellectual, my brother, who thanked God or some *locum tenens* that he was not a Pharisee, a Philistine, or, as a matter of course, an intolerant person. Or Oliver Cromwell's plea to members of the Nominated Parliament that in the bowels of Christ they should consider *they* might be mistaken. A Grand Inquisitor could only say "amen."

History encounters its special difficulties in dealing with human affairs because it attempts to recapture moments of the past. That past is not something still out there. It has vanished and must be recreated by our minds, imaginations, words, and story. But we are also bearers of the past. Our genes, our bodies, and our psyches bear it and change it. Our societies and cultures carry it as institutions, techniques, values, and traditions. The individual is doubly laden with the past: with the personal inheritance and the legacy of a culture that gives the individual form and direction and an angle of vision that, as it were, enables one both to see and to fail to see.

We as interested parties provide some of the obstacles to any attempt to recreate moments of the past. The moments have left marks and evidence of their passing. Of parts of the past — that is, all times past — we have memory and traditions. For long periods, memory and traditions have apparently been satisfactory links with the past. When they are not, and when witnesses of the past — documents, inscriptions, and participants — are available, the first historians appear to claim that their subject, history, is the "life of memory."

The new subject acquired many meanings. The word *history* signifies both its subject, the past, and the study of it: It denotes the inquiring search for past realities as well as the presentation of the results of that inquiry.

Before it has historians, a society has a history, that is, a past which is presented in tradition or myth as something given and not as a subject for inquiry. Inquiry is the essential activity of the historian in moving beyond the repetition of traditions, in studying evidence of a past reality, and in reconstructing it by making a story of it. This presupposes the art of writing and a belief that some happenings in time are matters to be mindful of.

The historian in pursuing his inquiry looks among the relics of the past for evidence. At any particular time some remains may not be accessible, and the stage of culture and technology may inspire or make possible the use of some evidence and for later ages may explain the failure to use others. Similarly, the state of culture will suggest, if not provide, explanations of motivation and causality as well as the form of the history and the author's view of the uses of history.

Historical writing, then, is rooted in its time and culture. It varies from age to age, prizing now one group of sources, later another group, and from age to age providing different explanations of actions and their motivation. Historical writing itself, which deals with finite beings, time, and change, manifests the very change that it describes. Every age may seem to provide an unexpected consequence or a new conclusion of some major past event and may, therefore, require a new construction of its story.

To study the history of historical writing, then, particularly to read the classics of historical writing, enriches our vision of a past with the visions of that past seen by writers of earlier times and other cultural outlooks. The same study provides caution against the ever-present inclination to turn our own view into an absolute. This is to say that our own histories and visions of the past are bound to be as incomplete and inadequate as are the works of earlier historians. Herodotus, who knew that truth was difficult to reach, professed that he preserved the memory of great deeds and expected his work to endure. Thucydides, his young contemporary, believed that his work would be a possession forever. But Herodotus' inquiry and Thucydides' science have not captured any particular past once and for all, to everybody's satisfaction and agreement. Nor has the work of any other historian.

This argument in favor of tentativeness requires the black-listing — one cannot ban the irrepressible — of all such phrases as "the lessons of history" and "the teachings of history." Whenever those phrases are used, one may be sure that Clio, the muse of history, has been stepping out with sailors and salesmen again.

The study of history and historical classics, for all the tentativeness I emphasize, performs its function: to make us conscious of a past, of an otherness outside ourselves but with which we are kin. The study gives us a sense of the texture of our knowledge of human affairs, a sense that may warn us against the temptation, which issues from our very selfishness and pride of knowing, to believe that the approximation is absolute, the tentative is the certain, and the transient is the unchanging. This is not the sum of wisdom but a beginning of it.

2. Herodotus:
History and Inquiry

THE HISTORICAL WRITING of Western civilization begins with two masterpieces. The histories of Herodotus (c. 484-429 B.C.) and Thucydides (c. 460-398 B.C.) were responses of Greek culture to a spectacular triumph and a devastating failure of fifth-century Greek political life. Such a start at the top set a standard that could not be maintained. It also challenged the predisposition of many historians to find long periods of preparation for innovations. Historians have, in fact, found considerable fragments of antecedents, but this history of history has strengthened rather than reduced the reputation of the founders of Western historical writing.

The histories of Herodotus, his account of the events and geographical and cultural backgrounds of the Graeco-Persian wars (494-479 B.C.), established the form of history based on inquiry. The Roman orator and philosopher Cicero called him "the father of history." Some ancient critics jeered that he was the father of lies. This name-calling, at any rate, reveals the importance historians and their critics have attached to accuracy of representation. Both critics and historians have professed their attachment to truth in history, but this agreement may be the very source of contention. For this there are two principal explanations: the first is that historical writing can never present the whole truth and incompleteness can be charged to every historian; the second is that societies and historical writers may use history for certain functions — reassurance, pride, praise, or moral teaching — that encourage distortion and even misrepresentation, that in short work against the presentation of such truth as may be attainable.

6

The historian of the Persian wars was born between 490 and 484 B.C. in the Greek world of southern Asia Minor. Halicarnassus, his birth place, a wine-exporting harbor town governed by a tyrant who had the support of the Persian emperor, was the outgrowth of a Dorian Greek conquest of Carians. The latter were herdsmen, and the Dorian Greeks were farmers. In time some of its people came to use the Ionic dialect, the speech of most Greek communities in Asia Minor and the language in which Herodotus wrote. Herodotus is often critical of the Ionians, who were the major Greek presence in Asia. Lyxes, Herodotus' father, bore a Carian name, indicating that the historian himself embodied the meeting of East and West, which he made his subject.

Around 470 B.C., presumably after a political change at home disadvantageous to his family, Herodotus went to the island of Samos as a refugee. Between 460 and 454 B.C. he returned home. By 454, at the very latest, the city had a change of fortune: it became a democracy and a tributary member of the Delian Confederacy that had been instituted for the defense of Greek cities against the Persian Empire and, in its turn, became an empire of Athenians over Greeks.

The years from perhaps 460 to about 443 B.C. are the period of Herodotus' major travels and inquiries. What he then learned, he put together for public readings and his book. Some Athenians warmly welcomed this Asian visitor. Athenian influence gave form to his work, but his observation of Athens as an imperial oppressor of Greeks added to the melancholy tone that sounds through his brisk phrases and never wearying sentences. He celebrated the great deeds of barbarians, Greeks, and, in particular, the Athenians: "Greece was saved by the Athenians" (7.139: 487).[1] But while he was praising the savior city, the leadership it had won cast for it a role similar to that of the Persian Empire it had defeated.

The Athenians reciprocated Herodotus' admiration, but not to the point of granting him citizenship, a requisite for owning real property in Athens. Perhaps inability to acquire property in Athens accounts for his participation in the Panhellenic colonization of Thurii (444-443 B.C.) in southern Italy. The colony was one of the most ambitious enterprises of Athens at the peak of its imperialism. A number of Herodotus' references to early

events of the Peloponnesian War (431-404 B.C.) indicate that
the historian lived until at least 429 B.C.

Herodotus' experiences were with cultural diversity. He was
a Greek republican without much political experience. His first
community was a tyranny, which meant that he had neither
the intense political education of Thucydides nor the opportunities and duties of an Athenian citizen. Thucydides was inspired by his culture to seek a science of politics and power; he
even boasted that he did not write to entertain. Herodotus, of
the preceding generation, was spiritually on the winning side
of the story he chose to tell, but he also observed the later power
rivalries of Greek cities whose self-inflicted decline Thucydides
presented. With the first part of that later train of events in
mind, Herodotus told the story of the Greek triumph.

In the very first sentence, which serves as a title of the work,
Herodotus described it as researches or inquiries presented so
that the memory of the great deeds of Greeks and barbarians
and the causes of their quarrel would be preserved. The
medium of presentation is prose. An agrarian age of warriors,
professedly devoted to fighting and honor, had used poetry and
(as its supreme literary form) epic poetry to celebrate great
deeds. The past was remembered as myth presented in poetry,
the sacred language of the sacred order of the world. To the
Homeric society there succeeded transformed societies using
money, engaged in commerce, manufacture, farming for
markets, and colonization—activities that made necessary the
arts of record-keeping and writing and new social qualities,
calculation and adaptability. It was a world that, on occasion,
required the shaping human hand and new departures. These
actions might not have the warrant of myth or a clear sacred
origin. The historian, among others, might be necessary to explain their significance. Even warfare no longer served as a
stage for the clash of heroes—as it were, an epic cast of stars.
It required the massing of citizens cooperating in the self-
disciplined groups of the phalanx formation, that is, hoplites,
as the warriors and the low-class crews of ships of war. Nevertheless, Homer comprehended so much that his survival hero,
the wily Odysseus, could serve as a model for the age of city
men. The new Greek societies took the form of many city-
states, which had grown in rivalry one with another, gaining

strength and trade not by conquest at home but by colonization. During the formative centuries, from the eighth to the first part of the sixth, there was no major empire in Asia, Egypt, Greece, and the western Mediterranean to threaten the growth of a divided Greek world.

In the new societies, especially in Asia Minor where the plurality of cultural myths and the clash of traditions encouraged questioning and new formulations, Ionian myths that legitimized authority and explained the cosmos were found inadequate. Philosopher-scientists, rejecting the old myths, advanced their own explanations which had to be presented and defended in discourse. This intellectual development Herodotus himself identified with a higher form of life: civilized discourse.[2] This questioning of elements and sky, this searching of men's customs and the land in which they lived, provided the background of Herodotus' historical work. Before him there had been *logographoi*, that is, prose writers who compiled local histories, genealogies, geographies, and some accounts of areas and countries. Dionysius of Halicarnassus, a rhetorician and historian in the Rome of Emperor Augustus, judged the works of the *logographoi* to be lacking in general views and the coordination of one part of an account with another.[3]

The fragments of one such writer, Hecataeus of Miletus, whose name Herodotus cited four times, produce a livelier effect. One of his books was a going round the world. He introduced another, *The Genealogies*, with the patronizing revisionism so often professed by historians: "The following is . . . an account that I think is true: for the Greeks, as I believe, tell many ludicrous stories."[4]

The relationship of people to environment, their customs and monuments, fascinated Herodotus. From his youth in Asia Minor and from the Ionian philosophers he had learned to distrust myths and to question. Beyond that he judged their search for general explanations excessively single-minded, and at odds with the details and variety of human living. His search accordingly became an inquiry into people and their actions, the study of men in time, space, and groups, history that embraced geography, anthropology, and morals. When did Herodotus make this transition? The question cannot be answered forthrightly from the sparse details of his life or by textual analysis. Estimates in a considerable literature inspire admiration for scholarly ingenuity more than they persuade.

To inquire about men in time and space was to travel around the world of the eastern Mediterranean, Europe, western Asia, and Africa. For presenting his account of a particular people, he settled on an order determined by when that people had come into contact with the Persians or, as was usually the case, had been conquered by them. Lydia is treated first because it conquered some Greek cities and then was incorporated into the Persian Empire. The long description of Egypt is also an exception, perhaps because Herodotus originally wrote the section as a separate study or because the traveler found his Egyptian stories and observations too interesting to eliminate or even to abridge.

Travels, inevitably arduous, in southern Russia, Mesopotamia, Persia, Egypt, North Africa, and Greece suggest that a hardy constitution supported his curiosity. On land and sea he followed merchant trails, inquiring his way along them in search of evidence and things to observe. He was untroubled to find that many people might tell many stories about the same matter. When the stories interested him, he sometimes retailed several of them, on occasion without reconciling them. Where a matter was controversial, he presented the views of each side. Sometimes (and then he is misleading) he did not know how partisan a particular position was. The stories, including those about barbarians, were presented for their own sake, for entertainment (4.30:280), or to illustrate a Greek moral.

He used chronicles and records. In barbarian lands, since he did not know the language, he had to depend on those who could tell him about the records. This evidence consisted of what he saw or what he heard about what he saw, and in the main that was in Greek. Wherever he traveled, for example, in Egypt and Scythia, he was a lively and sympathetic observer with eyes and mind both awakened and limited by Greek culture. Foreign stories lost something in Greek translation, and Greek moral views often provided the point of his stories.

Herodotus' concern with truth is noteworthy when the reputation of the Greeks is considered. Thucydides regarded Pericles as great because he understood what had to be done in a situation, he could persuade people, and he was honest and patriotic enough to advocate the policy that his understanding indicated to be appropriate. Herodotus praised Cadmus of Cos, who had a reputation as a just man, because he had returned the money with which Gelon of Syracuse had entrusted him, an honest action, a deed "most remarkable" (7.164:499). Indeed, the word Herodotus chose for his work in gathering materials and making them coherent is from the Greek courts. The *histor* has seen an action and can serve as an eyewitness. *Historie* is knowledge or information gained by inquiry.

In the very first sections Herodotus briefly and wittily presented myths that explained the Asian-European conflict. Of the distant beginning, he recognized, there was neither evidence to examine nor witnesses to question. As the ultimate beginnings were beyond his reach, he chose "to rely on my own knowledge, and to point out who it was in actual fact that first injured the Greeks." The story would feature both great and small cities, because "human prosperity never abides long in the same place." The humble of the past achieve eminence, and the great become small (1.5:43). This seesaw of generations composes finally a pointless tale beyond philosophizing.

Human life, the Athenian sage Solon told the king of Lydia, is a treading through uncertainty, and a man's entire life must be considered if he is to be judged happy. The jealous gods so like to trouble man that until his death, when all the returns can be counted, he cannot be said to have had a happy life (1.31-32:53). That Lydian king, Croesus (c. 560-546 B.C.), was first among the Asians to conquer the Greeks. His ancestor's usurpation of the Lydian throne, in itself a punishment for the arrogance of the overthrown ruler, had scheduled the doom of Croesus, who confirmed it for himself by his inability to understand Solon's stories about the modesty required of man. In Herodotus' account Croesus figured as an attractive and generous man, but he failed to know himself as a man and to know his place before jealous gods. To boast that he was the happiest or most fortunate of men made Croesus guilty of human arrogance, what the Greeks called *hybris*, and is the working out of a destiny, itself the consequence of the murder. Sardis, his capital, however had its prime of glory and to it came "all the great Greek teachers of that epoch" (1.29:51).

In Lydia these were of no avail, not even Solon, whose lessons were ineffective against an operational doom. To Croesus the fates had allotted an inescapable fall. The very success of Lydia in conquering Herodotus' ancestral world in the Near East stirred Croesus to large ambitions that brought him down.

Croesus ruled over one of the four major states, Egypt, and the kingdoms of the Medes and the Chaldaeans, which became rivals after they had destroyed the Assyrian Empire (612 B.C.). The Medes lost out to their kin, the Persians, who finally created a consolidated empire with an experienced bureaucracy, a greater empire than that of the Assyrians. The rise of the Persians confronted the divided Greeks with a new power and troubled Croesus, who is presented as thinking in power-political terms rather than with the personal motivation of the figures in the first six books of the history; Croesus wondered "if he might be able to check Persian expansion before it had gone too far" (1.46:57).

His intelligence-gathering extended to the gods. Before deciding on war, the Lydian king tested the quality of several oracles. The priestess of Apollo at Delphi passed the test, but Croesus misinterpreted the oracle's ambiguous response that in a Lydian war against Persia a great empire would fall, and he warred against Persia (545 B.C.). Here Herodotus used an account edited by the Delphic oracle to obscure its dubious role. The expedition, at any rate, did not prevail; while Croesus was preparing a strengthened force, Cyrus, the Persian king (559-520 B.C.), attacked: "Indeed, he was his own messenger — for so swift was his advance into Lydia that Croesus had no news that he was on the way" (1.79:72).

The Persian rulers had conquered their kin, the Medes, who considerably augmented Persian power. Babylonia, the realm of the Chaldaeans, was also subdued. The Persians, then, were heirs of eastern empire. Their origins in a spare land and a culture that discouraged self-indulgence made them formidable and successful. Later, they readily borrowed foreign ways: Herodotus, far from being a simpleton enthusiast for cultural borrowing, cited as examples luxurious living from the Lydians and Greek pederasty, added to their own polygamy (1.135:97).

The rulers of Egypt had not acted to forestall Persian power, which was turned against Egypt in 525 B.C. Cambyses, the son of Cyrus, initiated the conquest, after he had asked Amasis of Egypt for an eye doctor, who was obligingly sent to Persia. The doctor, resenting his forced exile from Egypt, urged Cambyses to ask for the daughter of Amasis as his wife. The Egyptian ruler, fearing to refuse the Persian emperor but reluctant to lose his daughter, decided upon the dim-witted stratagem of sending as his daughter the beautiful offspring of King Apries against whom Amasis had successfully rebelled. In Persia the substitute princess talked. At the root of these traditional stories probably lie some marriage diplomacy and Persian claims to inherit Egypt. At any rate, while Cambyses was wondering how to get his army across the Egyptian desert, he received a deserter from Egypt, Phanes of Halicarnassus, a Greek mercenary who had knowledge of the Egyptian land, its resources and defenses. The conqueror captured Psammetichus III, who had briefly succeeded his father, thereby initiating the Twenty-Seventh Dynasty, the first of three dynasties in the period of the first Persian conquest (525-404 B.C.). Cambyses himself died in 522 B.C. on his way back to Persia to face a widespread rebellion from which Darius I emerged as emperor (522-486 B.C.).

In Egypt Herodotus found the priests a major source of information. Cambyses, therefore, is presented as the perpetrator of harsh and impious deeds, among them the spoliation of temple treasuries and the cremation of the mummy of Amasis as warrant of the divine king's immortality. The former is based on the conqueror's prohibition of payments to the temple treasuries, a measure designed to soften the impact of his tribute exactions from the Egyptians. Dishonoring the body of Amasis was probably the consequence of the Persian emperor's claim to be the rightful ruler of Egypt, a claim that required him to treat Amasis as a usurper.

With Egypt's subjection to Persia, Herodotus turned to a long account of Egypt. As more than one-third of the pages devoted to Egypt deal with its topography and customs, Herodotus has been described as a geographer who became a historian.[5] The hypothesis of an Egyptian travel book that Herodotus had written earlier and then incorporated into the history of the Graeco-Persian wars is designed to explain the lengthy account of Egypt, out of proportion with Egypt's role in the war, and the mode of treatment of its people. The hypothesis is plausible, but Herodotus provided the simple ex-

planation that he dealt with Egypt at length because it was so
remarkable and had so many things that defied description
(2.35:142). Its attraction for the Greeks is evident in his many
references to "clever" Greek opinions concerning Egypt. His
own opinion, in moderate form indisputable, was that climate
and geography shape differing cultures. The uniqueness of
Egypt's position, therefore, explained the distinctiveness of
Egyptian ways. The indisputable nevertheless yielded to controversies about the extent of Egypt and whether it is part of
Asia or Libya. Herodotus argued that Egypt consists of all the
land south of Aswan, created or flooded by the Nile. Even the
oracle of Ammon at Siwa affirmed that in this area, the "only
true boundary between Asia and Libya is formed by the fron-
tiers of Egypt" (2.17:135-36). As it is made by silt, it is the
very gift of the Nile, whose floods regulate the life it renders
possible.

The flooding of the Nile in summertime, "which made the
Nile behave in the opposite way to other rivers," was a classic
problem. Herodotus dismissed the theory that the summer's
north winds caused its flooding by blocking the river's flow.
The theory that the flooding Nile originated in the ocean that
encircles the world he dismissed as mere imagination. The
third, most plausible and all the more erroneous, affirmed that
melting snow — what snow, Herodotus asked, in the river's tor-
rid source lands? — caused the flood. His own complicated
theory was that the seasons and the nearness of the sun differ
in Egypt and in the Nile's sources so that the Nile brings winter
rains to Egypt in summer. That was notable as the opposite of
what happened in other rivers. Herodotus then listed Egyptian
practices that were the contrary of Greek customs or those of
other people. His exaggerations here (2.35-37:142-44) — and the
faults are primarily exaggerations[6] — inspire a grateful response
that the man from Halicarnassus did not seriously apply
geographical determinism to the whole of his Egyptian work.

Although the Egyptians, Herodotus stated, long believed
themselves to be the world's oldest people, in his own time they
thought that the Phrygians were senior. The changed opinion
was in consequence of an experiment by the pharaoh Psammetichus designed to determine the oldest people by the
language children totally isolated from other human voices

would use. Apparently Herodotus was not convinced. The Egyptians, he noted, had records and talked of things and times thirteen hundred years and even more than eleven thousand years earlier. From them the Greeks had even learned the names of the gods (2.142:186; 2.49-54:149-51). Characteristically Herodotus disclaimed any intention of treating religion except as his story required it, because "I do not think that any one nation knows more about such things than any other" (2.2: 130). His exception is as monumental as the tolerant pragmatism implied in the reason he gave, which, it should be emphasized, is not a profession of incredulous agnosticism.

The enlarged time perspective of the Egyptians directly affected Herodotus, inducing or confirming his religious relativism and doubt about major Greek myths. Thus, he affirmed belief in the Egyptian priests' version of the story of Helen of Troy. Fleeing with her, Paris reached Egypt, where they were detained until Menelaus arrived after a hollow victory at Troy. In claiming that she was not in Troy, the Trojans, Herodotus believed, spoke truth, because in spite of Helen's face they would not have endured the siege of their city for her. The Greek refusal to believe a patent truth "came of divine volition in order that their utter destruction might plainly prove to mankind that great sins meet with great punishments" inflicted by the gods (2.115-20:171-74).

The Egyptian time perspective affected Herodotus, but a historical time sense, a sense of the texture of social change in time and in a particular time, was beyond him. In *The Histories*, the Old Kingdom and the pyramid-builders, the Middle Kingdom, the Empire, and the New Kingdom until nearly his own time appear in temporal disarray and without any suggestion of those divisions, the conventions of modern scholarship.

A reaction against the burdens imposed by the pyramid-builders may be preserved in the story of the pharaoh Cheops and his resourceful daughter. The costs of the pyramid drove Cheops to send his daughter to a bawdy house, telling her to demand a specified sum from each Egyptian customer. She did so and, hoping to build a memorial for herself, asked each for a block of stone as well as her fee. With "these stones was built (the story goes) the middle pyramid of the three which stand in

front of the great pyramid. It is a hundred and fifty feet square"
(2.126:179). Whether or not the story originated as a political
criticism, it is a good story.

Between the defeat of the Assyrians and the conquest of
Cambyses, the pharaohs cultivated the Egyptian priests. In
spite of this nativist reaction the number of Greek merchants
and mercenary soldiers increased. These were major sources for
Herodotus when he visited Egypt, then under Persian domination. Some echoes of the shock of Persian conquerors upon en-
countering the pantheon and zoo of Egyptian religion sound in
Herodotus' stories about Cambyses. He is plausibly presented as
contemptuous of Egyptian veneration of animals, but an in-
scribed tablet found in the Serapeum of Memphis refutes
Herodotus' anecdote about Cambyses' slaughter of the sacred
bull calf, Apis.[7]

Perhaps an age of foreign domination in Egypt posed difficulties for understanding the divine rulership of the pharaoh.
Herodotus did not even mention it, but his judgment that the
Egyptians "are religious to excess, beyond any nation in the
world" (2.37:143) tells us much about Herodotus as well as
about Egypt. He loved stories about religious and cosmological
beliefs, although he agreed with Pindar that custom rules all
men. "Everyone without exception believes his own native
customs . . . to be the best: and that being so, it is unlikely that
anyone but a madman would mock at such things" (3.38:
219-20).[8] The conclusion has not been a Western experience.

Cambyses' conquests led Herodotus to the history of the
island of Samos, an early sea power, where he had lived as an
exile. At the end of The Histories' first account of Samos he explained that he had presented so much about the island because
the Samians were responsible for three of the greatest construction feats in the Greek world: a mile-long (actually more than
one-half mile) water tunnel cut through the base of a hill; a
breakwater of about a quarter of a mile extending into water
twenty fathoms deep; and the largest of Greek temples, the
Heraeum (3.60:228-29). Polycrates, the tyrant, carried out the
first two feats of construction with forced labor and finished the
temple of Hera.

Samian naval power, sometimes used for piracy, became a
major element in Near Eastern politics when the Persian Em-

pire took over Miletus on the mainland. Herodotus noted that the might and good fortune of the island's tyrant, Polycrates, made him the talk of Ionia and Greece. Cambyses and Polycrates initially agreed to work together against Egypt, but after the Persian emperor gained the mainland as well as the use of the Phoenician navy, Polycrates joined forces with Egypt.

In this recital of bad faith, survival, and conquest, Herodotus recounted two celebrated anecdotes. The first involved those who opposed Polycrates and sought Spartan aid. The Spartan response exemplified, neatly, and perhaps improbably, their proverbial "no nonsense," "men of few words" reputation which has given meaning to the adjective for Spartan, "laconic." When the Samians made a lengthy plea for assistance, the Spartan magistrates replied that they had, by then, forgotten the beginning of the speech and could not understand the conclusion. Thus clued to pithiness the Samians, presenting a sack, said that the sack needed flour. The Spartans, agreeing to help, observed that the word *sack* had been unnecessary (3.46:222-23).

The second anecdote, about the ring of Polycrates, perhaps recalls a sea power's ritual marriage to the sea by casting a ring into its waters. The story centered on the usual good fortune of Polycrates. It had been so consistent that his ally, the pharaoh Amasis, urged the Samian to balance his "excessive prosperity" with a controlled misfortune. He therefore advised his ally to throw his most precious possession into the sea. Later, Polycrates, having thrown a treasured ring into the sea, received the present of a particularly fine fish. Upon cutting open the fish, the royal servants found the ring. They joyously brought it to Polycrates, who announced this apparent providence to Amasis. The pharaoh, like a Greek sage, recognized that no one could save a man from his destiny, especially the miserable one allotted to Polycrates. Although Polycrates had been responsible for breaking the alliance with Amasis, the latter, in the Herodotean account, took the initiative in renouncing a partner whose inevitable misfortune would cause the pharaoh too much distress. For a good story's full effect, no more—particularly apologetics or moralizing—is necessary. Later, Herodotus recorded, a Persian satrap tricked Polycrates, put him to death, and affixed his corpse to a cross (3.40-43:220-23; 3.120-26:252-55).

The quarrels of claimants to the succession later took the shape of a massacre of Persians in Samos and, in retaliation, the extermination of the island's population by the Persians. Subsequently Otanes, the Persian general responsible for the slaughter, ordered that the island be restocked with human beings. He made this reparation because his vengeance was hateful to the gods, who had punished him with a genital disease (3.149:265).

The sequence of the narrative dealing with the early years of Darius' reign is confusing and inaccurate. After the rebellions against Darius, Herodotus turned to his campaign against the Scythians (c. 512 B.C.), a mainly nomadic people in southern Russia. Some of these nomads looked on other people as slaves, and the grain tribute they received from tribes settled in Russia's black earth region was passed on in trade through the Black Sea ports to Athens. Herodotus followed these trade routes into Russia to gather material for an account of Scythian customs and geography.

About them he rejoiced to report surprises, including a story about Amazons. But he almost silenced the voice of correction when in a sophisticated throwaway he reflected that it is the ends of the earth that produce matters rare and curious (3.106:247). Becoming the philosophical traveler, Herodotus mentioned Scythian mistrust of foreign customs and cited as an example their antipathy to Greek Dionysiac orgies: "No Scythian can see sense in imagining a god who drives people out of their wits" (4.79:297), a maxim for sanity rather than for the theologian's gropings. Darius, Herodotus implausibly wrote, decided on war against the Scythians to avenge their attack on the Medes at the end of the seventh century B.C. and to get information about Europe as a preliminary to Persian expansion. In this campaign Darius (513-512 B.C.) revealed the same human arrogance that marked the Persian attack on Greece which ended with Salamis and Plataea (480-479).

The Persian emperor proclaimed his intention to bridge Asia and Europe. To join what was originally parted he had a pontoon bridge built across the Bosphorus by a Greek from Samos. Another such bridge was constructed over the Danube. Darius further had every member of his forces march before him and deposit a pebble. The heaps of these made up large hills.

The speeches and summarized discourse of this section supply information on the area that explains the course of the invasion. As a country of nomads, Scythia had no tilled fields to lay waste and no towns and forts to take. Defeat by the Scythians was not to be feared, as the Greek commander of Mytilenean forces advised Darius; the danger was in failing to find them and in the fatigue and casualties of endless and pointless marches (4.97: 303). As some Scythians refused to resist Darius, the commander of the Scythian forces planned to lure the Persians into the interior of their land. Darius, in pursuit, angrily challenged the Scythians to a pitched battle—that is, a fight on Persian terms—or surrender. Finally Darius recognized that withdrawal was the prudent course.

Even in retreat the Persians had no trouble from the Ionian Greeks, although some of them had pledged cooperation with the Scythians. The rulers of these Greeks were tyrants supported by the Persian emperor, and consequently they feared that an anti-Persian rising, requiring popular support, would mean the loss of their hegemony. The Scythians, Herodotus wrote, said that when the Ionians are free men, they are base and craven, and when slaves, they love their master and do not seek to escape (4.142:317).

Some ten years later the Ionians did rebel (500-494 B.C.) and, having done so, sought assistance from the cities of the Greek mainland. Persian rule, which extended across the Bosphorus and to the Black Sea, had greatly reduced Ionian commercial opportunities. The personal fears of Aristagoras, tyrant of Miletus, Herodotus wrote, prompted this Ionian rebellion. This rebel ruler had earlier won Persian support for an attack on the Aegean island of Naxos which had succeeded to a part of Samian naval power and trade. The attempted conquest failed, partly because the Milesian ruler had antagonized the Persian commander under him. Fearing that Darius would punish him, Aristagoras sacrificed his tyrannical power by proclaiming for his city equality under the law, a form of constitutional democracy. He pressed the same course upon the other Ionian cities, even arresting some rulers who had been with his fleet. They were given into the hands of their democratic subjects.

The people of Mytilene on the island of Lesbos immediately
stoned to death Coes, their former tyrant, but only they
resorted to such violence. The rebellion that Aristagoras had so
initiated roused the Ionian cities as well as many Aegean
islands. A rebel force, invading the Lydian province of the Persian Empire, burned Sardis, its capital.

Aristagoras persuaded Athenians with the argument that, as
they did not use shield or spear, the Persians were pushovers
and with extravagant claims of the kinship of Athenians and
the Milesians. The appeals prevailed on the masses, the
democracy, Herodotus sharply observed, and would not have
been effective with sober individuals because Aristagoras was
"a poor spirited creature" and the sailing of the Athenian "fleet
was the beginning of trouble not only for Greece but for other
peoples" (5.126:387; 5.97:379).

Nevertheless, some Athenian citizens favored war because
they feared the restoration of the former Athenian tyrant Hippias, to whom Darius had given refuge and support. The
tyrants, as their record shows, with Herodotus and Thucydides
agreeing, were sometimes careful about burdening their
citizens with taxes and difficult projects. Instead, as Herodotus
noted, the Athenians proved in war, imperialistic activity, and
in all respects how excellent freedom is. The same Athenians,
when under a tyrant or oligarch, were no better than other people and "deliberately shirked their duty in the field, as slaves
shirk working for their masters; but when their freedom was
won, then every man among them was interested in his own
cause" (5.78:369).

As the separate Greek states did not work closely together,
Darius more than regained his conquests in the Aegean and
Asia Minor. Desire to avenge the burning of Sardis led him to
seek the subjection of mainland Greece. As long as Greece was
independent and, therefore, likely to aid anti-Persian dissi-
dents, Darius had to recognize that he would not securely rule
Thrace, the Aegean islands, and the Ionian cities, even though
by then the cities had been enslaved three times, once by the
Lydians and twice by the Persians.

This Herodotean generalization, like his account of Samos, is
exaggerated, and the historian himself later qualified it. The
Persian commander and son-in-law of Darius, Mardonius,

swept away the restored tyrants and set up democratic institutions. Although the context makes it likely that Herodotus understood this democratic restoration to be a political move in the interest of the empire's security, he did not make that point. But the restoration was not universal, as any Chian, Samian, or Halicarnassean knew very well (6.32:398; 6.43:402).

Mardonius, with fleet and army, regained Thrace and won parts of Macedonia only to lose many ships in the stormy waters off Athos and part of the army to a Thracian tribe. He returned home, and a new Persian campaign was slowly prepared to punish Athens and Eretria on the island of Euboea, to complete the subjugation of mainland Greece, and incidentally to assist Hippias against the Athenians. Eretria was captured, and "Greece is the weaker by the loss of one fine city" (6.106:425), as the Athenians vainly told the Spartans. The Athenians had many factions, but one of their leaders, Miltiades, who had long controlled a Thracian area on the European side of the Dardanelles, arguing for decisive action against the Persians, used prophetic words, or Herodotus chose them to emphasize the significance of the Athenian decision: "If we fight and win, then this city of ours may well grow into pre-eminence amongst all the cities of Greece" (6.109:428). The plea was successful and, when the Persian forces landed at Marathon, some twenty-four miles from Athens, probably hoping to encourage Athenian divisions and treachery, the ensuing battle cost them heavily. When Miltiades, the victor of Marathon, then hastened to the defense of Athens, the Persian commander gave up the invasion and the fleet returned home.

Darius, who was determined to continue the hostilities, died in 486 B.C., leaving the war as a legacy to his son Xerxes (486-465). The latter, presented as a barbarian acting out a Greek tragedy, suffered at least from overconfidence compared with his experienced and able predecessor. The new emperor spoke in terms of an activist struggle that may echo Zoroaster's injunction to join the struggle of the truth against the lie. As a punishment Athens must be burned. Herodotus' language here has a special irony, for he has Xerxes say that a god leads him. As the Greeks understood it, divine leading frequently meant leading to destruction. Then, his intention to bridge the Hellespont — yoking the sea, as Aeschylus put it — and to march into Greece was the arrogance of excessive power which proposed so to "extend the empire of Persia that its boundaries will be God's own sky, so that the sun will not look down upon any land beyond the boundaries of what is ours" (7.8:444). His enmity with the Greeks allowed no middle course (7.11:449).

Persian preparations and the initial marches of the army advanced the drama. Several anecdotes revealed Xerxes as forgetful that he was a man: he ordered the whipping of the Hellespont for obstructing his army's passage and in his pride caused a canal to be cut across the peninsula at Mt. Athos. As the ships could more easily have been dragged across the isthmus, Herodotus thought this construction the monument of an arrogant vaunter of power (7.24:454). The emperor and Artabanus, who had tried to dissuade him from invading Greece, exchanged speeches about the mortality of all things and the dangers ahead. Xerxes allowed that life was full of dangers but added that to take account of every danger would be timorous futility. Arrogance appeared again when Xerxes, crossing into Europe, failed to rebuke a man who hailed him as Zeus and asked why to destroy Greece he had "assumed the shape of a man of Persia. You could have destroyed Greece without going to that trouble" (7.56:464).

As a tragic protagonist, Xerxes was unable to take good advice. Pride disabled him from understanding the Spartan Demaratus, who said that the Spartans, fighting together, are the best soldiers in the world. As free men they have but one master, the law, and they fear it "much more than your subjects fear you" (7.104:477). Nevertheless, Herodotus allowed Xerxes fellow feeling when, to add to the emotional effect of the emperor's review of fleet and army at the Hellespont, he had the emperor weep. To a questioner he explained that he had been lamenting the brevity of life: within one hundred years not one man of his myriad forces would be alive (7.46:460-61).

The roll of the naval forces as well as the military contingents on the Persian side recalls a similar catalogue in the *Iliad*. Listing them conveyed a sense of the immensity of this Persian act of war. The Greeks knew the forces in detail because Xerxes was assured that his force was fearsome. He therefore permitted captured Greek spies to observe and report on the imperial hordes. Herodotus also detailed the names of Persian commanders but not those of the native officers leading tributary contingents. As they were the pawns of great events, their names would tax the reader's attention and, a rare note from Herodotus, are not required for his story (7.96:473).

The Persians captured Athens, whose leaders nevertheless helped to hold the Greek forces together. The Greek navies assembled at one end of the island of Salamis, but even here Greek unity barely survived. Detachments of the Persian fleet closed off the channel approaches, on either side of the island of Salamis, to the Bay of Eleusis. Themistocles, the Athenian leader, called this "good news" because the Greeks had to fight, even if they only sought escape. The Persian fleet finally launched their attack in the narrow channel where the heavy, oared Greek ships had the advantage. In the ensuing Greek victory, the navies of Aegina and Athens stood out. As long as there was Athenian sea power, Themistocles recognized, the Athenians, even though the Persians held their city's buildings, had in the fleet a means of survival and a city.

An omen prefigured the Greek victory, as did the advice of Queen Artemisia of Halicarnassus, for whose capture the Athenians, angered that a woman should propose to fight them, offered a reward (8.93:554). After defeat Xerxes decided that his fleet should return to home ports but that a large army under Mardonius should remain in Greece.

Themistocles, among others (including the Spartans of legendary caution), performed yet another service for the Greeks, counseling moderation in success. To some Greeks wishing to pursue Xerxes, he recommended that they be content with victory and refrain from cornering the Persians, who would then fight as desperate men. Another victory was not assured, and "it was not we who performed this exploit; it was God and our divine protectors, who were jealous that one man in his godless pride should be king of Asia and of Europe too" (8.108-10: 560-61). By this course the Athenian also sought to gain credit with Xerxes, an explanation that may have seemed plausible to Herodotus, who drew his information from aristocratic opponents of Themistocles, and to his first readers, because of the later unpopularity of Themistocles, his outlawry, and his seeking refuge among the Persians. Those who reject Herodotus' explanation as unthinkable do not understand the Greeks.

Herodotus enriched his account of the Battle of Plataea (479 B.C.), a decisive defeat of the Persians, with a story told by Thersander of Orchomenus. A Persian guest at a Theban banquet before the battle told him that soon few of the Persian soldiers present would be alive. God had so ordained, yet no one would believe the warning. The Persian concluded with a sentiment that is required of both observer and participant in tragedy: "The worst pain a man can have is to know much and be impotent to act" (9.16:582-83).

A Persian remnant was wiped out at Sestos, where *The Histories* end. Some think they are unfinished and merely break off. But a continuation would have dealt with the background of another war caused by arrogance—in short, another history on the theme he had just concluded.

At the height of their success some Persians urged that their people move from their "small and barren country" to one with rich resources. In this Herodotean fable Cyrus refused the temptation of prosperity. If they moved, Cyrus said, they must prepare to be ruled by others because soft countries, not hard ones, breed soft men (9.121:624). From this it follows that hard countries breed the hard men who conquer soft countries, finally to be weakened by their plunder and to yield to yet others.

So ends the work of the father of history. It was widely read, accordingly drawing critical and disgruntled comments. The moralizing biographer, Plutarch, found Herodotus' treatment of Boeotia, the "sticks" of Greece and Plutarch's birthplace, evidence of the historian's malignity. "Everyone," wrote Josephus, a historian of the Jews, "criticizes Herodotus."

He reacted to his world of empire and war by devoting himself to writing the history of the struggle between the Greeks and the barbarians. To get his information, he undertook research or inquiry, and the Greek word for inquiries gave history its name. Much of his oral history search garnered information at several removes from eyewitness accounts. Nevertheless, for all the emotionalism and inequity of critics, Herodotus' veracity can be demonstrated: there is perhaps not a single instance where Herodotus wrote "I saw," as he did very many times, and was contradicted by later findings.

He presented his purpose as threefold: to preserve the memory of the great deeds of the warring parties and, as he is the principal source of information about his subject, he succeeded; to mention such interesting matters as he had encountered (4.30:280), an avowal that he would entertain his readers by pacing his work with "digressions," moments of comedy and wonder, so that his auditors and readers would not tire from a surfeit of great actions; and to recount how the Greeks and the Persian Empire warred one against the other.

The history is a study of actions rather than policy. It does not probe the source of actions, which are explained in brief speeches. Herodotus' account, it should be evident, is not analytical. Events fit together as part of a narrative that holds the reader but is not linear, not part of a strictly defined process. Each event, each item, is separate and yet part of the overall history. A good example is the account of Xerxes, vaunting his power, forgetting the modesty that humans, because of their transience, should observe, and then weeping as he recalled the mortality of his fighting men, the occasion of his arrogance.

In Thucydides almost every event forms part of a logical, psychological, and narrative structure. The twofold design in Herodotus' *Histories* is not so imperious and formidable. The *Histories* initially recount the fall of the Lydian empire at the hands of Cyrus. Herodotus then proceeded to Persian affairs because, as he noted, his story then required him to tell who Cyrus was and how the Persians gained predominance in Asia (3.95:81). In the rest of the work he followed the easygoing order of dealing with countries and people as they come in contact with the Persians. The second element in the design is the Greek view of power, freedom, and arrogance (*hybris*), which holds the work together and gives it meaning.

Herodotus touched on many subjects but, as a Greek, he was concerned with public life and war. In public life, power is the prize; and power, making for arrogance, "is a slippery thing, and has never lacked lovers to woo it" (3.53:226). The powerful by their excesses cause the gods to pass judgment on them, long-term dooms that provide part of the continuity of history. This continuity is partial, because history does not make for an edifying story in which every crime is punished.

Power may seduce anybody, although Herodotus believed that aristocrats were more likely to avoid excess: despotic

power seduced the despot from self-control; freedom, in remov-
ing restraints on the energies of citizens of a democracy, also
left them unprotected against their own willfulness. The ruler,
nevertheless, must be active, and his soundness is nurtured in
conflict. There is then a struggle for empire, prosecuted by Persian and Athenian, a struggle involving the innocent and the
guilty about who "shall bear the yoke of servitude" (7.8:445).
Providence itself provided the human fodder for this war, for
it "has made prolific every kind of creature which is timid and
preyed upon by others, in order to ensure its continuance"
(3.107:248). In his own century, Herodotus knew, Greece "suffered more misery than in the twenty generations before Darius
was born — partly from the Persian wars, partly from her own
internal struggle for supremacy" (6.98:423).

Herodotus had a pessimistic view of life, a point not recognized by commentators who are misled by the breadth of his
sympathy and his lively curiosity. There was once a tradition
of describing Herodotus as naive. That mistaken judgment was
a triumph of Herodotus the supreme artist or, as Thomas Mann
would put it, confidence man. More than most artists, Herodotus is inimitable.

3. Thucydides:
History, Science, and Power

THUCYDIDES AND HERODOTUS are separated by about twenty-five years, less than a generation. There are, however, short generations when changes are few, and long generations when every year appears new and the decades *seem* to sever links with the past as though the earth were bringing forth a new creation. The long generation between these two historians sets them as contrasts in achievement. Herodotus, writing to preserve the memory of great events and to entertain his readers, told of the repulse of the Persian emperor by his intended victims, Athens and the Greek cities. Thucydides (c. 460-398 B.C.) described the protracted warfare of Greek against Greek, in a work that was more than a history, for its narrative and speeches made up an analysis of the war as the disorder of Greece and an account of recurring human behavior.[1] Their differing achievements, shaped by contrasting outlooks and temperaments, point to large social changes in fifth-century Athens that imposed on its citizens the ordeal of rapid cultural adaptation.

Unlike Herodotus, the native of a despotism, Thucydides lived an active public life. He was responsive to the intellectual currents of his time, especially to the tragedians' exploration of human nature and to ventures toward a science of nature, human nature, and politics. For him the achievements of his own time were so remarkable as to create a sense of modernity that made the past archaic and alien.

This consciousness expressed the moral change that went with the commerce, empire, and democracy of Athens. Old guides, religious sanctions and taboos, aristocratic honor and

27

moderation, oligarchic caution, all had been weakened. Was man free to measure and to regulate all things? Or was he in public actions subject to limits which, if exceeded, brought down the vengeance of furies as inexorably as human crime and arrogance once called forth the retribution of gods and the fates?

Athens had already become a commercial city before the Persian invasion. As such, it had sea power that maintained itself and the Greek cities against the Persians and created the later Athenian Empire. This future imperial city had virtually become a democracy. In its Athenian form, democracy signified no human brotherhood: it was an exclusive club with membership restricted to the adult males who were citizens. Athenian citizenship, jealously guarded and bestowed, said nothing of human rights.

The democracy had been limited because earning a living prevented many citizens from participating in the privileges and duties of citizenship. The practical limitation was eliminated in an imperial-democratic program sponsored by Pericles, aristocrat by heritage and the principal citizen of Athens as a democracy. During his ascendancy, citizens were paid to discharge such civic duties as sitting in the assembly and serving on juries or in council. The costs of this salaried democracy came from the empire, as did much of the cost of the buildings on the Acropolis. In the history of Athens, empire made democracy possible, and to Athenian predominance in Greece the democracy provided energies, interest, and will.

The empire had its beginnings in 479 B.C., when the Greek states sought to maintain their pledge of resistance to Persia and to aid the Greek communities still under Persian rule. This Confederacy of Delos, the mainly Aegean-Greek treaty organization, became an Athenian empire. The power that supported Athenian interest was enhanced because many members of the confederacy, preferring not to render armed service, contributed to the Delian treasury. The league became an empire when Athens refused to allow cities to withdraw from the confederacy, compelling them to pay tribute, to make their government acceptable to Athens, and to submit trade disputes to Athenian courts.

The citizens of Athens were parties to these violations of Greek civic autonomy. Until approximately 460 B.C. Athenian power and transgressions provoked no challenger. Sparta, military leader of the Lacedaemonian League, being reluctant to undertake campaigns far from home, was at first content to have Athens carry on against Persia. Although some Athenians described Sparta as their inveterate enemy, the Spartan garrison state, maintained by servile laborers, the helots, was so slow to act that coexistence seemed possible and even desirable. After 460 B.C., however, Sparta developed an increasing fear of growing Athenian power and the forward and aggressive policies of Pericles.

Thucydides lived his formative years in the climax of Athenian democracy, imperialism, and rivalry with Sparta, provocatively encouraged by Athens' neighbor and commercial rival, Corinth. As a citizen of Athens he found politics an absorbing subject for reflection and analysis. When in 431 B.C. the rival alliances went to war, he resolved to write on what he believed to be an inevitable conflict and the greatest of wars. The history became a work of memory and learning shaped in form and tone by prolonged reflection and analytical thought. Its spareness and austerity, its lack of romance and beguiling anecdote, he boasted, were the price of relevance and accuracy. The very things presented as done, said, and thought formed the descriptions that finally made possible diagnosis, that is, explanation of the process at work. He wrote, then, not primarily as a historian but as a scientist of Greek political life, of the government of the city and its relations with other cities. In these matters he sought to rise above civic partisanship, and no doubt what he regarded as the extremism of democratic Athens promoted a sense of being apart from his city. He was exiled from it for twenty years of the war and so was able to consult with the combatants of both sides (5.26:364).

He was an Athenian, as he wrote, the son of Olorus. His father's name indicates that the family was from Thrace, a frontier of the Greek world whose people Thucydides described as barbarians, that is, non-Greek. When he was exiled, he probably lived in Thrace where, ancient tradition reported, a mine provided him with income. Presumably his familiarity with the area had won him election to command a naval expedition there. His expedition (424 B.C.) was fruitless: its expectations were thwarted when the enemy's successful enterprise prepared the Athenians for what turned out to be an interim peace. The historian-general, nevertheless, was exiled, which he recorded without a hint of bitterness.

His Athenian connection was with the descendants of Marathon's hero, Miltiades. In Athens, then, Thucydides had imposing aristocratic connections. This relationship placed him in the class that before the age of Athenian imperial democracy filled the major positions in city life. Aristocracy, he believed, saved the imperial democracy of Periclean Athens from destructive folly, for under Pericles Athens was a principate, ruled by the aristocratic best citizen. Pericles had all the qualities a statesman should have: he perceived what was necessary, he could persuade the people, and he was patriotic enough to espouse the necessary course. Pericles sided with the democracy and expansionism that made Athenian power hated. For the ensuing and inevitable war, however, he proposed a policy of aristocratic moderation.

Oligarchies, Thucydides wrote, usually pursue modest policies at home and in external affairs. Since the interests of the few can be destroyed by the "popular" many, oligarchic governments usually avoided boat-rocking courses that might engulf their tenure of power.[2] They favored oligarchies elsewhere, not out of a passion for ideology, but because they had good reason to fear the dynamic course of democracies. Even in 411-410 B.C., when Athens had overreached itself and was facing defeat, Thucydides opted for the Periclean mixture of aristocratic and democratic rule, which surprisingly he found in the Constitution of the Five Thousand. More surprisingly he added that during its short lifetime Athens had had the best government he had ever known. It blended aristocracy and democracy and thus promoted the city's recovery from wretchedness. Not enough evidence survives to confirm or refute this judgment.

In the first book of the history, Thucydides presented his grounds for describing the war as the greatest enterprise of the Greeks, a greatness and defeat not to be celebrated but to be understood. The greatness of the war is established by materialist arguments which form his major political outlook. Ancient times, characterized by subsistence and poverty, could not have prepared any great expeditions, even though epic poets and romancers falsely depicted old wars in exaggerated proportions.

The Greek war against Troy amply demonstrated this: the war took so long because the Greeks could not amass supplies and provisions. State centralization, commerce, sea power, and money made possible vast expeditions. Not until the Persian wars, however, had large fleets and armed forces become possible.

Thucydides' objective, to describe the war and rival policies and actions accurately, was at odds with the desire to entertain (and with credulity). The recounter of the war queried each side in the war as well as the factions of a city. Research into events and policies was necessarily directed to speeches, the principal medium of public life and one peculiarly difficult to recapture with any precision. Thucydides' account of his procedure in this matter is problematic despite its apparent simplicity and common sense. In every case he sought to learn what was said, where possible the exact words. In all cases as well, he had the speaker present the general sense of the situation, "what the situation required" (*ta deonta*) (1.22:47).

Many of the speeches contain personal and particular allusions unlikely to have been invented by Thucydides. The speakers used arguments calculated to appeal to interest, fear, and honor as basic psychological motivations, and similar views of psychological motivation were common enough among Thucydides' contemporaries. The speakers argued on the grounds of likelihood and profit, as did the characters in contemporary tragedies. His version of the speeches, therefore, could have been given by contemporaries. When he claimed that he presented as far as he could the actual text of speeches, his assurance may be accepted, although we cannot know the extent of *as far as*. The central difficulty comes in determining the meaning of "what the situation required."

All the leaders speak of "what the situation required," but in life, as we know, men often mask their brutal egoisms in lofty words or fail to rise to the thoughts and words fitting to an occasion. As for Thucydides, his idea of "what the situation required" was dictated by a grim conception: man is moved by fear and interest; and when centralization, money, commerce, and empire help him make the breakthrough to a materially easier and secure society, man can also think in loftier terms of honor. But power and especially paramountcy attract the rivalry and suspicion of others who as jealously pursue their interest and as readily know fear. Dominance eventually must meet the challenge of war which provides a stern test to any people: a battle and, more likely, a campaign may frustrate human preparations and calculations. Men are thereby stripped of the civic and material props that may lift human character above competition, fear, and brutality. Human character, in words reminiscent of Thomas Hobbes, is reduced to the level of its circumstances. "What the situation required" is determined within the context of those views (3.82:242).

In this history—which, as Eric Voegelin has noted, he called "write-up"—men spoke from a Thucydidean script. The rival parties, being bound by solemn pledges of peace, were unwilling overtly to initiate war against each other. But each was ready to act in behalf of allegedly vital interests that might at the same time provoke the rival to active resistance. Eventually the rivals of Athens held a meeting at Sparta where the Corinthians pointedly emphasized that Sparta's slowness in reacting and caution about going to war put her allies at a disadvantage against the promptness and daring that often characterized Athenian response (1.68-71:73-77).

Each side had injured the other, and each had a multitude of complaints. When the Spartans yielded to the urging of their Corinthian and other allies, each side took up the religious and other complaints: Athenian alliance with Corcyra, a Corinthian colony; Athens' exclusion of Megara from Athenian Empire markets; and Spartan encouragement of defection in the Athenian Empire. Thucydides distinguished these complaints from the truest cause of the war, "and that the least talked about," the Lacedaemonian fear that Athens was becoming too powerful, for the largest part of Greece was subject to Athens. If the Greeks really talked little about the root cause, did not Thucydides have to supply a great part of "what the situation required" (1.24:49; 1.88:87)?

A section of book 1 described the origins and growth of the Athenian Empire, the power complex that Sparta felt compelled to diminish. Implicit in the Thucydidean analysis is the war's inevitability, but he presented a rather sanitized account of the role of Pericles in the coming of the war. In barring Megara from Athenian-controlled markets, did Pericles deliberately provoke a war that he believed inevitable? Thucydides made no mention of the financial corruption with which tireless Athenian gossip, the mark of community, and comic writers taxed Pericles' warmongering.[3] Instead we have the figure of an Olympian statesman deploying prestige and talents to persuade his fellow citizens that they must adopt and sustain his policy — that is, what he foresaw as necessary because of his understanding of "what the situation required." Imperial Athens should avoid land engagements, because her enemies were numerous and, in part, superior in land forces. Even if the Lacedaemonians were to invade Attica itself, the Athenians were counseled to withdraw into the city and allow the Lacedaemonian forces to waste their resources in devastation that could not gravely injure Athens. Athens could be the master of its fate if the Athenians avoided diversionary adventure and used their sea power against targets that might seriously affect the enemy's resources and will.

Book 2 reported the events of the first three years of the war. Thucydides dated the beginning, 431 B.C., by reference to established lists of priests and archons. He divided the year into summer and winter, time spans not at all equal because, for Thucydides as well as for the Greeks, the fighting season coincided roughly with the summer months including spring from the end of February and autumn till about November.[4]

The account of these few years brought in the main themes of the history. A Theban attack on Plataea revealed immediately the incalculable strains and desperate devices of the Greek world polarized in war: Pericles' Funeral Oration presented the speaker's idealization of what Athens was and could be, as it were, a Gettysburg Address by and for those who eventually lost the war; and the rapid decline under stress of Athenian character, a disintegration that was prefigured by the plague.

The attack on Plataea, an ally of Athens, was undertaken even before war broke out. Geopolitical and power considerations made the city a target. It commanded the principal road from Boeotia to the Peloponnesus, and its alliance with Athens outraged the agrarian oligarchy of Thebes, the leader of the Boeotian Confederacy's cities, all linked to Sparta. In order to control the road, Thebes plotted with some Plataeans, who arranged to admit at night a small Theban band which, if necessary, would be reinforced the following day by a major force.

Surprise initially gave the attackers success, but when the Thebans were discussing terms for the city, and the defeated saw how few the victors were, the Plataeans attempting a counterstroke killed or captured the Theban force. Athens counseled moderation but, as Athenian forces were not on the scene, the Thebans within the city were put to death. Thereupon the Thebans with Spartan reinforcements besieged Plataea (429 B.C.). The city surrendered in 427. The Spartans then followed with the inevitable reaction: they executed Plataea's male population and enslaved its women. No adequate help came from Athens, which had been gravely weakened by the plague.

On an earlier occasion a Corinthian speaker had enumerated the worst errors in warfare: stupidity, cowardice, and carelessness. At Plataea something else appeared, a sharpening of temper and the play of the unexpected. The calculating statesman, then, had to prepare for surprises and reverses, and he had to ready the minds and spirits of citizens to bear them, "for it is just as possible for the course of events to move perversely as for the plans of men" (Smith trans. 1.140:241).

Pericles appeared as the patriot and persuader in the oration (2.35-36:144-51) delivered, when the war was in winter quarters, at the funeral of Athenians who had fallen in the first year of the war. The speech has been read as a eulogy of the democratic form of government, but in its Athenian self-regard ("Happy, happy we") there is no brotherhood of mankind or even of Greeks. Pericles praised the imperial democracy of Athens and the training that brought eminence to the Athenians, their institutions, and the manner of life that made for Athenian greatness.

The Athenians trained for war but, unlike the Spartans, did not train as a way of life and to one end. Spartans were predictable and not at all versatile. The Athenians could know ease and yet display courage that was shaped by the city's way of life rather than by compulsion. The city was a democracy — that is, it was government by the many rather than the few — but Pericles was more emphatic about the equality of law and opportunity its citizens enjoyed, and even more emphatic about the prevailing competition in civic service and the individual excellence and wealth in private life. Instead of leveling, Athenian democracy released the talents of all citizens.

For such a city the soldiers had sacrificed their lives. What claims could Athens make on the rest of Greece? Two, assuredly: first, Athens was a model for the instruction of Greece, the claim of the benefactor; and second, the Athenians took the lead against the Persians. The preeminence so won was transformed into an empire but an empire remarkable in the contrast between its power and the light burdens it imposed.

The empire so conceived required a spirit of moderation to restrain its expansive energies and will. In the war, however, many found moderation irksome. The recklessness that was to doom the imperial city was foreshadowed in the discontent with the abandonment of the fields of Attica to Lacedaemonian invaders. To Athenian murmurings Pericles responded in a speech different from his earlier political pastoral. The devastation of Attica, he said, was exactly what had been expected. Citizens had suffered personal losses that were decidedly minor compared with the sea and land power of Athens that could be expected to make the losses good.

Pride in the unprecedented power of the imperial city was the new Periclean note. Athenian power, he now said, was a tyranny, conceivably wrong to have exercised but dangerous to give up (2.63:161). Willingly to yield a part of the empire would be disgraceful as well. The Athenians were hated, but in aiming at the highest empire they would be well advised to accept the odium inseparable from power. The Athenians accepted his arguments and in characteristic fashion fined and removed him from office. Shortly afterwards they reelected him as general.

Meanwhile Athens experienced a plague which, originating in Ethiopia, had spread to Egypt, the Persian Empire, and finally to Athens itself. Curiously, the affliction appears not to have penetrated the Peloponnesus. Thucydides described it as unprecedented in extent and destructiveness of lives, just as he judged the Peloponnesian War to be the greatest conflict of all time: he experienced the war and contracted the plague. In describing the disease's onset, fever and thirst, ulceration, and finally diarrhea, the doctors' unfamiliarity with it, their inability to treat it, and the despair of the afflicted, Thucydides

presented the plague as a paradigm of Greek society under the
strain of war. The plague, like the war, took the props of
decency away from men so that their character was reduced to
the level of their circumstances. The life of man rapidly
became, to borrow some of the words of Hobbes, "poor, nasty,
brutish," lacking both the decencies that custom prescribed and
the conveniences by which calculation made society tolerable.
Thucydides' own words are: "the violence of the attack being
in each case too great for human nature to endure" (Smith
translation, 2.50:347). "I myself shall merely describe what it
was like, and set down the symptoms, knowledge of which will
enable it to be recognized, if it should ever break out again"
(2.48:152). The plague was an ordeal, like the war: he came to
see the war as comparable to a disease. He described the symptoms, cause, and course of the war as well as those of the
plague. The method used was that of Hippocratic medicine.
The disease could be recognized, but the knowledge did not
permit the manipulation of nature and the avoidance of
catastrophe.[5]

Both sides were involved in the civic and moral deterioration
that in war became the disease of the Greek cities. Sparta
helped Thebes to exterminate Plataea. In a parallel case, that
of Mytilene on Lesbos, Athens for a moment revealed harshness that completely negated Pericles' boast that the Athenian
Empire was beneficent and light even in its burdens. The
Mytilenian oligarchs, believing that the plague had seriously
weakened Athens, procured Lacedaemonian assistance for an
attempt to free the island from Athenian overlordship. The
venture failed.

In Thucydides' narrative the popular leader Cleon urged the
extermination of the male population of Mytilene: to feel pity
and to be influenced by clever arguments and claims of decency
went against the interests of an imperial power (3.40:216).
Cleon won his case, but on the following day the Athenian
assembly reversed itself. From all the talk we are given only the
speech of Cleon and the case for sparing the rebels delivered by
Diodotus. The latter was not a speech for mercy. Diodotus
refused to challenge the justice of the verdict, and his appeals
were all to interest and calculation. The debate centered on the
rights of power and the value of moderation, which the mass

passions of Athens made a less likely course. The Athenian response was portentous because recklessness meant squandering the resources of a nearly incalculable power, one that could therefore afford to be more than selfish and less than harsh. But the political and moral disease affected all the warring parties.

Thucydides described this civic affliction after recounting a sequence of events in Corcyra. There the war made the party and class struggles ferocious, especially after several rapid turns of fortune ended with the victory of the democratic forces. Their prevailing meant the extermination of the oligarchic party, or so they thought, and acted accordingly. In Corcyra each side acted desperately, as do people without hope. Moderation and prudence were condemned as cowardice. The best test of loyalty was the espousal of extreme courses. As the war went on, oligarchic and democratic factions in each state were prepared to welcome or seek Athenian or Lacedaemonian intervention, and each party became more willing to intervene. (3.82-85:242-45).

In his ambition and quest for power, man had become a wolf to man. The center could not hold because each side silenced or killed off the moderate element. Thucydides saw the process affecting both oligarchies and democracies: each party rejected the restraints of justice or concern for a common good. But he is more emphatic about the democratic deterioration: "And indeed most people are more ready to call villainy cleverness than simple-mindedness honesty. They are proud of the first quality and ashamed of the second" (3.82:243).

If the Athenians were hard to defeat, they behaved, Thucydides thought, unworthily in victory. Their arrogance was manifest when they gained a notable advantage at Pylos and Sphacteria. The former is a peninsula that the Athenian general Demosthenes occupied. From it the Spartan lands could be attacked, and, even more important, the helots could be encouraged to rebel. The Spartans, therefore, strenuously sought to nullify the Athenian gain. After a long siege of Spartan forces on the island of Sphacteria, adjacent to Pylos, a siege in which Cleon played a major role, there came the stunning surrender of the heavy-armed Spartan troops. Athens then had hostages for whom Sparta was prepared to pay a high price.[6] The Spartan initiative for peace was rejected through the influence of Cleon, who played the role of expansionist war hawk, the anti-Pericles, dialectic opposite of reason and moderation, a principal carrier of the Corcyraean disease to Athens.

The year 424 B.C. saw the unfolding of unsuccessful Athenian imperialist efforts in Megara and Boeotia. Then the Spartan commander Brasidas captured Amphipolis and withstood an attempted recapture. Amphipolis and the other failures gave Athens an incentive to seek peace. Truce was made in 423 B.C., and the peace of Nicias, a recognition of stalemate and therefore a restoration of the prewar situation, was negotiated in 421. Amphipolis had marked the death of the war prosecutors, Brasidas and Cleon.

Thucydides explained that Cleon wanted war because it gave him leadership whereas peace would reveal his villainies and render his calumnies implausible. If this seems difficult to credit, Thucydides attributed willingness to seek peace to personal motives, in this case moderate and praiseworthy. The Spartan Pleistoanax, who in days of reverses was blamed for tricking the Spartans into allowing his return, thought that peace, a time of no reverses, would free him from the constant threat of spitefulness and calumny. The Athenian Nicias, likewise, wanted to get out of a boat endlessly rocking. So far, his record had been free of disaster. The longer a run of good fortune, the more likely it was to end in proportionate adversity. Nicias no longer wanted to tempt fortune and sought quiet for his fellow citizens as a means of assuring security and reputation for himself.

These events and considerations are presented in book 5 up to section 25, which appears to have been the conclusion of the history that Thucydides put together a couple of years after the Peace of Nicias and a fifty-year alliance of the warring parties. He resumed the history with a sentence about writing up the events from the armistice to the end of the Athenian Empire. Before the peace, the future had already appeared in the Corcyraean paradigm as well as in Athenian engagement in Sicily against the dominance of Syracuse. For about seven years a dubious peace prevailed, but only an erring judgment would "consider the interval of the agreement as anything else except a period of war" (5.25). It was at best a peace of bad faith, for neither party implemented its terms, and each continued to inflict on the other as much damage as possible. The war's periods add up to twenty-seven years (5.26:364).

Both the weakening of the protagonists, who had thereby been induced to make peace, and the peace itself, in lessening for some states the necessities of alliance, meant that politics became more fluid. Some old contests were resolved: Athenians finally captured Scione, massacred its male inhabitants, sold the women and children into slavery, and gave its land to the remnants of the Plataeans. This horror is a small operation mentioned but briefly by Thucydides.

The war itself acquired momentum in the Peloponnesus. There the young Athenian leader Alcibiades favored an alliance with Argos, Elis, Mantinaea, and, at one moment, Corinth against Sparta. This bellicose policy, from which Nicias and the Spartans sought to dissuade the Athenians, collapsed before the solidity of Spartan discipline at the battle of Mantinaea (418 B.C.).

This collapse is the prelude to the gigantic Athenian expedition against Syracuse. In the prelude the tactics and diplomacy of Alcibiades had revealed a trickiness, attributed to very personal motives, that excelled the wiles of Themistocles. Meanwhile, before the armada was projected and in consequence of their failure in the Peloponnesus, the Athenians sent forces against a Dorian colony, the island of Melos, which had remained neutral in the war. The Melian action was a display of power. When the Athenian generals approached the Melian rulers, the latter did not call a general assembly; the few, the oligarchy, discussed surrender almost intimately with the Athenians. The Athenians ironically noted the situation and presumed that the Melian leaders were fearful that Athenian reasoning would prevail with the populace. They therefore proposed that, in place of a long, argumentative speech followed by a lengthy rebuttal, the Melians reply to each argument as the Athenians advanced it.

The dialogue was presented as the idea of the Athenians. It is an expression of pure reason of state. The Melians were ironic about the instructiveness of a debate, which, if they should win, would mean war, and if the Athenians should persuade them, would mean Melian servitude. The Athenians, limiting themselves to the obviousness of their superiority in force, excluded niceties about the rightness of Athenian empire or Athenian retaliation against Melian offenses and simply described justice as a matter involving equals. Because the Melians and Athenians were not equals, the governing rule was that "the strong do what they have the power to do and the weak accept what they have to accept" (5.84-116:400-8; quotation, 402).

The dialogue is so spare, pointed, and universal in significance that it could be from Euripidean tragedy or from a poet-philosopher's dialogue on power. Could any historical actors speak so to the point, if their words were not the work of an artist? Is this not the clearest case that "what the situation required" was dictated by the vision of a writer who, while attempting a scientific account of political pathology, was driven to the form and vision of tragedy, although he never adequately came to terms with the compulsion?

The dilemma of the weak before the strong remains, intensified by the advent of Christianity — "the meek shall inherit the earth" — and confused in modern times by the pejorative label of imperialism. In the dialogue the Melians, noting that the Athenians in their strength had excluded appeals to justice, were driven to argue that advantage for the Athenians coincided with the Melians' interest in their own neutrality. If the Athenians should crush Melos because of its neutrality, and thereby should rouse other neutrals to fear a similar fate, would not Athens be widening the war by increasing the number of its enemies?

The Melian condition, the Athenians argued, afforded no basis for hope. They would have to recognize that the Lacedaemonians were slow to take risks. As to their professed expectation of good fortune or divine favor, the Melians comforted themselves groundlessly, for the Athenians insisted that their proposed action violated neither divine requirements about human behavior nor divine self-interest. Among men, those who have power necessarily ruled, and the Athenians believed that the same law applied to the gods. Rule was not an Athenian invention, but they used it just as the Melians would use it, if roles were reversed. The Melians' character, in effect, should respond to the extremity of their circumstance by ignoring justice and honor and concentrating on self-interest, that is, survival. The Athenians asked that they be spared the execution of the law upon the Melians, who were warned that for them the greatest folly would be to resist out of fear of disgrace. Action so prompted would surely end in greater disgrace.

The Athenians won the dialogue because the Melians never argued that, if they should surrender, they could not live with themselves. The men were massacred and their wives and children were enslaved. Athenian colonists soon came to replace the Melians. Over their bones could be blazoned the earlier Athenian reproach that the Melians were unique "in your ability to consider the future as something more certain than what is before your eyes, and to see uncertainties as realities" (5.113:407). Hope was either irrelevant or a cardinal sin.

In 416 B.C. the Athenians voted to send an expedition against Sicily. In their ignorance, we are told, they did not know that the Sicilian enemy commanded resources comparable to the war potential of the Peloponnesians. The Athenians expected to conquer all of Sicily, although they speciously claimed to be aiding their kinfolk and allies, the citizens of Egesta. The latter principally urged on the Athenian effort in order to gain assistance against the Selinuntians who had secured the Syracusans as allies. It was argued that the Syracusans, if unchecked, would control all Sicily and, in joining forces with their fellow Dorians of the Peloponnesus, might topple Athens. Lest Athenian power calculations, as well as greed, be thought to be in decline, the Egestaeans had tricked their allies into believing Egestaean wealth to be more than sufficient to cover their pledge to pay the expedition's costs. At Athens the assembly voted to send sixty ships to aid the Egestaeans and then the city of Leontini, and to establish the best conditions in Sicily for the Athenians.

At a later assembly the elected but unwilling co-commander of the expedition, Nicias, vainly argued the folly of seeking to create a distant and inevitably rebellious empire while war threatened in Greece itself and there were unpunished rebels in the original Athenian Empire. Finding his counsel unheeded, he called for and received ships, men, and supplies on a scale that seemed to secure against disastrous chance the promise of victory.

The departure of such an expedition might have inspired an epic poet to catalogue the men and ships. For Thucydides it was a comparable civic occasion. The young were restless, while parting friends and relatives were silent in anxiety, though some wept. The expedition was the largest ever sent out from a Greek city. Reality had eclipsed romance. Thucydides contrasted the feelings of the Athenians with those of the foreigners in Athens and the people in the rest of Greece. The foreigners observed the expedition's departure to admire the spectacle and to marvel at the ambition that inspired it. At the time, the rest of Greece thought less of the goal of the armament than of the armament as a demonstration of Athenian power and greatness. The Athenians (Thucydides used their word of reproach against the Melians) had "hopes for the future which, when compared with the present position, were of the most far-reaching kind" (6.30-31:428-29).

And already Athenian folly had jeopardized the expedition's chances. Nicias' colleague in command, Alcibiades, a near veteran golden boy, inevitable and sometimes brilliant enemy of calculating moderation and discretion, intensified the suspicions with which fellow citizens recognized his high abilities and ambitions. At this time the suspicions involved an oligarchic plot, desecration of votive statues, and parodying the Eleusinian mysteries. He was not tried forthwith as he and sense demanded. His enemies, some hoping to act when he was absent, publicly decided to defer trial until the general's return. This, in Thucydides' judgment, doomed the ill-advised campaign.

At Syracuse the speakers presented statements contrapuntal to those of the Athenian leaders. Hermocrates, eventually the successful leader of Syracusan resistance, emphasized the news of Athens' venture because he had to allow for his fellow citizens' unwillingness to believe that the Athenians would undertake an operation on the Persian scale. Large expeditions dispatched to distant objectives, he affirmed, rarely had success, and Syracusans could hope that in repelling Athens, their city, like Athens upon the repulse of Persia, would rise to dominance. Athenagoras, described as a power with the people, spoke with all the simplist rationality of a demagogue: the threat from Athens was talk to cover oligarchic plotters against the people. The clever Athenians would certainly not leave their homeland with enemies unsubdued to take on another war and another empire.

The Athenians had done so and soon summoned Alcibiades to stand trial at Athens. He then became war consultant to Athens' enemies in Sparta, with whom he took refuge. The theme of disaster is *sostenuto*, for upon arrival in Sicily the Athenian leaders lost momentum by failing to attack Syracuse, and their resolution was shaken when they learned that Egesta was no wealthier than any other city. The delay correspondingly cheered the Syracusans.

Belatedly the Athenians launched a winter attack on Syracuse. With a battle impending, Nicias addressed his troops in words that possibly no other artist could have drafted. For the prospect of victory he invoked the many Greek peoples who formed his great host. The latter should draw resolution from the fact that they were in an unfriendly land. For them the decisive argument was the reverse of the Syracusan cry "defend their country": "the struggle in front of us is for a country which is not ours, and . . . unless we win, we shall not find it easy to get away" (6.68.452). The combination of realism and concern with safety through moderation, which had gained Nicias high repute, made him unfit for the daring enterprise he commanded.

The Athenian attack was resumed in the summer (414 B.C.). As Syracuse is on a promontory that shelters its harbor, the city was particularly vulnerable to being cut off by the walls that the Athenians had begun to build. During this attack, siege positions were reversed. By an irony that sometimes denied the comfort of fatalism to the defeated, the Syracusan assembly was debating a cessation of the war when the first of the Peloponnesian reinforcements reached Syracuse and put an end to such deliberations. More ships soon arrived, as did Peloponnesian land forces and Sicilian allies. The surrounding wall attempted by the Athenians was nullified by a Syracusan counterwall so that, as Nicias explained to the Athenians, the besiegers had become the besieged. The morale of his fleet had declined, and the Syracusan advantage in cavalry restricted his

action. By messengers and letter Nicias therefore asked the
Athenians to relieve him of command because of ill health and
to provide reinforcements on the lavish scale of the original expedition. Nicias insisted that Athenian forces and leaders had
been adequate to their original task, but at the time of writing
a coalition of all Sicily menaced the Athenians, who also expected presently to face Peloponnesian reinforcements. The letter, we are told, was to make sure that the Athenian assembly
got the message. Nicias feared that the possibly bad memory,
guile, or lack of courage of his messengers would distort an oral
report. Again the Athenians responded with ships and men on
a scale comparable to their original expedition.

The war's hurt came closer to the Athenians when, on the advice of Alcibiades, their enemies built a permanent fort at
Decelaea, some twelve miles from Athens. The enemy post interrupted almost all supplies by land to Athens, providing a
place of refuge for runaway slaves and instilling so many fears
of attack that Athens, in turn, became a garrison. The Syracusans, meanwhile, in bold and ingenious resistance, successfully withstood Athenian attacks only to fear Athens as a
wonder-city when the new Athenian forces under Demosthenes
arrived to nullify the impact of Athenian reverses. Demosthenes, seeking to avoid Nicias' error, engaged the Syracusans
and was defeated. Thereupon he urged a return home, while
the Athenians were still strong enough to prevail against the
enemy who had taken positions in Attica.

Nicias opposed such decisiveness, not out of boldness but out
of a surface optimism in the service of an immobilizing fear.
Principally, Nicias dreaded the vengeful reward of his city to
a failed leader, preferring to die as a soldier, if nothing better
turned up. If this is tragedy, it is without *hybris*. In history and
politics, as Thucydides knew, even the moderate, the safe-
playing innocent, may be destroyed.

Even Nicias' piety contributed to ruin. When additional
Peloponnesian forces joined the enemy, he agreed that the
Athenians should leave Syracuse. On the eve of departure an
eclipse of the full moon disturbed the soldiers and caused Nicias
to wait out the twenty-seven days that the prodigy required. A
full-scale battle in the harbor followed, and again the Athe-

nians were defeated. Afterwards the Syracusans blocked the
harbor entrance with sunken hulks.

Before the final sea battle the respective commanders addressed their forces. Readers, as though they are a theater audience, are briefed by the actors. To the allies Nicias recalled
that victory meant that they would see their home cities again;
as for the Athenians, they could define their fate in terms of
their own original intentions toward Sicily and should recall
that they were, in effect, all that Athens had. They were its
navy, its army, the name of Athens, and what was left of the
state (7.64:519). The Spartan general Gylippus contrasted the
Athenians, beaten at sea and dispirited, with the confident
Syracusans and their allies: they should relentlessly go in for the
kill of an enemy who would have enslaved them.

The Athenian forces, the navy and then the army, were
defeated. Syracusan harshness increased with the victors' success. The doleful Nicias, once peacemaker with Sparta, surrendered to the Spartan Gylippus, hoping that all would not be
lost. For his part, the Spartan would have gloried in bringing
the Athenian commander to his garrison city. Some Corinthians, however, feared that Nicias might yet harm their city,
and some pro-Athenian Syracusans feared that under torture
Nicias would talk. He was therefore executed, "a man who, of
all the Hellenes in my time, least deserved to come to so
miserable an end, since the whole of his life had been devoted
to the study and practice of virtue" (7.86:536). The fate of
enterprising and arrogant Athens destroyed even a paragon of
moderation, scrupulous to the point of excess about outraging
fortune. For him irony, indifferent to the reward of virtue,
prepared the precise role of the wrong man, by his moderation
the architect of the failure of his city's arrogant enterprise.

The captives, about seven thousand out of some forty thousand, were imprisoned in a Sicilian quarry where, subject to
cold at night and intense sun by day, they died. This was the
greatest event of the war and, in fact, of Greek history — "to the
victors the most brilliant of success, to the vanquished the most
calamitous of defeats; for they were utterly and entirely
defeated; their sufferings were on an enormous scale; their
losses were, as they say, total; army, navy, everything was

destroyed, and, out of many, only few returned" (7.87:537).[7]

When news of the failure in Sicily reached Athens, the first reaction was incredulity followed by panic fears that the victors in Sicily and Athens' adversaries in Greece would immediately descend upon Athens, where they were certain to be abetted by the Athenian Empire on the brink of rebellion. The worst did not happen. Athens again raised forces for resistance, and the democracy in its panic was ready to "put everything in order" (8.1:539). Against it was a hostile force including Sparta, Alcibiades, and the Persians, a trio that could properly be look-ed for amidst the unexpected developments of war, however it might outrage sense and decency.

The play of fortune stalking the ultimate pages of the un-finished history is failure of reason. Reason could not make events meaningful, although it would not have occurred to Thucydides to complain of history's meaninglessness. The play of chance is striking in the case of the people of Chios, who mistakenly judged the time for joining the enemies of Athens. Apart from the Spartans, Thucydides judged that the Chians were the only people to be wise in prosperity and in their time of greatness to provide for their security. "And if they were thrown out by one of the surprises which upset human calcula-tions, they found out their mistake in company with many others who believed, like them, in the speedy collapse of the Athenian power" (8.24:551).

So much for the design and content of Thucydides' work: intellectually powerful, unforgettable, and characteristically Greek in exceeding the limits of history. He used history to meet needs presented to him by Greek culture and his eminently Grecian mind. The point must be made insistently because a more than century-old tradition has described Thucydides as the father of scientific and critical history, as an ur-Ranke.

His capacity for critical penetration is evident in the account of early Greece, in the story of Harmodius and Aristogeiton, and even in the discussion of the years from Salamis to the Peloponnesian War. But his sharp mind had little interest in the small-time and pretentious heroics of earlier and benighted ages. Ancient critics complained that his work lacked variety. This is fair enough, because his attention was riveted upon his own time, an age of breakthrough for the economy, the city, and the character of its citizens, and for the mind in understanding the making of policy.

Thucydides presented a war, its origins and course, explained with intellectual power and artistic propriety. It is nevertheless proper to ask what kind of history it is and what its limits are as a true history. Thucydides did not unequivocally describe his work as inquiries, researches. Instead, he professed to be "writing up" the war between the Peloponnesians and the Athenians. Like Herodotus and, since then, the long, though often interrupted line of Ocdipean historians, he claimed decisive superiority for his work; and for Thucydides this meant that he used scientific analysis which his actors and their speeches illustrate in forming part of "a possession forever."

In a sense, Thucydides anticipated Aristotle's criticism of history as lacking the general philosophical significance to be found even in poetry, for Thucydides sought to present the war as an analysis of an ordeal of politics and character under plague, revolution, and disintegration. Fifth-century Greece had found a new plateau of group living, challenge, and understanding, but the last revealed man's limits: he is motivated by interest, fear, and honor, and his character is determined by the level of his circumstances. Man so conceived, at any rate imperially democratic man, cannot sustain the ordeal of war without losing the saving grace of balance and moderation. The moderation and foresight of Pericles, Thucydides observed, became clearer after his death. Could Pericles, if he had lived through the war, have averted catastrophe? The question was not answered, and the point is that Pericles died, leaving the conduct of the war to politicians, not commanding the first position, but struggling for it. As they were inferior to Pericles, they resorted to demagogic means and mistaken ventures. But it was Athenian in-fighting that accumulated mistakes into self-destruction. Thucydides brooded on this suicide, and in a celebrated passage that blamed inadequate Athenian support for the failure in Sicily, he went against his own analysis. Nevertheless, the subsequent catalogue of what went wrong after Sicily is impressive (2.65:163-64).

The History of the Peloponnesian War presented this
analysis, and its extraordinary unity was wrought by the selection of incident and, where necessary, the composition of
speeches. No historian of comparable stature has had so much
freedom to write his own scenario. The invention of speeches,
appropriate to each occasion in a way loose-ended history rarely allows, helps to explain the power of Thucydides' work.
Without philosophy and philosophical criticism, history is im-
poverished; but it is also destroyed when it is made a
philosophy or science. In seeking to make history more than
itself, Thucydides made it less as history, that is, as a humanity.

The composition of speeches — like his limitation of history to
war — was a baleful legacy to later historians who could not
make men speak so pointedly. His dialogues on interest and
power are stark and wearing: they sear and then numb because
in their constriction they first impress as satisfactory explanations and then finally leave us with a sense of inadequacy and
hopelessness. Rarely in historical writing have power considerations been so sternly isolated and presented in one narrative. Throughout the twentieth century, Thucydides' readers
have regularly noted parallels to the events of their year or
decade. Although his science has not won its way as science,
readers have found that the history or something like it has happened again and again.

The work is "a possession forever" not because it is history,
although it is the principal source for the Peloponnesian War.
Thucydides was concerned with what happened, but not for
the primary sake of factual truth and narrative, although he
was notably accurate about dates and the texts of decrees and
treaties. He was a political scientist concerned with policy,
power, war, and civic degeneration.

The speeches provided the proof, and Thucydides' defense of
his method supplied the key. The speeches were designed to
reveal the disturbance, the progress of the illness of intercity
nonheroic war in Greece. They did so effectively with an apt-
ness that only art, and not what actually was said, allows. The
speaker presented "what the situation required," and the situation required the revelation of the disease's progress. Is it likely
that Pericles spoke so comprehensively — and aptly for the
historian's vision — in the Funeral Oration? Or that the Corin-

thians would have so neatly given a similar account of the Athenians? The pithiness of the Melian dialogue is unique. Not even Shakespeare in his different way created anything more right and moving than Thucydides in the last speeches of Nicias. It is not likely that Thucydides could have heard verbatim reports of them.

The motivation of his characters is as true as we are, by no means, always as selfish and evil as we can be. Oligarchy may add a kind of check and balance of the passions. Yet Thucydides, especially in his account of the plague, suggested that knowledge, in this case knowledge through suffering, could lead to a higher form of behavior.

Against the grimness of selfishness and power we may summon the figure of Christ, in some measure those who always inadequately seek to imitate him, the biblical prophets, the image of the Compassionate Buddha, and perhaps the teachings of Gandhi. The summoning can dispel the sense of hopelessness issuing from an analysis that leaves us one with human character reduced to the level of its circumstances.

Thucydides expressed the basic dilemmas of power politics. In spite of the oratory of Pericles, most of Greece, Thucydides wrote, favored the Spartan side because it professed to stand for the liberation of Greece, that is, the autonomy of each state (2.8:129). The two and one-half millennia since he composed the history have merely added a bleak patina to a bleak book. As W. H. Auden wrote, "If what is to happen occurs according to what Thucydides defined as 'human,' we've had it."[8]

4. Tacitus:
The Mind of the Moralist Historian

CITIES AND EMPIRE ARE the themes of Greek and Roman political history. The Greek cities defeated the Persian Empire, later defeated the dominant city Athens, which had organized some of the Greek states into an empire, and still later were brought into Alexander's and then Rome's empires. The latter, for some centuries, was not acknowledged by its own creators, who would not adapt the government of their city republic to the requirements of the empire. So it was that the first imperial Roman centuries marked the ordeal of the Republic.

The empire also retained the moralizing of republican Rome. Historians were expected to teach morality, and in the main they were honest enough to record much to condemn. In fact, no Roman historian except the scholar-propagandist Livy would have described his own age as the best of times and the worst of times. Imperial pagan Romans were too morally pessimistic about history to be able to say more than what Tacitus in effect said of the age of Trajan: it was the best of the worst times.[1] His patriotism in no way encouraged him to say yes to his age, as Livy and the poet Vergil had done to theirs. Instead it strengthened the moral severity with which he passed judgment on men of an iron age.

Tacitus, a Gallic Roman provincial, who accordingly had the piety of a Roman, wrote histories with the classic power of illuminating and expanding our own experience. The Roman world had changed profoundly in his lifetime (A.D. 55-117) and in the preceding century. The change transformed Roman institutions and social classes as well as civic roles and character. The ordeal of transition from republic to empire, or better, the

50

years of this transition that he chose to describe, abounded in horrors, crimes, and periods of terror.

Experience, rather than his studies, had compelled Tacitus to develop a philosophy of survival. To teach survival, nevertheless, would not have been adequate for the grand moral function of Roman historical writing. Nor was Roman Senator Tacitus tempted to abandon republican and senatorial standards, the criteria by which he judged the formative period of his new age. He was caught between two worlds, the imperial world of his maturity, in which he developed his philosophy of survival while continuing to serve Rome, and the Republic, with its aristocratic code of behavior and a political philosophy that questioned the durability of a beneficent empire.

To live somehow in two worlds, the ordeal of transition, is the task of modern man, and of men in all periods of change. As Tacitus enacted it, the role was dramatic, even wounding, in tensions and contradictions. If his values were out of joint with the times, he served the latter without surrendering his conscience. Like all Roman moralists he did not readily accept change and was, therefore, predisposed to harshness. This harshness he shared with the searingly savage Sallust. But Sallust's life indicates that he was a bounder, whereas Tacitus, for all his snobbery and complicity of silence before the crimes of despots, was at least a decent man and a moralist of integrity.

Cornelius Tacitus was born around A.D. 55, probably in the south of France. His biography may be briefly told; he was reticent about himself, and his friends and other ancient authors provide little more. An education in rhetoric and early success, including marriage in A.D. 78 to the daughter of Gnaeus Julius Agricola, indicate that his family had substantial means. His outlook was aristocratic. Common men were mainly objects of contempt in his works and usually appeared as the mob or mutinous soldiers. They were, of course, not his main concern, which was with exemplary or shameful deeds of powerful men. The whips of his criticism, therefore, flailed emperors and the members of his order, the Senate, who figured as self-servers and flatterers of despots. Tacitus had the proud rigor of the successful provincial; he, his family, and friends were not new to

Roman service, but they were relative newcomers to the
Roman Senate.

He became an orator and advocate. His career began under
Vespasian (A.D. 69-79) and Titus (A.D. 79-81) and was advanced under Domitian (A.D. 81-96). In Vespasian's reign he
served as a financial officer, a quaestor, in the provinces and
probably as the officer of a legion. Under Domitian he was a
praetor, holding an administrative post that usually led a
senator to a provincial governorship and the consulate, which
he held in A.D. 97. Between A.D. 89 and 93, when he was away
from Rome, he may have commanded a Roman legion. A letter
of Pliny the Younger (A.D. 100) mentioned that he and Tacitus
won acclaim for their case against Marius Priscus on behalf of
the people the latter had misgoverned in Africa. About A.D. 112
he held the lucrative governorship of Western Asia Minor.

The Asian proconsulate was the climax of a career that had
already abandoned political advocacy, become meaningless
under the empire, and had turned to literature, in Tacitus'
case, history. The choice of a new vocation was suggested in the
Dialogue on Oratory, which he did not publish until A.D. 102.
The work was dedicated to Fabius Justus, a consul in that year.
In it Tacitus professed to present a conversation he had heard
while quite young (A.D. 74-75).[2] The *Dialogue* proposed to
answer a friend's question: Why did former times have many
great orators, and their own age few?

The discussion began with Marcus Aper upbraiding Maternus, a poet and his host, for devoting himself to poetry, thereby
wasting his great oratorical talents. Exaggerating in the manner of an advocate, Aper claimed that oratory was useful to the
republic as well as for winning fame, influence, the capacity to
help friends, and wealth. Poetry he dismissed as a private and
unrewarding pursuit driving its undignified devotees to solitary
lives in the woods. Subsequently, he scorned any estimate of
modern orators as inferior to those of the past, and supported
his point by describing the devices and tricks of earlier orators
that his own age would simply not accept.

Vipstanus Messala then bound himself to explain the decline
of oratory during the sixscore years following Cicero's death.
When he advanced evidence of decline, Maternus reminded
him that he was not to lead to the conclusion that the ancients
were superior. That was to be taken as an established fact

which he was asked to explain with old-fashioned candor. So charged, Messala enumerated changes in Roman customs and education: the young were no longer trained and educated by their parents but by a maidservant, probably an illiterate and frivolous Greek, and a male slave; later they were entrusted to teachers who flattered them; finally they were instructed by rhetorical technicians instead of learning civil law, philosophy, and the capacity to make emotional and moral distinctions. In this last stage the old practice of observing great orators and advocates, when they argued cases actually in process, gave place to displays of virtuosity by men with nothing to say.

Maternus was not satisfied. Why, he asked, were we no longer motivated to efforts comparable to those of the past? Because there were no great matters to be affected by oratory when, as under the emperors, "political questions are decided not by an ignorant multitude, but by one man of preeminent wisdom." A well-ordered and law-abiding society no more needed orators than an always healthy people needed doctors.

This historical explanation, so problematic for the politics of Tacitus, enabled Maternus to assure his eloquent friends that in earlier centuries they would have commanded the highest eloquence. Oratory, so ran the argument, flourished in times of trouble, for example, in fourth-century Athens and in the great commotions of the Republic: "the great and famous eloquence of old is the nursling of the licence which fools called freedom." Since the divine Augustus had pacified the Roman world and eloquence as well, Maternus concluded with an injunction to cultivate one's garden as the times allow: "seeing that no one can at the same time enjoy great renown and great tranquillity, let everybody make the best of the blessings of his own age without disparaging other periods" (*Dialogue* 40-41:768-69).

Maternus then presented the point of the *Dialogue* and, accordingly, the views of the future historian Tacitus, who had given up advocacy for writing history and was, like Maternus, in the Roman view engaged in a form of poetry. But this withdrawal from oratory meant no neglect of civic duty, because for the Romans history was, above all, cautionary, moral, and civic.

His subject was the out-of-joint time between Nero and Domitian, whose successors "blended things once irreconcilable, the principate and freedom." The history would be a

testimony to the "present happiness" prevailing after Domitian's reign, when "we should have lost memory as well as
voice, had it been as easy to forget as to keep silence." That last
period (A.D. 81-96) saw many die of ordinary casualties and the
ablest fall to the emperor's rage. Some survived, but they have
"lost these many years which brought the young in . . . silence
to old age, and the old almost to the verge and end of existence!" (*Agricola* 2, 3:678).

Shortly after Domitian's murder, Tacitus, as consul, had
delivered a panegyric on Verginius Rufus, a duty which may
have inspired him to write a tribute to his father-in-law, who
had died before Nerva relieved Rome of paralyzing fears. In the
preceding reign, panegyrics of some great men had been made
capital crimes and burned, as though "in that fire the voice of
the Roman people, the freedom of the Senate, and the conscience of the human race were perishing. . . . So true is it that
merit is best appreciated by the age in which it thrives most
easily" (*Agricola* 1, 2:677).

Tacitus professed to find the task of praising Agricola difficult. If he had merely to indict the evils of such an age, he
would not have had to crave his readers' indulgence as he did
because of his lack of experience in praising a man who served
that state in a dark time.

Agricola's victories and governance in Britain won him glory
that attracted the envious fear of Domitian. For survival,
Agricola's many virtues required something additional, a
discretion and a moderation that allayed the rivalries of his
equals and superiors and tempered the passions of his imperial
Lord and God, a title the emperor preferred. Tacitus presented
Agricola as a model of the new Roman bureaucrat, schooled in
moderation early at Marseilles, "where refinement and provincial frugality were blended." Later his mother taught him to
restrain his love of philosophy in order to conform to Roman
anti-intellectualism (*Agricola* 4:679).

This worked. Agricola, who died in A.D. 93, was like his
panegyrist neither a martyr nor a suicide. And he retained his
integrity:

> Let it be known to those whose habit it is to admire the disregard
> of authority, that there may be great men even under bad

emperors, and that obedience and submission, when joined to activity and vigor, may attain a glory which most reach only by a perilous career, utterly useless to the state, and closed by an ostentatious death.

Agricola was spared the worst scenes of Domitian's reign when, because the guilt was universal, "our hands dragged Helvidius to prison" and "we were steeped in Senecio's innocent blood" (*Agricola* 42, 44-46:703, 705).

In the same period when Tacitus wrote *Agricola*, he also wrote a treatise on Germany that has had a curious history. Since the Renaissance, for example, some German nationalists have found it an inspiring scripture. Its title, *On the Origins, Geography, Institutions and Tribes of the Germans*, adequately summarized an ethnographic work. The occasion for writing was Trajan's campaign against the Germans, a return to Roman expansionism, and thus a reversal of what Tacitus regarded as the contemptible policy of the later Augustus and Tiberius.

The essay was largely a reworking of former writings, particularly the Elder Pliny's book on the German wars, and in some matters Tacitus failed to update his sources. The Germans won his commendation for their freedom even where they had kings, their chastity, their rearing of children, their preference for fighting with their women and infants nearby as reminders of the battle's stakes, their lack of "natural or acquired cunning" — which tells us something about Tacitus and the Romans — and the simplicity of their economy, although the Romans had "taught them to accept money also" (*Germania* 22, 15:720, 716).

"No one in Germany laughs at vice" or thought corruption fashionable (*Germania* 19:718). The Germans were free of the vices of sophistication and cities. They were nonetheless barbarians, indolent, slothful, excessive drinkers, in the main wanting in directed intelligence. Like all barbarians, they could not withstand unexpected trials and were fit only for sudden exertions, not for sustained labor.

Their customs might perhaps inspire Romans to return to their own earlier austerity and rigor, but the reversion was more desirable than likely, because the Roman world, secure

under one rule, was exposed to the temptations to "sloth of prolonged peace and repose." As the Germans were a fighting
race, Tacitus prayed that they would continue to hate each
other, because fortune could give imperial Rome no greater
boon than the discord of her enemies (*Germania* 14, 33:716,
725).

At various times Tacitus proposed four historical works in
all: the *Histories*, from January 1, A.D. 69, to the death of
Domitian; a later treatment of the happy times of Nerva and
Trajan; the *Annals*, covering the period from the accession of
Tiberius to the death of Nero, A.D. 14-68; and an account of the
reign of Augustus. Two were not written, and the major works
survive only in part. The *Histories'* author, who believed that
chance ruled or disarrayed many human plans, owed the survival of this classic, four books and part of a fifth (of fourteen),
to a copy made at Monte Cassino in the eleventh century. The
first six books of the *Annals* survived in a single copy made in
a Saxon monastery. Books 11 to 16 were with the Monte
Cassino manuscript of the *Histories*. The rest have disappeared.

The *Histories* began with three prefatory paragraphs of
masterful terseness with a flawed last sentence. Of the days of
the Roman Republic, when there was a *res publica*, a public
thing, to discuss, many historians had written with eloquence
and freedom. The later life of the Republic was full of commotions concluded by the one-man rule that issued from the Battle
of Actium (31 B.C.). Thereafter historical writing changed.
Under one-man rule, first of all, many men simply did not
know what was done or why. The same subjection impaired
historical faith, because men publicly flattered their rulers and
privately often vilified them. Later, flattery could be readily
recognized or suspected, but — and here we have self-
knowledge that did not help Tacitus — detraction and malice,
because they seem to betoken independence and integrity, are
the more easily credited and thereby distort the record.
Tacitus, then, presented himself in the character of a man
without anger or partisanship; his advances took place under
the emperors whose reigns he recorded. He had no narrow personal cause for a vendetta against them. He used the same point
when he described the strange political deliberations in Alexan-
dria about whether Vespasian should attempt to heal a blind

man and a man with a withered hand. Vespasian yielded and, believing that with his good fortune everything was possible, healed the afflicted twosome. The imperial miracles, Tacitus wrote, reaching for credibility, were attested by eyewitnesses, "even now when nothing is to be gained by falsehood" (*Hist.* 4.81).

For a Roman moralist and patriot, vocations scarcely separable, this historical enterprise was fearsome: a time of wars, civil strife, the killing of four emperors, the burning of the capital, the profanation of sacred rites, the sea crowded with exiles, and nobility victimized by informers or destroyed by enemies or friends. Portents and prodigies cosmically paralleled the civic disorder. Not all was moral squalor, however, because there were instances of loyalty in families and among servants. Then Tacitus indulged his bent for the denigrating climax, this time at the expense not of men but of the pantheon: Rome's calamities proved that the gods think not of our happiness but only of our punishment. If this is true, if all is divinely and malignly ordained, what is the use of moral historical writing? For Tacitus, as well as his contemporaries, an answer would not admit contradiction and confusion but would point to the Greek levity of logic. Indeed, the remark itself may be taken as Tacitean pity for mankind.

The year of four emperors, A.D. 69, witnessed the breakdown of the Principate, the achievement of Augustus. The latter had routed and destroyed his rivals and on that military base held the position of command, *imperator*. With his own wealth and the revenues of Egypt he supported the people of Rome. The fate of his assassinated uncle, Julius Caesar, warned him against monarchy. Augustus, therefore, cooperating with the Senate and Roman magistrates, presented himself as *princeps*, first citizen and restorer of the Roman Republic.

Nero (A.D. 54-68) undermined Augustus' grand hypocritical design by alienating all elements except his own fawning entourage. When he killed himself, there was such general relief that speakers in Tacitus assured the soldiers that in turning against their imperial master, they were not deserters: Nero had deserted them. The relief was momentary, however, because its occasion meant civil war. With no clear successor, the secret of Actium that Augustus had disguised — the same secret divulged when Caligula was killed and Claudius became emperor, the disturbing secret of empire that an emperor could be created by the army and away from Rome—was made public in the atrocities of A.D. 69.

The aged veteran soldier Galba, governor of Spain, was Nero's first successor. His short reign revealed all the irony in the famous Tacitean judgment: Galba would have been thought capable of ruling, if he had not ruled. The new emperor, grave and thrifty, acted as though he were indubitably legitimate. To promote stability he adopted a successor, Piso Licinianus, whose moderation could not save him in the few days of eminence that he described as more dangerous than times of adversity. Galba's efforts were in vain. The civil war was advanced by rebellions: of soldiers in the provinces, of soldiers strange to Rome and thronged in the city, "materials for a revolution, without indeed a decided bias towards any one man, but ready to a daring hand" (*Hist.* 1.6), and of the emperor's special forces, the Praetorian Guard, dissatisfied with the pace and magnitude of Galba's largesse. Before Galba was brutally killed and a handful of soldiers saluted the trembling Otho as emperor, Galba, as a final irony, was engaged in sacrifice, "importuning the gods of an empire which was now another's" (*Hist.* 1.29).

Galba and Piso made high-minded speeches, but Otho, affable, with a style more congenial to the soldiers, argued directly and destructively to their interests. The soldiers rode high; later some one hundred and twenty memorials asserting special service in the atrocities against Galba were found. Otho's successor, Vitellius, followed traditional policy in having these reward seekers executed to protect the incumbent by the certainty of revenge (*Hist.* 1.44). On the day of atrocities, however, the passion of civil strife overwhelmed any thought of policy or posterity, and the ultimate horror was that men rejoiced in the horrors (*Hist.* 1.47).

Otho understood that, as Galba and Piso had to suspect him, his hope was in revolution. He was, we are told, possessed of luxurious tastes that would drain an emperor's treasury and of poverty barely endurable by a subject. In an interior monologue he argued that, as the "same lot awaits the innocent and guilty, the man of spirit will at least deserve his fate" (*Hist.*

1.21). He became, nevertheless, the shuttlecock of soldiers and rivals for the empire. His eventual successor, the highborn Vitellius, was the beneficiary of legionary risings in Germany. These forces were dispatched to Italy. Otho's low view of human nature enabled him to see that evil-doing required daring. He therefore sought the initiative in battle. For his part, Tacitus presented, as it were, the public voice complaining that in a conflict between Otho and Vitellius, he could be sure only that the worse would win (*Hist.* 1.50).

Otho's forces were bested, whereupon Otho resolved to end his life and the civil war. The *Histories* (2.47-49), as Sir Ronald Syme has explained, present a virtuoso account of a Roman suicide, which was the best thing a man as bad as Otho could do.[3] His speech, principally the composition of Tacitus, explained that he and fortune had become familiars and with that resignation he had no complaints against gods or men, because such complaints were only for those wishing to live. Tacitus concluded Otho's history characteristically: his tomb was unpretentious and therefore likely to stand (*Hist.* 1.47, 49).

Vitellius' imperial days have Galba's irony but an incomparable, disastrous ending. The emperor, addressing the Senate and people as though they were the people of a foreign state, praised his own energy and moderation. Popular acclaim, thereupon, hailed him as Augustus. Some time before that occasion he had visited in triumph the plains of Bedriacum, near Cremona, where some five weeks earlier his forces had defeated those of Otho, to see the rotting corpses of Roman soldiers. Finally, when Vespasian's legions were before Rome, Vitellius vainly tried, several times, to abdicate. His soldiers would not accept the decision, and in the ensuing struggle the Capitol itself was burned. Rome was stormed, while Vitellius struggled amidst the destruction of his imperial statues and, as he was being slain, could see the spot where Galba fell (*Hist.* 2.70, 90; 3.68-73, 85).

Tacitus found Vespasian more acceptable. As an Italian soldier he had lived the serious and austere life of a republican Roman and yet had been subtle enough to survive the dangerous frivolities of Nero's court. In the civil war he had the armies of the east and careful counselors. One of them, Mucianus, whose ever-ready slogan was that money was the sinews of war, levied contributions from the rich. It was Mucianus who presented the case after Vespasian's estimate of the imperial situation had been made. His argument embraced the interests of the state and of Vespasian: "To be chosen successor to Vitellius would be more of an insult than a compliment" (*Hist.* 2.76). If Vespasian was to emulate Augustus and Tiberius, he must first seize power as his only refuge against suspicious rivals. His power and sources of support would benefit the state and offered the promise of Vespasian's victory as surely as did the vices and weaknesses of the enemy.

After victory Vespasian delayed a year in the east, a possibly secure base, before going to Rome. His agents made the first ventures in the new emperor's policies of restoring finances, allaying the local rivalries that had free play in the civil war, quieting the provinces, extending courteous treatment to the nearly shameless Senate, and cultivating the support of the army not by purchase but by winning its respect.

The surcease from civil war with the return of order was Tacitus' theme. In the civil war Roman soldiers had plundered their country and stripped the corpses of fellow soldiers. One Spanish soldier unwittingly killed his soldier-father in battle. Upon recognizing his dying father he exclaimed that a soldier is but a small part of a civil war in which all in fact are guilty (*Hist.* 3.25). On the larger scene dangerous hopes and prophecies circulated about the transfer of universal empire from the Romans to the Druids and to Judaea (*Hist.* 4.59, 5.13).

The imperial power was formidable and could be menacing, especially when the emperor felt threatened. Vespasian exiled and executed some critics—for example, Helvidius Priscus, who claimed for the Senate the right to discuss the imperial succession. In A.D. 71 the emperor exiled some philosophers from Rome. Although Tacitus knew that in extensive power there could never be complete confidence, he served Vespasian, who alone among his predecessors improved when he had power (*Hist.* 2.92, 1.50).

In the *Annals*, a story of the Principate from the death of the divine Augustus, the author's intent was to provide some facts concerning Augustus, notably those about the end of his reign, and then to recount the reigns of Tiberius, Caligula, Claudius, and Nero. Their histories, so he justified his enterprise, had been falsified during their lives by fear, and after their deaths by resentment. These works, as well as the witnesses of the period, some of them contemporaries of the author's youth, were remote enough to permit Tacitus his profession that he would write a faithful history without anger or partiality. This means that Tacitus was bitter, but not for reasons of personal interest. He was not a member of the earlier factions, but he used their sources; and their bias, which he had not the means to correct, helped to shape his presentation.

Augustus defeated his rivals and then established the Principate. He won the army "with gifts, the populace with cheap corn, and all men with the sweets of repose, and so grew greater by degrees, while he concentrated in himself the functions of the Senate, the magistrates, and the laws" (*Annals* 1.2). The Augustan Principate was one-man rule without monarchy, deftly secured by concentrating many offices in Augustus' person. It was difficult to maintain because the prestige of Augustus was not transferable, and the Roman practice of adoption did not work, inasmuch as Augustus survived various adopted heirs.

The *princeps* normally could look for the acceptance of the Roman people. They were the beneficiaries of the first citizen's donations. From the Senate they could look for nothing. If the *princeps* lacked full legitimacy or felt insecure, his rivals were in the Senate, or so he feared. Against the senatorial order Caligula, Nero, and Domitian waged campaigns in which the treason law, *maiestas*, was most effective. The Senate did not resist; in fact, in the terrorized atmosphere of each man for himself, individual senators, drawing on the resources of Rome's fast-growing service, informers, pursued whatever feuds they could. In using treason charges recklessly they enlarged the *princeps'* armory.

The verdict of Tacitus is that under Augustus the state had been subverted so that there remained nothing of the ancient and healthy morality. But this is mild compared to his handling of Augustus' successor. The Tacitean treatment of Tiberius (A.D. 14-37) is notorious for its almost unrelenting hostility, which nevertheless includes mitigating factors and material contradictory to the dominant tone. Tiberius is presented as a shamelessly dissolute tyrant whose worst crime was possibly diffidence. He pretended a hesitation about ruling that left senatorial toadies without a clear course, and this ambiguity shrouded even his end. Tiberius declined for a long time and finally appeared to have died. But he recovered and mightily alarmed the supporters of Caligula, one of whom, Macro, once Tiberius' man, ordered that death be made definite by smothering the old man with clothes.

Senatorial sources and histories were, in the main, severely critical of Tiberius. From those sources Tacitus composed an acid portrait of a man feigning the refusal of power which he could not but use. The Senate did not have Galba's later certainty that one man should rule because the Romans could not live in freedom and would not live as slaves. Senatorial authors and witnesses gave free vent to the sophisticated malice of an aristocracy being displaced. They had some cause. There were dark features in Tiberius' personality and character: arrogance, impatience, and resentment. The last had been intensified by Augustus, who dictated to Tiberius a divorce, a choice of wife, and adoptions without disguising the mistrust that delayed Augustus from making the preliminary arrangements for his succession.

In politics, Tiberius displayed no concern or talent for gaining favor. Absence made Rome and its atmosphere unfamiliar to him. A general rather than a politician, he was ill prepared for dealing with senatorial anxieties in the immediate post-Augustan period.

These points Tacitus passed by, but two others he made emphatically clear. First, Tiberius professed that he would follow Augustus' course, thereby creating a dilemma for the Senate. Tiberius used the consuls "as though the ancient constitution remained, and he hesitated about being emperor" (*Ann.* 1.7). But did he not have the position of the first citizen? The dilemma plunged the Romans into slavery; indeed, the "higher a man's rank, the more eager his hypocrisy" in taking the oath of loyalty. Tacitus reported Tiberius as accustomed to say on leaving the Senate: how ready they are to be slaves. Nevertheless, his constitutional profession was held against him. When Tiberius, after fixing the price on grain for the people of the city, refused again the title of "father of the country," Tacitus concluded: "Consequently, speech was restricted and perilous under an

emperor who feared freedom while he hated sycophancy"
(*Ann.* 3.65; 2.87).

The second point was corruption by power. Here Tacitus
was sometimes palpably — even inexplicably — unfair, as in the
matter of endowing senators of reduced circumstances with the
means necessary for the senatorial order. This, we are told, was
one of the good uses of money in which Tiberius took pride. A
feckless senatorial pauper, Marcus Hortalus, the grandson of a
senator who had been encouraged by a grant from Augustus to
avoid the extinction of his illustrious family, staged an appeal
for an imperial handout. Tiberius rejected the plea as unseem-
ly, because Hortalus had brought private business to the public
discussion, and as inexpedient, because aid in this case would
be given not as a matter of grace but in response to the impor-
tunity of one who would not fend for himself. In a sentence
that, in effect, confirms the imperial judgment, Tacitus wrote
that Tiberius showed no pity, when that "house of Hortensius
sank into shameful poverty" (*Ann.* 2.39).

Despite references to the crimes of the new regime, Tacitus
called the years to A.D. 23 (neatly covered by the first three of
the six books on Tiberius) a time of tranquillity for the state.
Then bad luck set in for the state, the emperor, and his family.
The villain here was Sejanus. When Sejanus acquired power,
intrigue and prosecutions flourished. In A.D. 26 Tiberius retired
from Rome, eventually going to Capri and leaving the Principate without a visible first citizen. Sejanus' power increased
to a point of overreaching, when Sejanus acted against his
belief that the substance of power is more satisfying and safer
than the appearance of power.

The summary obituary of Tiberius does him more justice
than the detailed history. Tacitus recalls the many changes in
the emperor's fortunes and the ordeals of his early career.
Character changed with circumstances: first apparently virtuous, then reserved with a crafty pretense of virtue, in a third
stage a compound of good and evil, in a fourth (under Sejanus)
cruel, though veiling his debaucheries, and finally, when on his
own, freed from fear and shame, wicked and disgraceful as he
indulged his own inclinations (*Ann.* 6.5).

No annals remain for the following years of Caligula (A.D.
37-41), and the missing four books also covered the period to

A.D. 47, the first six years of the reign of Claudius. Caligula's cause had been fostered by his grandmother, the daughter of Mark Antony, and some Oriental princes. The spoiled young man, inexperienced and arbitrary, was, as though these defects were not enough, at least slightly mad. Hailed as a liberator upon the death of Tiberius, he soon began to quarrel with the Senate, the generals, and his family. His tyranny worsened, and finally a conspiracy of the Praetorian Guards and some senators ended in Caligula's assassination. Tiberius' unfavorable estimate of Caligula's inexperience, his subjection to Greek and Oriental influences, his upbringing and savagery had been vindicated at public expense (*Ann.* 6.46).

The Praetorian soldiers found Caligula's uncle Claudius (A.D. 41-54) hiding in the palace and saluted him as *princeps*. The Senate considered restoring the Republic but lacked wide support, not to speak of sustained will. As Tacitus' account of the first six years of Claudius' reign is missing, we cannot read his treatment of this episodic key to the reign. The emperor had cordial relations with the senate and governed the empire with some care and knowledge. But Tacitus cannot admire or like him. He is the puppet of his servants, the imperial freedmen who probably inevitably supplanted the aristocrats and knights in the central administration, and of his imperious wives. The first of these grasping and destructive ladies was Messalina, who had been married to Claudius when she was fifteen and was killed at the age of twenty-four (A.D. 47) without her husband's orders, an irregularity that did not discompose the emperor.

Thereafter, in a sophisticated comedy, the freedmen held a council on the choice of a wife for Claudius. They settled on his niece Agrippina, who exercised a "masculine despotism." The emperor's consort compelled Claudius to adopt her son, Nero, who eventually killed Claudius' other son. For her part, Agrippina assured Nero's succession by poisoning Claudius. The verdict of Tacitus is that she could give the empire to Nero "but not endure him as emperor" (*Ann.* 12.64). Perhaps the best comment on Claudius and his succesor is that Nero delivered a panegyric, written by Seneca, in which his praise of the foresight and wisdom of Claudius drove a solemn audience into irrepressible laughter (*Ann.* 13.3).

The first victim of the new regime was Junius Silanus, pro-consul of Asia. Agrippina, not Nero, ordered the murder to secure Nero's title, because Silanus was of the Claudian line. Once again, this time by Nero, the Senate was to be strength-ened. And, in a short time, Nero was thwarted by family and palace rivalries. Frequent funerals crowded a depopulated Rome, while Tacitus in dealing with the monotony of death almost exhausted his ingenuity in finding words for murder and suicide.

Agrippina was done in at the urging of Nero's new sweet-heart, Poppaea, a death that had to be contrived to disguise the matricide. She was almost as hard to kill as to live with. Suetonius reported that Nero rushed to view his mother's corpse, "handling her legs and arms critically and, between drinks, discussing their good and bad points" (*Nero*, 34). Tacitus limited himself to saying that some tell this story and others deny it.

Nevertheless, the impropriety of the esthetic Nero as emperor is the theme of Tacitus. Fear, flattery, and shamelessness prevailed, but not to the exclusion of some virtue. Ordinary rivalries could motivate threats to Nero, but an emerging challenge had the support of patriotic indignation and wasted loyalty. One of the plotters, Subrius Flavus, finally gave a frank confession of motives. When asked why he broke his oath of allegiance, Subrius protested that no one had been more loyal than he as long as Nero acted worthily. "I began to hate you when you became the murderer of your mother and your wife, a charioteer, an actor, and an incendiary" (*Ann.* 15.67).

In the crescendo of tension and horror, the pregnant Poppaea died as the result of a kick from her enraged imperial spouse. (16.6). Nero's last two years are missing from the *Annals*, and accordingly we do not have Tacitus' account of the rebellions and Nero's suicide that prepared the civil wars which formed the beginning of Tacitus' *Histories* and marked the end of the Claudian dynasty. Its first figures belong to world history, but later members, to the misery of Rome, were weak before the temptations of power and short of the qualities their roles demanded.

For Tacitus, it is evident, history is not a demythologized past or, as with Thucydides, a scrupulous account and explanation of human behavior that will be a possession forever. Although Tacitus tersely dismissed some Roman legends as fictions, Romans did not aspire to science and in philosophy trailed the Greeks, who, in the general Roman view, should be kept in their place as slaves, pedagogues, sages, and panderers to luxury. Somewhat in the manner of British imperialists, the Romans saw themselves as practical men, sensible enough not to be bound by logic. This meant that they saw no rational order of the world or history (*Ann.* 3.18), and the protagonist or writer when he contradicted himself might be the most faithful witness of men and events.

Rome, though a great empire, did not encompass the world and all time, although Tacitus made it his focus and obsession, even in the *Germania*. He knew about the long astronomical year, the great cycle of recurrence, but it meant nothing to him. Sometime before Rome there was a golden age, when the human condition was relatively equal and men lived without seeking to exploit others. Real time began with the founding of the city, a mythic date. Thereafter, as Roman institutions developed, time was measured from the foundation and identified by the consuls in whose year the Senate did some particular thing. After men became unequal and had something to struggle for, there ensued the second golden age, the time of the Republic, when the power of men took the form of the competition of an elite, an aristocracy disciplined by a code of honor. The struggles and actions of aristocrats provided a theme for good history.

Men responsive to considerations of honor and fame justified a moralistic approach to history, which preserved fame and infamy. This was a civic version of the epic; and, like the epic, history had to be formulated in a moral pattern and rhetorically fashioned to interest and captivate the reader. Tacitus searched for his story among such sources as he could find and weigh, not out of a desire for scientific accuracy or a passion to know what really happened, but so that he would be taken as a faithful witness. Alternative explanations, rather than a simple one, might be advanced to establish his faithfulness. The work he presented would be shaped to a pattern by conventions the mind accepted, but it would not be a logical design. At its best it would allow for the role of fate as well as chance while it illumined the subtlety of things, "their relations and causes" (*Hist.* 1.4).

How thoroughly did Tacitus search? Extensively, to judge from the evidence of the *Annals* and the references in them. But much apparently depended on the subject and his purpose. For the *Germania* his research was limited, and his knowledge of the Jews and Christians, the merest currency of governmental Rome, displayed a lack of understanding as profound as his disabling lack of sympathy. The same may be said of the Egyptians and their worship. To a Senate debate proposing that four thousand Jews and followers of the Egyptian rite be sent to Sardinia to reduce brigandage there, Tacitus added his own comment: "a cheap price should they die from the pestilential climate" (*Ann.* 2.85).

His digressions and other evidence indicate that he had a special interest in moral legislation, Roman antiquities, Roman priestly offices, Gaul, the emperors, the Senate, and the play of motivation and feeling in complex events. His discussion of the Roman army is invaluable for its account of the organization and outlook of the legions. He cannot be called a military historian, because he is vague and careless (as almost all Roman historians are) about numbers on battlefields, the disposition of forces, and geography.

The narrative is enlivened and advanced by the speeches. These brilliant compositions, so mercifully and artistically brief, provide explanations of courses of action, portraits of character, and accounts of motivation. Many of the speeches are versions of talks actually presented. The style varies with the speaker, and among the more revealing are those of Tiberius and Claudius, whose pedantry and pomposity as rendered by Tacitus make delightful reading. Some of the speeches are virtuoso compositions—for example, the speeches of barbarian enemy leaders which voice what he called the usual sentiments expressed in such wars against Rome. In general, the Romans had much better collections of speeches and records to consult than Thucydides had.

The views that constituted Tacitus' historical vision are those of a man of authority. People, he believed, needed government and authority to which they owed dutiful obedience. A mutinous army is "headstrong, cowardly, and spiritless, as a

mob without a leader always is" (*Hist.* 4.37). One prefect, in
fact, ended a mutiny by a policy based on the soldiers' "instinct
for obedience": he commanded all officers to refrain from issuing the orders that regulated the routine of the soldiers' day.
The soldiers milled about aimlessly and soon clamored for their
orders. The incident, of course, served as a parable: most
mutinies ended with the restoration of authority but only after
brutal violence (*Hist.* 2.29).

Men need government because they seek advantage over
each other and lust for power. The same lust might inspire
challengers to the ruler and invite trouble. It could also appear
as a love of servility: many Romans sought power by fawning
upon its possessor. The lust for power stirs the forceful passions
of actions explained by Tacitus, envy and jealousy. In the
Histories he calls them instincts or traits of human nature
which prompt men to look sharply at the good fortune of others
and "to demand a temperate use of prosperity from none more
rigorously than from those whom they have seen on a level with
themselves" (2.20).

The first golden age was one of near equality, and the second
golden age, the Republic, saw a kind of balance of contenders
in inequality. Republican inequality itself was tempered by
discipline and rigor. Later experience showed that wealth as
well as excessive power might destroy self-control: wealth made
luxury possible and, in a chain reaction, idleness, sensuality,
and debauchery; power made for willfulness, crime, and tyranny, along with all the enfeeblement of wealth.

In a masterful Tacitean letter to the Senate, Tiberius made
this very point while refusing to assume for the state the care
of morals that should be sought in each individual's heart: "Victories over the foreigner taught us how to waste the substance
of others; victories over ourselves, how to squander our own."
Under Tiberius, Tacitus then said in his own right, luxury of
the table (which was a fashion from the time of Actium until
A.D. 69) gradually declined. His explanation of the change is as
remarkable as is the apparent diffidence, which made him worthy of his own Tiberius. Formerly, he wrote, many Roman
families ruined themselves in the extravagances of a passion for
splendor. Vespasian, old-fashioned in dress and diet, encouraged strict manners. His effect had been anticipated by those

who took the places of the ruined, "new men who were often admitted into the Senate from the towns, colonies and even provinces, introduced their household thrift, and though many of them by good luck or energy attained an old age of wealth, still their former tastes remained." Characteristically Tacitus did not leave the matter with a definitive explanation. Perhaps, he added, there was a cycle in manners just as there is in the seasons. At any rate, his own age could provide examples for posterity to imitate: not everything in the past was better (*Ann.* 3.53-55).

For good behavior in their own time, men need faithful histories that, with exact discrimination, will reveal worthy actions that were obscured by the flattery and malice of men who lived under despotism. Few people are prudent enough to distinguish right from wrong and the sound from the harmful. Accordingly, and here Tacitus described his function, most men learn from what happens to other people (*Ann.* 3.65; 4.11, 33).

The discrimination and fairness of Tacitus have been obscured by the asperity of his style — terse, deliberately shocking in reaction to bland Cicero — and his practice of concluding subjects with an overpowering denigration. When, for example, Tiberius sat at one end of the Praetor's Tribunal to oppose improper influence in the Senate's judicial proceedings, he was credited with promoting justice while ruining freedom (*Ann.* 1.75). The foreign policy of Tiberius was crafty and aimed at peace instead of being straightforward, expansionist, and bellicosely decisive to impress barbarians. The annalist apologized for the "wearisome monotony" of his subject matter which was attributable to, among other matters, "peace wholly unbroken or but slightly disturbed" (6.32; 4.32).

Matters were more satisfactory under Vespasian, but again Tacitus made distinctions. Under the Flavians, historians distorted their representation of the rivalry of the partisans of Otho and Vitellius. The source of the falsification was in assigning to them patriotic and pacific motives when in truth they were opportunists, shameless, jealous, and unfaithful (*Hist.* 2.101).

Expansion and the rivalries of the first century before Christ had undermined the Republic. The Principate had been at first

a veiled despotism which was unmasked in terror under the
Claudians from Tiberius to Nero. The Flavians' attempt at
restoring ancient ways foundered in the tyranny of Domitian.
Under Nerva and Trajan, Tacitus professed to see a solution,
the combination of princely rule and liberty. He apparently
found it so and hoped that it would continue.

What were the grounds of his hope? They were twofold: the
resolution of the succession problem by abandoning family succession and adopting the practice of co-opting a worthy successor; and the disposition of the emperor toward liberty and
acceptance of the services of men like Tacitus. Nevertheless,
both his experience and historical work enforced recognition
that excessive power, which the emperor had, could not inspire
confidence or guarantee security.

Tacitus accepted this situation unblinkingly as the pitiless-
ness of his vision required. There could be no hope in the resistance of the Senate. His position was expressed by Marcellus in
a speech in the *Histories*:

> I do not forget the times in which I have been born, or the form
> of government which our fathers and grandfathers established. I
> may regard with admiration an earlier period but I acquiesce in the
> present, and, while I pray for good emperors, I can endure whom-
> soever we have (4.8).

Tacitus' works, describing the emerging new reality, the empire, judged it by republican and senatorial standards. But
something else appeared in the tension between the republican
myth and the detested empire. As the immortality of the city
was then to be the care of the emperor's foresight (*providentia*),
which might mean tyranny, the individual value of survival
was affirmed. This individualism appeared in Tacitus' dispar-
agement of suicide. This practice might impress a flourishing
aristocratic order but was sheer waste, an abetting of the
tyrant, in time of terror. And Tacitus could no longer be clear
about the audience to whom he addressed his moralizing histories. The Senate could not act on the code that the *Histories*
exemplified. Tacitus had to act and survive in the old-fashioned
terms that his individual conscience maintained against a
changed world.

The *Histories* presented a lively, brilliant, and incisive account of a great historical change. Tacitus' principal defect was the exaggeration of a great merit. His views and his moralistic psychology combined to produce works that are close to histories with the good left out. But the merit is the vivid awareness of human selfishness and of the stratum of evil in people. He looked on it so directly that he prepared the mind for the texture of human affairs we experience and read about. His writings may be an affront to liberal hopes, and indeed his view was too much even for the author of *Candide*. Of the account of Nero's matricide by Suetonius and somewhat qualified by Tacitus, Voltaire in his *Philosophical Dictionary* made a nearly Panglossian remark: the interests of humanity compel us to believe that such horrors are exaggerated, because they reflect too much shame on human nature.

The differences between Voltaire and Tacitus define the latter's achievement. Voltaire, looking to human betterment, found ages of violence and religion wearisome, unimproving, and unworthy of the attention of an enlightened person. Tacitus singled out virtuous actions for praise and misdeeds for infamy. In his snobbish refinement he was ingenious in devising euphemisms, literally to the point of not calling a spade a spade. Nevertheless, he was resolute as a faithful witness of a Roman senatorial season in hell. He did not censor it to elevate human nature and, because he did not do so, he learned to serve Rome as the times allowed. With others of similar mind he made possible that second-century empire of Rome which Edward Gibbon celebrated for its civilization, laws, public administration, and peace.

5. Bede:

Monastic Historian
In a Barbarian World

NEAR THE END OF HIS life in 735, Bede, a monk in Northern England, completed *The Ecclesiastical History of the English People.*[1] In it he gave currency to the practice of dating events from the birth of Christ, that is, the Incarnation, which with the Redemption is the central moment of history for Christians. Tacitus would have judged the event as regrettable as Bede's project of writing the religious history of a barbarian people. The two historians, setting themselves opposed tasks, were opposite in temperament. Tacitus bitterly described the horror-filled end of the Roman Republic; Bede celebrated a beginning and looked to a transcendent end. Tacitus, seared in spirit, described a manscape quaking in the land mines of his anger; Bede charmed readers with the style of a gentle and hopeful spirit. What was full of promise to Bede would have been the fulfillment of Tacitus' worst fears. But the greatness of Tacitus cannot be dwarfed by comparing him with a gentle wonder among the barbarians. The acerbic historian and the Anglo-Saxon saint, to give him his title, were of different cultures and with varying purposes they wrote different histories. When they wrote history, Christianized barbarians differed from their predecessors of the classical world because their beliefs and experiences provided new subjects, purposes, and outlook. By the eighth century Bede was heir to centuries of Christian historical experience, adaptations, and thought about history.

The new society of Christians, the Church, commanded their highest loyalty; before it, the claims of the state — the city of man, St. Augustine called it — and historical lessons in civic virtue dwindled in importance for those anticipating the Second Coming of Christ. For what was vital in the time before Christ, his followers took the biblical view of history: the Fall of Man and God's Covenant with the Jewish people. Diverging from Judaism, the Christians believed that the life and death of Christ had fulfilled the Covenant and initiated the age of a new humanity of persons called to imitate Christ.

The beliefs of the first Christians that Christ was crucified to redeem humanity, that he rose from the dead, and that his followers were members of a new society of God and with God, make up the fundamentals of a theology. This theology affirmed historical events and time: that a historical Son of God, not a mythical figure, lived and died. The Gospels recalled his life and teachings. The first years of his Church were recounted in the Acts of the Apostles (in Greek, their *Praxeis*).

This Church lived and witnessed Christ's mission to the world. To preach to mankind was the Church's duty to the world. But the world cannot be an idol, and its end was imminent. When the Roman Empire persecuted the Christians, apocalyptic Christians thought of Roman domination and power as the harlot, Babylon, under judgment and certain to fall.

The emperor Constantine (306-337) decreed toleration of the Church and favored it. Around 325 Eusebius (260-338), a learned bishop of Palestinian Caesarea, composed his *Ecclesiastical History*. For this work he had to impose an order on the many ways of dating that his sources from various times and places provided. This father of church history saw in history the providential biblical story and in the Roman Empire the divine preparation for the spread of the Gospel. In other writings Eusebius, dwelling more on the triumphs than on the sufferings of Christ, looked on Constantine as the new and providential Augustus of the empire and the survival of the Church as a story of divine triumph.

This triumphalism was challenged by a revived paganism when Visigoths in 410 sacked Rome, the imperial city. The pagans blamed the fall of Rome on the Christians, who had abandoned the city's ancient gods. The charge was formidable enough to inspire the tireless Christian teacher, Augustine (354-430), bishop of Hippo, to devote years to writing *The City of God.* His principal point was that Christians in pilgrimage through this world, a city whose self-love was idolatry and immoral behavior, gave their love to a heavenly city that after death would be theirs in fullness. The sufferings of humanity were the chastisements of a just and loving God, who mingled them with mercies and benefits.

In dealing with the pagans' objection, Augustine recalled the disasters Rome had suffered in its thousand-year pagan history. Not only were the traditional gods powerless to help, but their myths and festivals encouraged believers in self-indulgence and brutalities repugnant to serious moralists and deserving of punishment. This, however, was not the principal concern of Augustine, who wished to develop the "city of God" theme. He therefore asked the Spanish priest Orosius to compose a history of the disasters men had suffered or inflicted on other men. His *Seven Books Against the Pagans* (417) heavily discharged the tedious assignment. Its simple tale of violence and suffering, which Christian hope made bearable, was more readily grasped than Augustine's lengthy, overextended work, and its simple argument, rather like the pagan's charge put to Christian use, was an influence in much medieval historical writing. For the education of his people, King Alfred (849-899) translated the work of Orosius into Anglo-Saxon, and in the tenth and eleventh centuries the book was read yearly to the monks of the great Benedictine monastery at Cluny.

As the Roman Empire of the West declined, barbarians invaded its territories, and their conquests became barbarian monarchies. The barbarian conquerors were of distinct and separate tribes. The christianization of these tribes, however, provided a consciousness of unity that succeeded the imperial unity of Rome.

Bede (c. 673-735) was born to descendants of the Germanic conquerors of Britain in its northern English area, the Anglo-Saxon kingdom of Northumbria. When he was seven years old, his parents entrusted him to Benedict Biscop, a nobleman who had founded a monastery at Jarrow. Shortly afterward Bede was sent to a new monastery founded at Wearmouth. Each monastery had its own head, but together they were considered one, the monastery of the Apostles Peter and Paul at Wearmouth and Jarrow. Appended to Bede's *Ecclesiastical History* was a brief recapitulation of events to help the memory, a list of his writings, and some two hundred and fifty words about his life. "I have spend all my life in the monastery," observing the monastic rule and giving the parts of each day to singing the Divine Office, studying, writing, and teaching. In his eyes writing and teaching had the same end. His writing communicated and preserved what was worth knowing. If what he wrote or dictated was here and there the words of Scripture, of the Church Fathers, or of an author like Pliny, sometimes he mentioned the source, but he had no notion of the words of others or of himself as property or props to egoism. His labors, preservation and communication of what was worth knowing, were in an ultimate sense the work of God, to whom then was the glory — and God forbid that they be vanity.

In his studious love of the Scriptures, the Church Fathers, and the available fragments of classical learning, Bede was the most learned man of his age. He was a student of time and, in particular, a master of the means used to reckon time. Two problems prompted him to this study: to reconcile the many forms of chronology — those of republican Rome, the years of the emperors, biblical and Christian records, and the regnal years of the many kings in Anglo-Saxon England — and, much more important, to determine the date of Easter, the festival that provided the sequence for most of the Church's year, and to defend the Roman practice of reckoning Easter, particularly against that of the Celts of Britain and Ireland.

The liturgical calendar was used for recording memorable events, and this is the origin of monastic annals, a major form of medieval historical composition. The keeper of the calendar began with the Julian calendar based on the solar year, which was the same from year to year. To the days of this calendar were assigned the many feasts that were always celebrated on the same date. To these the keeper added materials about the saints whose feast days were celebrated and particularly about saints from the locality of the monastery or saints who were the object of particular local veneration. The Easter calendar had to be figured in cycles and fitted into the solar calendar. There were several of these cycles, but the principal one was of 19 years, a period in which the lunar and solar calendars coincided. For accurate, long-range computation, the cycle of 19 years was multiplied by 28 to produce a great cycle of 532 years. Into these cyclical calendars were written notes of memorable events, and these notations were the humble beginnings of that medieval creation, annals.[2]

Bede had a number of annals to consult as well as a larger collection of lives of holy men and saints. He had accumulated information from traditional sources and from many eyewitnesses. At his request the papal archives in Rome were consulted for material on the missionaries sent by Pope Gregory to preach to the Anglo-Saxons. He had also written on martyrs, on the lives of several saints and of the abbots of his monastery, and, in sum, "On the Nature of Things."

The Ecclesiastical History of the English People was in his mind all of a piece with his other works. As he chose to write a church history, he wrote not in the form of annals, but in a narrative. He wrote to preserve the memory of what was done, and along the way he would provide other information, especially on wonders of topography, which should inform some and please those who lived near the wonder.

The Ecclesiastical History narrated a meeting of what Bede saw as two unities, the Church and the English people, who thereby became a new people of God, at one with the Apostolic See of Rome. The Gospel conveyed the news of salvation, and as witnesses to its truth are the exemplary behavior of Christians and the wonders and miracles performed in Christ's name. The obverse of this Christian belief was the detestation of a relapse to paganism and a willingness to use force against those who would not convert, although faith was believed to be God's gift. Pope Gregory urged the king of Kent "to suppress the worship of idols," to destroy pagan shrines, and "to strengthen the morals of your subjects by your great purity of life as well as by exhortation, deterrence through frightening them, enticement, correction and the example of good works."[3]

The principal subject of book 1 is the conversion of the Germanic conquerors of Kent, the Jutes. Twenty-two of the book's thirty-four chapters provide a background, including the geography of Britain. For the latter the author drew from the works of Pliny, the sixth-century monk Gildas, and Orosius, among others. Here Bede made little use of his own observation: he thought the sentences of authorities were more important. Later he himself was regarded as an authority and was cited by the historian of the crusading kingdoms, William of Tyre (c. 1130-1184), as an authority on the Jordan River.[4]

Britain had been conquered by the Romans, and the first British Christians were Roman Britons. As Roman power declined to the vanishing point, the Britons were weak before dangers, inclined to vice in prosperity, and, in any case, divided in rivalries that assured their eventual defeat. A chief lord (the British word is *Vortigern*, the name Bede called him) sought the help of the pagan Saxons under Hengist and Horsa against the northern enemies of the Britons. The Saxons came, did their job, and sent home word of Britain's fertility and its unready defenders. A new contingent of Saxon home-seekers joining these in Britain began the conquest of the island.

Bede found this story providential. He was sympathetic to holy men, but in his story the Britons were a people properly punished for refusing to preach Christianity to their conquerors. This Celtic withdrawal gradually meant separation from the practices of the Apostolic Church of Rome, for example, the variant time of the celebration of Easter. The conversion of the Anglo-Saxons, thus, was undertaken by a mission sent from Rome, and Bede used some of St. Paul's words about the Jewish rejection of Christianity as making the Gentiles "chosen": "But God in his goodness did not utterly abandon the people [the Anglo-Saxons], whom he had chosen . . . and sent this nation more worthy preachers of truth to bring them to the Faith" (1.32).

The divine instrument was Pope Gregory, who sent Augustine and a band of monks to preach the word of God to the English. The missionary party, journeying to "a barbarous, fierce and pagan nation" whose language they did not understand, became fearful and halted their progress. Thereupon, Augustine returned to Rome to advise abandonment of the enterprise. Gregory greeted him with encouragement. The pope also gave him a letter reminding the missionaries that it would have been better not to undertake a good work than deliberately to lack constancy in it. Gregory then announced the appointment of Augustine as abbot of the monks, who "for the good of their souls should obey him." If their mission was difficult, the pope argued, the more difficult the missionary task, the greater their heavenly reward would be — and yet, of course, God did all and men were but his agents. To his concluding wish for their safety, the pope added the hope of seeing "the result of your labors in our heavenly home" (1.23).

Resuming their journeys, the missionaries acquired some Frankish interpreters. When they landed in Kent they were heard in the open air rather than in a building where, the barbarians feared, the monks might work magic on them. But they also had an ally in the Christian Bertha, a Frankish princess married to Aethelbert, king of Kent. When the monks settled in Canterbury, the king's city, for religious services they used a church building that Bertha also used. Their Church of St. Martin had originally been built by "believers" in the days of Roman Britain (1.25-26).

Aethelbert accepted Christianity and according to Bede's account favored Christians. He did not use force against his pagan subjects because he had learned from his teachers that the service of Christ must be accepted freely and not under compulsion (1.26). Meanwhile, Augustine consulted Gregory about pastoral problems arising from the differences between the Latin cultural formulation of Catholic teaching and practice and the Germanic customs of the Kentish people. Gregory's reply, extending over several pages of Bede's *History*, urged pastoral rigor in matters such as valid and invalid marriages, which Gregory believed to be essential, but recommended that in other matters Augustine should adapt to local customs and sensibilities. Idols should be destroyed, but temples could be consecrated to the true God (1.27).

This correspondence and Bede's later account reveal the twofold cultural change involved in the success of Augustine's mission: religious transformation and the reintroduction of writing and the Latin language and some of its literature. The religious transformation, which Bede exemplified, introduced a new group of people and a Visible Church into Jutish society. In its growth this Church went beyond the individual barbarian kingdoms to reveal the unity of the English people. But each kingdom had to come to terms with the clergy and church property. With his councillors, Aethelbert, king of Kent, therefore, established laws to protect those who had come with the teaching he had welcomed (2.5). The new customs enumerated the penalties and compensation to be paid for offenses against God's things and ministers. These and other prevailing laws were codified in the Roman manner but written in the Anglo-Saxon language.

Cultural differences figure prominently in Bede's hostility to the Celtic natives of what became England and Wales. Augustine sought to persuade them to reject practices that did not conform to those of Rome and to preach the Gospel to their Germanic enemies. Bede's hostility, nevertheless, softened when he presented a Celtic hermit. This holy man proposed a test designed to reveal whether the Roman missionaries were men of God. The British representatives were to delay their arrival at a forthcoming conference of the two parties until the Roman party had seated themselves, and should observe whether Augustine rose to greet them. Humility on such an occasion would mean that Augustine was a man of God. The Roman leader sat on his dignity, although Bede's account played the matter down by noting: *it happened* that he remained seated. Augustine pressed his demands for submission and British evangelization of the Anglo-Saxons in a formulation entirely unacceptable to the British. He is reported to have predicted that God would use the Saxons to punish the schism and the British refusal to evangelize.[5]

The battle of Chester (between 613 and 616), Bede recounted, was the fulfillment of the prophecy. The instrument of the destruction of the British forces was the pagan king of Northumbria, Aethelfrith, a lover of glory and therefore of conquest. The first victims of the battle were twelve hundred British monks from Bangor monastery, who prayed for the British. The Germanic leader explained: "If they pray to their God against me, they are fighting against us, even if they do not bear arms" (2.2).[6]

Book 2 centered on the conversion of Bede's own region, Northumbria. Even so, Bede began with the death of Pope Gregory (605) and proceeded to describe the life of a saint, a nobleman, spiritual hero, and the apostle of "our nation." The biography conveys what the culture of the religion newly accepted among the Anglo-Saxons could mean: in contemplation Gregory could transcend the barriers of the flesh; he was a perfect monk, who loved the spiritual life and was prepared to

welcome death as the entrance to the heavenly city; and meanwhile he passed much of his time pastorally serving the world.

Christianization required unwearying effort and, even so,
there were setbacks. Eadbald, son of the first Christian king of
Kent, rejecting Christianity, married his father's second wife.
Some of the ecclesiastics, therefore, went into exile fearfully ex-
pecting persecution from a ruler who restored pagan worship.

In 625 the Northumbrian King Edwin accepted Christianity.
Bede's account makes it appear that the change had been
prepared over many years. For example, in his days of exile,
Edwin had had a vision in which he unwittingly pledged himself to be a Christian. Later, upon marrying a Christian Kentish princess, he promised complete religious freedom for her
and her attendants and indicated a willingness to accept her
religion, if his councillors, after examining it, judged it holier
and more worthy of God than theirs. When the queen bore a
daughter she was baptized, "the first of the Northumbrian
race," as a pledge that Edwin would observe his promise made
to Paulinus, the queen's chaplain, that he would become a
Christian. He indicated that he would convert if he were victorious over the king of the West Saxons, whose agent had
wounded him in an attempted assassination.

Even after his victory, Edwin delayed, apparently because in
changing religion he wanted the wholehearted cooperation of
his warriors and councillors. Bede noted that Edwin would
spend long periods sitting in silent deliberation. A letter from
Pope Honorius pressed conversion on the king, and another
urged his queen to labor "in season and out of season" to the
same end. Then Paulinus touched the king in a fashion that the
king identified with his early vision (2.9-12).

Finally Edwin, some of his councillors, and the chief priest
of the pagans staged a conference. In its course Coifi, the chief
priest, said that he had served the gods faithfully but that many
at court were more successful than he. His judgment, therefore,
was that their pagan religion had no power and no use. A
leading councillor used the often quoted speech that described
the brief moment of a sparrow's flight across a hall where men
sat feasting, while outside storms of rain and snow rage. Its
passage across momentary shelter from winter to winter was

compared to the moment of man's life. We "know nothing about what went before this life, and what follows." If the new doctrine provided more certain information, he favored acceptance of it. After Paulinus spoke, Coifi too urged acceptance and the burning of the old altars and temples. Here Bede cut short his account with "Quid plura?" (Why write more?). The king accepted the Gospel and asked Coifi which of them should first profane the pagan altars. The chief priest took the lead, claiming that God had given him true wisdom so that he could set an example to all.

Paulinus' and the king's conversion had an extraordinary influence. When the bishop accompanied Edwin and his queen to a royal villa in the country, Paulinus was kept busy from morning till evening instructing and baptizing people for thirty-six days (2.13-14). Edwin even persuaded the king of the East Angles to be baptized. Soon afterward the new convert was slain and the East Angles relapsed. In doing so they had the precedent of the king's father and predecessor, Raedwald, whose state after conversion was worse than under paganism: in one temple he had adjoining altars, one for the sacrifice of the Mass and the other "for offering victims to demons." How close this was to Bede's time is evident from his source citation that Ealdwulf (d. 713), king of the East Angles, used to tell that he had seen the temple in his boyhood (2.20).

In 634 Pope Honorius appointed Paulinus to be archbishop with the proviso that when one of the two archepiscopal sees of Canterbury and York was vacant, the remaining archbishop could consecrate bishops and relieve new nominees from traveling to Rome. But in the meantime Caedwalla, a British king, joining with the pagan King Penda of the Mercians, fought against the ambitious Edwin, who was killed in battle at Hatfield Chase (633). In the bloody times of persecution following Edwin's death, Paulinus, Edwin's queen, two royal children, and others sought safety in flight to Kent. Caedwalla, Bede believed, was more barbarous in temperament and behavior than Penda, all the worse for being a Christian. Sparing no one, the British king would not respect the Christian religion among the Anglo-Saxons. Indeed, even to his own day, Bede wrote, the Britons despised the Christian religion of the Anglo-

Saxons, with whom they would no more work than with pagans (2.17, 19, 20). The Celts even had a disconcerting practice of refusing to eat with the Saxons and of requiring the purification of vessels Saxons had used.

The ecclesiastical differences, compounded in the years following Edwin's death, are the principal subject of book 3. Oswald, a son of Aethelfrith, gained the throne, but only after he had defeated the Briton Caedwalla, a victory that Oswald had publicly sought by using the cross of Christ. As Oswald earlier, in his exile among the Celts in the north, had been baptized and accordingly observed Celtic religious customs (including their reckoning of the date of Easter), he asked the Irish chiefs in Scotland to send missionaries for the instruction of his people. The sequel extended Celtic influence, learning, art, and customs in Northumbria. Nevertheless, the very first missionary failed because of the severity of his demands upon the prospective converts. Aidan, his successor, urged simpler preaching initially and a gradual revelation of Christian beliefs as the people were able to receive them. Bede happily told the story of Aidan's first period of preaching in Northumbria when the missionary "was not yet fluent in the English language" (3.3). King Oswald, having learned Celtic in his exile, interpreted Aidan's preaching to the warriors of his court.

Bede thought of Aidan as an almost perfect Celtic holy man. He was gentle, ascetic by his own example but moderate in his demands on others. He could teach others, including kings, although his speech at times must have been upsetting. When Aidan gave his horse, a royal gift, to a beggar, King Oswin asked why Aidan had given that horse, when less valuable ones in the stable would have been good enough. Is the horse more valuable to you than the Son of God? was Aidan's too sweeping reply. The king, after some reflection, threw himself at Aidan's feet, saying that he would never again question Aidan about the number and value of his gifts to the sons of God. The royal answer drew tears from Aidan, who explained that a king humble enough to take correction would soon die. He would be snatched from his people, who could not be worthy of such a ruler (3.14). In fact, Oswin died (651) at the hands of Oswy (642-671), who later founded a monastery charged with praying for the souls of the murderer and of the murdered king.

Oswy made possible the convocation of a synod to resolve ecclesiastical differences. The difficulties attendant upon the differences appeared within Oswy's own family: the king found
himself likely to celebrate Easter while his Kentish queen,
Eanfleda, observing the Roman date, was facing the strict fast
of Lent's last week. The king's son Alfred was guided by
Wilfrid, who had studied in Gaul and Rome and favored
Roman ways. The times, Oswy appears to have concluded,
favored unity, and unity under Rome was possible because the
Celtic bishops of his realm, Finan and Colman, did not enjoy
the affection and respect that Aidan had.

The synod (664) met at Whitby, in the double monastery for
men and women over which Hilda, the great-niece of King Edwin, presided as abbess. Oswy opened the synod with the
observation that those who served the one God should live
under one rule. Colman then argued that the Celtic practices
were those of their ancestors, of St. Columba, and of St. John.
Wilfrid told of his travels in which he found the Roman practice universal: "The only people who are stupid enough to dis-
agree with the whole world are those Scots and their obstinate
adherents, the Picts and Britons, who inhabit only a portion of
those two islands in the remote ocean" (3.23). Later, Wilfrid
asked which holy man could be preferred to the chief of the
Apostles, Peter, to whom, in Christ's words, the keys of heaven
were given. Both parties agreed that Christ had spoken such
words to Peter, and Colman further admitted to Oswy that
Columba had no authority that could prevail over the Petrine
claim. The king thereupon pronounced in favor of Peter and
the Roman practice. Then, according to Bede, all present
assented and renounced their imperfect rules for those they
recognized to be better (3.25).

The unanimity is questionable. Colman and some followers
retired first to the island of Iona, from which Columba and his
Irish monks had evangelized Scotland. The withdrawal greatly
reduced the monastic community at Lindisfarne. Subsequently
divisions, withdrawals, and shortages of clergy and bishops
were compounded by the deaths and dispersals of monastic
communities caused by the bubonic plague that reached
England shortly after the Synod of Whitby. High mortality
among the clerics in the kingdom of the East Saxons was the oc-

casion of a widespread return to paganism there. A visitation
of the plague in the early eighties reduced Jarrow at one time
to only the abbot and the boy Bede. The same plague took the
lives of Wighard and most of the party that went to Rome seeking his consecration as archbishop of Canterbury.

To the vacant see Pope Vitalian named Theodore, a learned
Greek of Tarsus, and instructed Hadrian, the scholarly abbot
of a monastery near Naples, to accompany and second the archbishop. Although Theodore was sixty-six years old in 668, he
was to serve in England for more than two decades. The papal
choice was designed to avoid putting Saxon or Celt over the
other, but the pope was also wary of another possibility:
Hadrian, Bede explained, was told to assist Theodore and ensure that he did not introduce Greek customs "contrary to the
true faith" (4.1). Book 4 covered the age of Theodore, and the
concluding book presented his successor and English missionary
activity on the Continent.

Bede saw the Synod of Whitby and Theodore, its imple-
menter, as the making of the church of the English people.
Theodore, "teaching the Christian way of life and the canon-
ical observation of Easter," visited every part of the island occupied by the English and was, in fact, "the first archbishop to
whom the whole English Church gave obedience" (4.2).

The archbishop ruled in a good time that his efforts made
better. Theodore's decades were "the happiest times since the
English came to Britain," because the worldly authorities, being strong Christian kings and the terror of barbarian nations,
were at one with zealous church authorities. Then, so Bede exaggerated, "all desired the joys of heaven of which they had so
recently heard" (4.2). Sacred learning flourished as Theodore
and Hadrian, among others, attracted students. They studied
poetry, astronomy, and the calculation of the ecclesiastical
calendar, and some of them, who were as proficient in Greek
and Latin as in their own tongue, were alive when Bede was
writing. "All who wished for instruction in the reading of Scriptures found willing teachers" (4.2).

Celtic influences appear in the life of Chadd, bishop of
Northumbria, who humbly accepted Theodore's questioning of
the validity of his consecration and submitted to reconsecration
and transfer to Mercia. Chadd, who had been Aidan's disciple,

found himself overruled when he wished to do all his traveling on foot. To expedite his evangelical labors the elderly but forceful Archbishop Theodore with his own hands lifted Chadd onto a horse.

Bede admired the humility and asceticism of Celtic monks but thought them impractical, as is evident in his story about an Anglo-Irish monastery founded by Bishop Colman in West Ireland. During the summer and harvest time the Irish monks became nomads, returning in time to eat the harvest that the English monks had gathered. Colman solved this cultural and caloric dispute by founding another monastery, thus separating one nation of the brethren from the other (4.4).

The interactions of Christianity and Anglo-Saxon culture are revealed in the celebrated story of Caedmon, a herdsman of St. Hilda's monastery at Whitby, the once quiet man at feasts. In a dream he was asked to sing. He protested and upon being pressed asked, "What shall I sing about?" The answer was that he should sing about the beginnings of created things. His song, when repeated, so impressed some learned men that Abbess Hilda, convinced that he had the grace of God, told him to become a monk and had him instructed in sacred history. The Scripture was translated for the new brother of Whitby, who "memorizing and ruminating over it, like some clean animal chewing the cud, . . . turned it into the most melodious verse." Of Caedmon's Anglo-Saxon poetry, Bede explained, he presented only a few Latin lines, a translation of the sense rather than the poem.[7]

In a hymn Bede contrasted Virgil, the poet of arms, with himself, a poet of peace and the gifts of Christ. Bede, however, had to record the actions of warrior kings and the achievements of a warrior society. Theodore, it is true, persuaded two warring kings, Ecgfrith of Northumbria and Aethelred of Mercia, to make peace (679). The same Ecgfrith, nevertheless, invaded Ireland in 684, attacking an "inoffensive people" and sparing "neither churches nor monasteries. . . . And although those who curse may not enter the kingdom of God, one may well believe that those who were justly cursed for their wickedness quickly suffered the penalty of their guilt at the hands of God their Judge" (4.26). The end came for Ecgfrith and most of his forces when in the following year they invaded Scotland.[8]

Although Bede celebrated the Church as a society of peace, he mentioned without a word of misgiving the spread of Christianity to the Isle of Wight. This was the work of Caedwalla, king of Wessex, who exterminated the isle's hostile pagans and replaced them with settlers from his own territory (4.16).

As he approached the end of *The Ecclesiastical History*, Bede noted the persistence of the Celtic Britons in ways that separated them from the fellowship of the Church and in their hatred of the English. He also noted that many Northumbrians, noble and common folk, had received tonsure and taken monastic vows, choosing that course rather than studying the arts of war. Elsewhere Bede indicated his disapproval of this misuse of monastic privileges and rules. In his *History* he wrote only that a later generation would see the consequence of the practice. One possible consequence of the decline of military readiness was the sacking of Bede's monastic church by the Vikings sixty years after his death, and the destruction of a culture that was a graceful fusion of church, Roman, Celtic, and Germanic elements.

The *History* was prized in the very years after its completion and Bede's death. Numerous eighth-century manuscript copies of the work that required the use of expensive materials and long periods of taxing labor are the best evidence of the book's reputation. Unlike Tacitus, whose works — *Histories* and *Annals*, based primarily on two manuscripts found and put into circulation in the fifteenth century — were long unknown, Bede has been honored in medieval and modern times. *The Ecclesiastical History* is the principal source for the first three centuries of English (that is, Anglo-Saxon) history. Its scope, the conversion of the English people to Christianity and their later history within the Church, is their major cultural experience.

On occasion, the reader may think that Bede has rambled — for example, when Bede passed from the life of Aidan in one chapter to the piety of Oswald in another, to the conversion of the West Saxons, and then to Earconbert of Kent, the first English ruler to order the destruction of idols and the observance of Lent in his kingdom, whose daughter having become a nun died while many in the monastery heard a heavenly choir and saw a light from heaven that carried away her holy soul (2.5-8). Where he appears to do so, the rambling is in the nature of the sources that deal with a space of many kingdoms, rulers, and peoples and a long time-span. Bede, like Herodotus, was an artist with a love of unity and a sense of pace, but his accounts of personal sanctity and miracles are properly part of his story rather than digressions.

The monastic historian drew sources from a lifetime of study of the Church Fathers and classical authors and historians, from monastic annals, saints' lives, the lives of bishops, and ecclesiastical records in England and Rome. Following the precedent of St. Jerome, who in turn wrote in the tradition of Herodotus, Bede recorded popular reports. These included the miracles and wonders, the favors and graces by which God revealed his presence in the world. Although a sense of wonder pervades Bede's history, he does not mention a miracle that he claims to have witnessed.

Bede compiled his sources into a narrative of events and of things done. He had to be concerned to present such truth as he could find, but he had also to present what others said. The world by itself was a kingdom or city of sin and error, but its events were ultimately under the governance of God. The historian had to be truthful in order to tell the story of God's governance. For Bede in England that story, until his time, was of the unworthiness of the Britons, first because of the sins that justified their punishment by the Anglo-Saxon invaders and then because of their refusal to preach Christianity to the conquerors, who in God's plan were converted by others.

Telling this story is also a form of moral teaching: the commendation of good actions and opprobrious treatment of evildoers can encourage people to goodness and to the avoidance of vice. For the monastic author, this moral service to the members of the Church performed a function similar to the good citizenship, the moral civic purpose, of ancient historians. There was, however, no teaching of prudence in Bede's history — life afforded little opportunity for it. Nor was there any serious interest in causality.

Bede's book enables the reader to experience the Northumbrian world presented through the eyes and spirit of a noble and saintly man. The monastic historian Dom David Knowles ranked Bede as a great Englishman of direct common sense, lucidity, and integrity, in the line of Chaucer, Thomas More, and Samuel Johnson.[9] Bede's learned achievements point to the large cultural role played by monasteries in the barbarian period. They made for survival, continuity, and diffusion of culture in a rural world of limited resources. Many monasteries were destroyed in the various invasions from the north, but they reappeared even before the ordeal was over. Not only did these places of withdrawal from the world remain cultural, even economic centers, but many of them composed from generation to generation the chronicles, (for example, that of Matthew of Paris) which were the characteristic historical form of the Middle Ages.

6. William Camden:
The English Renaissance and the Modern State

THE HISTORIAN WILLIAM CAMDEN (1551-1623) is an outstanding scholarly figure in the late English Renaissance. This cultural movement combined features of the Italian Renaissance and the Christian Renaissance, as well as patriotic English humanist values and learning. The veneration of classical antiquity, the prizing of service to society and kingdom as duty and self-fulfillment, and a measure of secularism developed into an English growth derived from Italian Renaissance transplants. The Christian Renaissance, a northern as well as Latin phenomenon, looked for renewal to study of the Bible and Church Fathers. The Protestant Reformation intensified this movement and gave it a polemical direction, but in spite of divisions in the church there persisted in some people, including Camden, a sense of Christendom as one. Finally, as a dutiful and interested member of the English commonwealth, the monarchy, and the English church, he worked for the reputation of his land among the learned of Europe and his brothers and sisters in patriotism.[1]

His particular achievements in historiography were a learned account of the geography, monuments, events, and distinguished people of the counties of Britain, his native island, and his remarkably researched and well-informed *Annals* of Elizabeth's reign, the tribute of a scholar and subject to his late sovereign. Like most medieval historians he was a learned man, a "clerk" of Oxford university. He was not, however, a monk or churchman but a Christian man of this world devoted to his country. He had a Renaissance and, therefore, wider knowledge of classical writers than Western medieval historians and a considerable knowledge of the Church Fathers. Finally, he collected and studied historians of England and historical materials about his country and extended that interest to a concern with his native kingdom and its relations with the rest of the world in his own day.

Camden was born in the old city of London; his first home made him the familiar of old St. Paul's Cathedral, Fleet prison, Sea-coal Lane, markets, and the most unsanitary streets of the Elizabethan city. As a boy of nine he saw St. Paul's destroyed by fire. In *Britannia* he used the memory of a boyhood scene to support the view that St. Paul's had been built on the site of a temple of Diana. "When I was a boy I have seen the head of a buck, fixed on a spear (which seems to agree with the sacrifices of Diana) carried about with great pomp and blowing of horns within the church" (Gough, 2:81).

His interest in ancient Britain Camden described as an early and enduring passion, evidently, therefore, the gift of God. His father, a painter, appears to have been unable to support the son's education, because for a time William was at Christ's Hospital, a school and home for orphans and foundlings. Having survived the bubonic plague in 1563, he entered St. Paul's school, founded by Dean Colet to banish "Barbary and fylthinesses." It gave him a solid secondary schooling. The search for a scholarship and support accounts for his nomadry among the colleges of Oxford University (1566-1571). There he made friends who shared or later encouraged his patriotic antiquarian interests, but Camden recalled later that at the university he gave to the studies he loved only the time he could spare from the prescribed work in philosophy.[2]

After leaving the university he traveled in England. His appointment as second master in Westminster School (1575) solved the problem of livelihood. The post gave him more than a modest competence in return for a heavy schedule of teaching; even more important, it put him next to the center of English government, the hearth of patronage in church and state, where an aspiring scholar could meet many people of high position and at least see most others, including foreign visitors.

Teaching Latin and Greek grammar to schoolboys was time-consuming in its long yearly routine, but works by the curriculum's classical authors were sources for his study of British antiquity. In London he found other students of that subject and collectors of its sources, many of them the contents of dispersed monastic libraries. The archbishop of Canterbury, Matthew Parker, and William Cecil, the lord treasurer, were collectors as well as patrons of antiquarian studies. Out of the meetings of like-minded men there developed the Society of Antiquaries (1586), a learned society which met regularly for the presentation and discussion of papers. For a time the society met in the office of the heralds and for another period in the quarters of Sir Robert Cotton, once Camden's pupil at Westminster, whose collection of antiquities formed the original basis of the British Museum.

England was, as Thomas Hooker argued, a commonwealth formed by the monarchy and the established church. At Oxford and Westminster, Camden moved in each sphere of that commonwealth. His patrons form a circle of state and church. In 1589 the bishop of Salisbury gave him a prebend at Ilfracombe worth £50 a year, a goodly reward for the services of an absentee layman. Five years later the queen presented him with a very Elizabethan gift: she required the dean of Westminster Abbey to admit Camden to the dean and prebends' table for life and to provide board for one servant. The royal document explained that because she had employed him and intended to do so again, she "wishes him settled somewhere near and eased of the charge of living."[3] Finally in 1598 he was able to abandon what he called "the toilsome task of teaching" because in the preceding year he had been appointed Clarenceux-King of Arms, a high and lucrative position in the College of Heralds, subordinate only to Garter-King of Arms and the earl marshal.

Clarenceux supervised matters pertaining to the bearing of arms for all of England south of the River Trent. To grant arms and to see that men bore only the titles and arms to which they were entitled by birth or grant, to record pedigrees and to make visitations to amass and supervise pedigrees and arms, and to supervise for set fees the funerals of gentlemen and nobles were the principal functions of the kings of arms. The duties, some of which were rewarding privileges, gave him an occasion for travel and researches to enrich *Britannia*. They also enabled him to move among men of power and wealth who might provide information for his growing concern with recent history.

A loyal functionary, he avowed his gratitude. Some critics made this seem a reproach. Men of humble birth and ambition like Camden, one argued, were prone to overdo their gratitude, and in his case partiality could also be attributed to his mildness and good nature.[4] The implication — and it is conventional malice — was that he served as mercenary to his patrons. At any rate, he rendered good service to them. He had discretion and a courtly facility of language. He understood the value of understatement, and his rhetoric was more temperate than the views he expressed. He was ambitious, but in a limited way, and he could work hard. Some of his students, distinguished men, wrote of him affectionately in paying tribute to his learning. Continental scholars were his admiring correspondents. Little more can be said about Camden, the man, apart from the point that he had musician friends and lived in a male world.

Camden's classical, antiquarian, and patriotic interests merged in *Britannia* (1586), his first major writing. The work is subtitled "a chorographical description" of Britain, which meant a view or survey of the counties and localities of Britain considered in themselves and not, as in geography, in their relationship to other places. At one time Camden had considered writing a Latin history of England. Such a history simply would have been an account of kings, councils, the church, some notables, wars, and civil discords. That enterprise, he recognized, would not adequately draw upon what he knew and would not satisfy his antiquarian and patriotic passion. His interest went beyond kings and wars to an account of the land and people of the kingdom.

Two words, *memory* and *restoration*, dominate his decision to write *Britannia*, more comprehensive and more formless than the history. Like Herodotus, Camden believed that his compilations served the cause of memory. His inquiries enabled him to learn many things that otherwise might have been lost to knowledge and memory. His work was also a restoration of a past unknown or incompletely known. Restoration was the advice of the Flemish geographer, Abraham Ortelius, to Camden, when he was twenty-five years old: restore antiquity to Britain and Britain to its antiquity.[5] This was to place Britain within the classical culture of the Renaissance.

This patriotic, even nationalist, impulse broadened the work. Shakespeare's celebration of this sceptred isle, this England, echoed the sentiment of even Elizabethan antiquaries and scholars. Camden described Britain as the product of rejoicing nature. There was a special worth to everything English, for England was the true Isles of the Blest and God had created men of answerable worth to live in such a paradise.[6] The bragging is love, not on oath. Englishmen who applied to the Privy Council for license to travel in Europe customarily had to face the lord treasurer, Burghley, who tested their knowledge of England. If an applicant was not familiar with it, he might be advised to stay at home.[7] At any rate, Burghley therewith had another reason for refusal.

The early pages of *Britannia* deal with the geography of Britain and the origin of the British people and their name. A venerable and arrogantly maintained legend derived the name Britain from its alleged founder, a Trojan refugee, Brut. Camden, taking his position with critics of the legend, argued that only the merest shred of evidence could be urged in favor of Brut. His own explanation was that the name of Britain originated in a description of its people as painted or colored. Language indicated that the British and the ancient Gauls were similar in race; they were the descendents of the biblical Gomer, whose name accounts for the Cimbri.

Camden could be dexterously discreet, a model of diplomacy. In his learning and ideas he is less sharp in mind than Robert Burton, author of *The Anatomy of Melancholy*, but nonetheless kin to him and to John Donne. He seemed to know all the issues of his subject and unselfconsciously to embody the tensions and contradictions of his time. Thus, he stated that in an early age men had enough to do without recording their history, that conjectures based on the origin of words should be made, that a marksman may have a lucky hit, that one must expect and tolerate patriotic myth in origins, that nevertheless truth is one, and that "the real name and origin of Britain is as uncertain as the opinions about it" (Gough, 1:lxvi). His gentleness could become a repetitious suavity that he used stubbornly and combatively against the abundant malice of critics and rivals. This point is worthy of mention because the reader may be overpersuaded by an author who concluded one section with "Such is my opinion, or perhaps my error, about the origin of the Britons and the name of Britain, which, if false, I wish the truth to appear" (Gough, 1:lxix).

Later sections deal with the Romans, the Saxons, and the coming of the Danes and Normans. The equable Camden, calm in the storms of history, recounted the destruction of Britain by the Saxons in the severely critical words of the British monk Gildas, "whelmed in tears." Addressing his fellow countrymen, Camden observed that "we must forgive" the invectives of Gildas against British vices, and likewise forgive the savagery of the Picts and Scots and the "insatiable cruelty of the Saxons . . . since . . . we are now all become one people, softened by religion and liberal arts, let us reflect what they were, and what we ought to be; lest for our sins the Sovereign Ruler of the universe should destroy us, and bring other nations, or give them dominion over us" (Gough 1:cxxxvii).

After some account of institutions such as the law courts of England, Camden turned to the face of historical Britain, which he described county by county with the counties grouped under the British tribes that in Camden's opinion had inhabited them: "In each county I mean to describe its ancient inhabitants, etymology of its name, its limits, soil, remarkable places both ancient and modern, and its dukes or earls from the Norman conquest, as faithfully, clearly, and briefly as I can" (Gough, 1:ccv).

Britannia, like a smorgasbord, is good for sampling. The items touch on every phase of living. There are worrisome points — for example, the foundries of Sussex, which produced iron more brittle than that of Spain. Those who used it to cast cannons made "no small profit," although Camden was less assured about its public utility. He was the ready moralist when he described the finding in Cornwall of ancient brass weapons wrapped in linen. Quoting Macrobius on Aristotle, that brass weapons inflict less dangerous wounds than iron weapons do, he observed: "But that age was not so ingenious at the destruction of mankind as our own" (Gough, 1:268, 4).

But nature, too, presented its challenges. For example, the north wind, "the tyrant" of Cornwall's northern coast, piled up the sand so that the town of St. Ives, named after an Irish woman of singular sanctity, had to change its site. And there is the story of seal-fishing at Huntcliff, near Whitby, by men dressed in women's clothes because the seals were less fearful of women. Finally, the lessons of history misled Camden on projects to drain the Cambridgeshire fens. The draining eventually was successful, but he had judged the projects to be designed for private rather than public gain, believing that the fens "would return to their original state, as has often happened in draining the Pontine marshes in Italy" (Gough, 3:252; 2:215).

The work reverberates with the note of time consuming all things, more an Elizabethan sensibility than convention. Conventionally Elizabethan is the prophecy of immortality for works of art and great scholarly labors. Edmund Spenser, who wrote on "The Ruines of Time," told Camden, "antiquity's nurse," "though Time all monuments obscure / Yet thy just labors ever shall endure." With *Britannia*, Camden had written a foundation book for the study of British antiquities and historical geography.

In 1597 Camden was invited to write the history of his own time, that is, an account of the reign of Queen Elizabeth. The invitation came from Lord Burghley, Elizabeth's principal councillor and Camden's patron, who made available his own and then the queen's papers. Burghley's death in 1598 cut off access to the state papers. Some ten years later, after the queen's death, the accession of James I (1603-1625), and enlarged editions of *Britannia* in 1600 and 1607, Camden returned to arranging the material for annals of the reign of Queen Elizabeth. He had collected books, documents, and oral information, and for many events and speeches he had his own memory.

His inspiration was the gratitude of a subject of the English commonwealth to the queen whose reign of forty-five years, times when ease was uncommon and serenity rare, had maintained the security of the kingdom. His work was also meant to commemorate Lord Burghley and some of Elizabeth's other servants in church and state. As he wrote for publication under the eyes of Burghley's son, Robert Cecil, and of King James I, he found that the effort to do justice to Scotland and England, to Mary, Queen of Scots, and to Elizabeth, who had her executed, taxed his sympathies and challenged his capacity for courtly rhetoric. His vision of tragedy in rivalry and conflict helped him to meet the challenge.

The function of history, as he understood it, was to preserve and to shape memory. Goodness, which included learning, was praised; evil, particularly disorder and treason, was held up for reprobation. Camden conformed to the moralizing convention in the obituary notices he usually appended at each year's end, but his principal interest was in policy and prudence, the sovereign teacher of a civic moral.

To emphasize policy and to feature prudence raised great difficulties for the writer of history in Tudor and early Stuart times. John Hayward, who had dedicated a life of Henry IV to the earl of Essex, was imprisoned for two years because it was charged that his description of the deposition of Richard II was a recommendation that Essex do the same to Elizabeth. This was to take in an impossibly rigorous sense the view that history teaches by example. Three years earlier, Thomas Dannet, in his translation of *The Historie of Philip de Commines* (1596), memoirs written some nine decades earlier, indicated to Burghley that he had been reluctant to publish the book because it treated of state secrets, and he cited a king who had been angered because Commines divulged state secrets.

Camden's problem was to deal with policy and to celebrate prudence without being "saucy to princes" and without causing King James to think that he was intruding upon the secrets, the mystery, the profession of ruling. His solution was to arrange material in the form of annals, a procedure that in other ways suited a mind that was neither systematic nor even tidy, and to address himself to responsible subjects of the English crown, literate men of substance, and to similar readers in Europe — that is, to write in Latin. He professed to follow Tacitus in arranging weighty events according to years. It would have been difficult to use his materials in any other way.[8] If he had composed a history of Elizabeth's reign, Camden would have had to choose topics within some large temporal division, disclosing his opinion on a scale that might have drawn the censure of King James, his servants, or surviving ministers of the queen.

Camden also followed Tacitus and his disciples among Camden's contemporaries in writing a politically instructive work. He declared that, as he wrote not for idle sport but for profitable instruction, he would consider how, why, and to what end things were done. He did speak his mind on many matters. But as an annalist he had precedent for stating here and there that he would not give an opinion; for presenting several explanations of an action; and for mentioning meteorological observations, wonders, the increase of drunkenness in England caused by soldiers who had fought in the Netherlands, government regulation of the length of swords, daggers, ornate dress, and the growth of London, and Elizabeth's skillful use of her women attendants as a source of information, especially about who loved whom. On some subjects the annalist could be apologetically brief, and he could sometimes hurry over religious matters because he was leaving the subject to the ecclesiastical historian, although he recognized that religion and state could not be sundered. Here and there, especially on Scotland and Ireland, he brought together matters drawn from several years in order, he wrote, to help the memory, but in fact to make them intelligible.

To justify himself to the reader, Camden had to indicate how he had gained his knowledge. A statesman and servant of the ruler would have had memories and a long experience, but Camden had been only in the shadows of power. He therefore justified himself by being explicit about the unusual range of his sources, including Burghley's papers. He had sought all kinds of documents so that he could see "the bright Lustre of uncorrupt Faithfulness shining forth in those Monuments and Records, which are beyond all exception: and peradventure I have attained no less Knowledge of those affairs than some others who have been deeply versed in State-Matters." Labor in many sources gave him knowledge that put him on a level with statesmen — he wrote with their eyes — and entitled him to hope that he had found "the truth hidden by stealth or hiding itself."

As was the case with his successors, his profession of method is loftier than his practice. He boasted that he would not declaim against the enemies of England and thereby gain applause as a good commonwealth man at the expense of his reputation as a historian. He disclaimed fear of those who think that present power can wipe out a later age's memory. In writing without partisanship or prejudice to raise minds to honesty and prudence, he stated ingenuously that scarcely anyone of those he would mention in the *Annals* had injured or favored him.[9]

At her accession, Elizabeth was twenty-five years old and had been schooled by experience and adversity, "effectual masters" (p. 12). Consequently, she had learned that decision was to bet on one course in a dangerous world. She preferred to keep options open, even at the cost of the danger that lurked in delay, of being tortuous, and of exasperating her well-selected advisors. Camden described Elizabeth as a mild princess, gentle and courteous, insistent upon her due revenue and more than prudently reluctant to spend it. Lack of resources and her sex made her mistrustful of war. She had resolved to be her own mistress, and she was an able, even shameless, actress with suitors for diplomacy's sake and for the fun of it, ultimately mistrustful of men — at any rate, of the pushing, colorful men she liked. She was a Protestant by birth, conviction, and interest.

After she had been proclaimed queen, it was up to her to maintain the crown by governing her kingdom. In her Privy Council she retained some of the councillors of Queen Mary and to them added Protestant advisors, notably William Cecil, who, under Mary, had conformed to Catholicism, that is, "humored the times" (p. 557), a "most prudent man, worth a company of other people" (p. 13).[10]

Elizabeth soon moved to end England's reconciliation with Catholicism and Rome. She and her first parliament reestablished the Protestant religion. Clergymen, officials, and candidates for degrees, among others, were required to take an oath recognizing the queen as governor of the church in England. There was a weariness in the beginning. Camden mentioned that "most" of the Catholic clergy who refused to take the Oath of Supremacy had taken it in Henry VIII's reign. This time, most of the bishops refused to take it and were replaced. Among the lords temporal, the earl of Shrewsbury also refused. Viscount Montacute made the solitary objection that with Parliament's authorization he had arranged for the

recent restoration of England to the unity of Rome. Recanta-
tion, he argued, would be dishonorable and dangerous. Those
who did not go to Sunday services were to be fined. Most of the
clergy conformed; most of the Catholic priests did so, according
to Camden, to protect themselves and to keep out Protestant
replacements, a course they regarded as piously prudential and
meritorious (pp. 19, 31). Over the years, if there would be so
much time, conformity and fines might wither Catholicism.

That she was a woman in the male world of church, council,
and war was long to put to trial Elizabeth's determination to
be her own mistress. To establish her position meant providing
firmly for succession to the throne, but marriage, whether to a
foreign prince or to a subject, was likely to curtail if not destroy
her independence. Nevertheless, the queen favored the vigorous and well-shaped Robert Dudley, earl of Leicester, as
much as his father and grandfather had been hated by the people. Camden professed himself unable to explain Elizabeth's
quarter-century of favor to Leicester: Could it, he asked, have
been their common experience of imprisonment under Mary?
Or his virtues, of which there was a semblance? Or did hidden
causes, the stars and planets, bring them together?

In 1565 the matter of the queen's marriage seemed likely to
provoke violence at her court. Armed followers of the earl of
Sussex, who urged that Elizabeth marry the brother of Emperor Maximilian, and Leicester, who opposed the proposed
union, menaced each other even at court. After a few days the
queen "reconciled them, and buried their Malice rather than
took it away." The queen's infatuation even inclined her to
accede to Leicester's request that he be named her lieutenant in
England and Ireland. Burghley and Sir Christopher Hatton
successfully opposed the bid. Burghley often opposed Leicester,
who, in Burghley's mind and Camden's account, was a dangerous adventurer. Happily for the kingdom, his selfishness and
overreaching ambition somewhat reduced the danger of the
man because they inspired disgraceful charges. The defamation
was, as Camden maliciously put it, "not without mixture of
some Untruths" (pp. 45, 79, 326, 419-20).

When the final card had to be played, nevertheless, the
queen was mistress of herself and could put on an impressive
act. Thus, when in 1578 one of the women of her bedchamber

urged Leicester as a husband, Elizabeth replied: "Do you think that I am so unlike myself that I would prefer for a husband my minion, whom I myself raised up, to the greatest princes of the Christian world?"[11] The annalist's final word is that on his death Leicester's goods were sold at auction to pay his debts to the queen, who almost never forgave what was owed to the royal treasury (p. 420).

Camden presented Lord Burghley as a contrast to Leicester, as the ideal servant of the queen and the new politics, a prudent and moderate councillor, and where possible a man of peace. His eminence attracted the envy of great lords, including Leicester, whom he overcame "more by patience than by obstinacy." As master of wards he was so skillful and upright, according to Camden, that he served the queen and the wards well, to his own middling profit and to the greater profit of his followers. Later, as lord high treasurer, he was strict but not rigid with the tax collectors, endeavoring, "not without good Success, that both Prince and People might grow rich." In 1598 he urged peace with Spain against the opposition of the earl of Essex, Leicester's stepson, rasher, more dangerous, and more ill-fated than his stepfather. Burghley died soon after, honored by the queen, without debts, having made bequests for good works, and with his son as lord treasurer (pp. 556-59).

Burghley and his queen may have preferred peace, but for what they believed to be her interests and England's they waged decades of war. Even so, the divisions and distractions of rivals and enemies were perhaps of as much service to Elizabeth as her military effort was. First of all, she weathered a diplomatic revolution in which Spain took the place of France as England's traditional enemy. Religion, English interest in the passage through the English Channel and the Dover Straits, and security against an attack from the Belgian and Dutch provinces of the Spanish king were principal points in a re-alignment of powers that challenged the growth of English sea power and favored the beginnings of English empire. When the Dutch rebellion against Spanish rule began, Elizabeth firmly and successfully supported the Dutch against Spain. Camden devoted many pages to Dutch affairs, which "often joyned and twisted with English matters and Counsels" (p. 120). He recorded Elizabeth's order to Leicester, commander of her forces in the Netherlands, to study the Dutch art of raising and depressing the value of money ("herein they . . . are skilled above all other men") so that her "Souldiers might not receive their Pay at one Rate, and spend it at another" (p. 326).

France, which through Mary Queen of Scots, widow of a French king, might have been even more troublesome than it proved to be, was soon to experience eight spells of religious wars. In those civil wars there were sometimes three parties: the Catholic Guise faction, often working with Spain; the Protestant (Huguenots) nobles and professional people; and a mainly Catholic faction (*politiques*) concerned with the political unity of France and prepared to recognize the religious division of the kingdom. Early in her reign Elizabeth aided the Huguenots, who briefly turned against the English. Camden recorded that Elizabeth then "resolved to take no longer Care of other men's estates with peril of her own" (p. 194). But the requirements of later politics caused her to abandon even that decision. The *politiques*, among whom Camden had friends and correspondents, won out, but with a surprising turn. The Protestant Henry Bourbon of Navarre outlasted his rivals to become Henry IV of France, who decided to adopt the Catholic religion of the large majority of his subjects and the *politique* position, toleration for the Huguenots. Elizabeth, leagued with him and the Dutch against Spain, expressed her aversion to his change of religion and to his consideration of peace with Spain. Henry consulted, as Camden put it, "his own concernment" and argued "urgent necessity" in pursuing the peace (1598), "which shortly after he concluded, to the general great Good of France." For that the common people of England made him a byword for an ungrateful prince, although Henry also sought to make peace between England and Spain (pp. 546, 548-49).

Camden's *Annals* describe Elizabeth's journeys through the kingdom and many scenes, pageants and tournaments that Elizabethans thought significant but that may not be found in modern histories. Camden, for example, thought the public executions of noblemen and some others accused of treason to be worthy of detailed description. He knew the sad truth of the cynical Elizabethan verses about treason's inability to prosper because no one dare call successful treason by its name. But treason put down was a civic and a moral triumph to be dramatically rendered. Here justice was seen to be done and the victim, just before facing judgment in another world, usually cooperated until the last twitch.

The first peer of the realm, the duke of Norfolk, made a classic case of Elizabethan treason. This Protestant duke was implicated in a plot supported by advocates of an active foreign policy in behalf of Protestants and by some favorers of Catholicism. The plotters intended to replace Secretary William Cecil as Elizabeth's principal advisor and to provide for the royal succession by the marriage of the duke to Mary, Queen of Scots. The English government foiled the plot. Norfolk was arrested, then released, and subsequently he took part in another plot. He pleaded not guilty to charges that he had planned to depose the queen and kill her. When his peers found him guilty, he was sentenced to be drawn on a hurdle through the city of London, then to be hanged, cut down half-dead, disemboweled, beheaded, and quartered. Eventually the duke faced an easier end: after he admitted that he had been justly judged and forgave his executioner, his head was cut off and shown "as a lamentable Spectacle to the sorrowing and weeping People" (pp. 170-78).

In 1572, Parliament imposed for the period of Elizabeth's reign severe penalties for attacks on her forts and ships and for efforts to release those imprisoned for treason before their indictment. The punishments, Camden wrote, were severe to meet the needs of the times. Nine years later both Puritan and Catholic suffered. To defend the Protestant religion, John Stubbs wrote "in a sharp and stinging style" a book against Elizabeth's projected marriage with the duke of Anjou. His unusual punishment for this seditious writing was the amputation of his right hand by striking a mallet against a cleaver placed on his wrist. Camden was present as a witness in Westminster marketplace when Stubbs awed the crowd by using his remaining hand to lift his hat as he shouted "God save the Queen" (p. 270).

The decade of the eighties aged in growing anxiety and fear as there was a convergence of threats from the Spaniards with their heavy, "Catle-like-ships," the imprisoned Queen of Scots, and the Catholics. Priest-missionaries trained at Douai Seminary and Jesuits came to minister to English Catholics, challenging the government's hope that persecution and lack of ministry would wither the faith and loyalty of the Catholics. When in 1570 Pope Pius V absolved Elizabeth's subjects from their allegiance, the English government had some ground for using a charge of treason against Catholics. Elizabeth, Camden wrote, did not wish to force men's consciences and refused to believe that most Catholic priests plotted the destruction of their country. But she was convinced that their superiors did. *Necessity* (the word is Camden's) compelled her to act against the Catholics lest she ruin her subjects and herself by yielding to their pretended claim of conscience (p. 271).

The Annals presented the government's position most explicitly in narrating the trial of Philip Howard, earl of Arundel. In it the sergeant-at-law quoted Arundel's prior statement that the thorough Papist must be a traitor. The sergeant argued that the earl had received the sacraments and that to do so he had to be reconciled to the pope. In the overkill usual in such prosecutions, Arundel was said to have acted out of disaffection rather than conscience and to have been the instigator of the papal bull of deposition (pp. 424-29, 506).

The scenes strain Camden's effort to use calm and judicious language. For example, he recalled the Jesuit Edmund Campion as a gifted and promising Oxford contemporary. After his arrest and torture, Campion took part in a theological disputation in which "he scarcely answered the Expectation raised of him" (p. 247). Camden's words on genuine conspirators in 1586 caricature him: the first seven were hanged, cut down, castrated, "their Bowels taken out before their Faces while they were alive, and their Bodies quartered, not without some note and touch of Cruelty" (p. 344).

Under the year 1594 Camden called Prince Henry, the newly born son of King James of Scotland, "the Love and Delight of Britain" (p. 483). This intrusion of hindsight into the *Annals* emphasized "the rare felicity of these times" (1607) and its providential opportunity in the union under King James of England and Scotland, so long divided (*Britannia*; Gough, 4:1). Camden pronounced it the design of God, but the tumultuous story of the union could be presented only, so goes the Spanish proverb, as God writing straight in crooked lines.

In the very long run Elizabeth's policy of intervention in Scotland, of seeking to influence King James, was successful. After Mary gave birth to the future king, she lost out to rebels and sought safety in England, where the troublesome refugee became a worrisome prisoner. The two queens were driven apart by personal antipathy and unacknowledged rivalry, and matters were worsened by the efforts of each to maintain her dignity. In his account of Scottish affairs, Camden used candid words for his cold eye's vision. Elizabeth, he wrote, did not oppose Lenox as regent of Scotland in 1570 because she knew that he would be kind to James, his royal grandson, she thought he would be mindful of favors received from England, and she had less to fear from Lenox "considering that she had his Wife in her power" (p. 142).

To the end of Elizabeth's reign Scotland remained a land of close calls for English interests. Elizabeth refused to name a successor until her last extremity. King James and the succession figured in the calculations of plotters and rebels, including the earl of Essex. In the last years Robert Cecil began a secret, dangerous, and necessary correspondence—Camden was not free to tell that story—to reassure the Scottish king, who was riled by impatience, and to arrange a peaceful transition of government upon the queen's death. As a herald, Camden was part of the company that greeted Britain's new king outside London, where plague raged.

Camden's *Annals* are remarkable for three principal reasons. The first is Camden's privileged position, with Burghley's favor and Cotton's friendship, in Westminster School and in the College of Heralds. He anticipated Leopold von Ranke, who demanded that the modern historian search for sources and practice a criticism as rigorous as that of the classical scholar. Camden was a scholar, not a statesman-author of memoirs, and as a near-contemporary historian had no peer in England for two hundred years. Although as an act of piety to Oxford and to the scholarly life, Camden founded Oxford's first history professorship, the professors were limited to ancient history and had little distinction.

Second, Camden wrote his *Annals* as a warm supporter of the queen's government, which on mercantilist grounds he saw as a modern state. He praised her for coining purer money—

debasement had been the medieval and early Tudor equivalent of inflation as hidden taxation — than England had had for several centuries. He knew and quoted the explorers, he had a knowledgeable interest in projects for colonies, and he approved the enterprise of merchants and government aid for their efforts. Ireland bulked large in his pages as a threat to England, the graveyard of English military reputations and the sink that drained English resources, a bad land for fighting, a land of ambushes and bad faith, guerrilla-haunted, full of damp hiding places. In 1603, he believed, Lord Mountjoy had suppressed the principal Irish rebellion.

The third distinction of the *Annals* is that the author reveals, in the main, with clarity and little embarrassment, the ethical dilemmas presented by the modern state, its interest and reason. Security may require domestic spying and knavish tricks. Political reason may require executions and determine their timing. At Smerwick in 1580 the English were short of supplies and men to guard the surrendered garrison. They therefore decided to spare the commanders and to put "the rest promiscuously . . . to the Sword for a Terrour, and that the Irish should be hanged up." The queen, disliking such cruelty, "hardly did . . . allow of the Reasons for the Slaughter committed" (p. 243). In governing her realm the queen, though sparing in her diet, often tried to have her cake and eat it.

7. Voltaire:

History Unexemplary and en Philosophe

VOLTAIRE WROTE IN THE name of reason and philosophy against the burden of the past, the intolerance of churches, the inhumanity of laws, the exploitation of the weak, and the vogue and power of folly. Religious intolerance had acquired new life when in the Reformation central and western Europeans divided into hostile churches. This intolerance added to the force and repression that were the instruments of state builders and absolute monarchs. International wars and domestic political struggles usually had religious aspects that were distorted to present the quarrels as religious wars.

The victims of the wars of religion and persecution had their revenge in the growth of a temper indifferent to the claims of particular churches. Others, too, adopting ancient materialisms, rationalism, or the outlook of physical science, rejected theology and abandoned religion altogether. For both, the Enlightenment meant a polemic against the Christian churches, as well as Judaism, and the articulation of new beliefs. Since religions touched in different degrees all spheres of life, the battleground included philosophy, morality, and history. Superstition and persecution were the themes of Enlightenment church history. God's hand, if there was a God, might guide history in some ultimate way, but not by direct intervention. As there was no "sacred history," the meaning of history or, at any rate, a way of looking at history, had to be sought anew. After the first quarter of the eighteenth century, this task attracted a remarkable and numerous response, to which the Romantic period added the dense and challenging Idealist philosophies of history. The *philosophes*, the gurus of enlightenment, presented history's meaning as not in the past but to come, as salvation from the irrational and the brutal, and presented it with a clarity as misleading as it was persuasive.

The age, in its critique of the past, became so self-conscious that it christened itself: the Enlightenment. Its ideas enjoyed a European triumph. In Germany, where it was called the *Aufklärung*, the Königsberg philosopher Immanuel Kant asked what it was and gave a memorable reply: his age required that all things be justified by reason, and that man be free to use his reason in all affairs. Spiritual authorities and established orders, whose privileges had been tied to functions the orders no longer performed, became objects of hostility. Reason threatened to overwhelm prescriptive title and historical right. In the writings of some, it appeared to promise a new order of the world: as it were, a new creation before which the old order and its history were proclaimed unexemplary and irrelevant. Voltaire's importance in historiography is that this prince of the *philosophes*, the new learned estate replacing bishop and priest, wrote biographies that exemplified Enlightenment taste and works that provided a new kind of exemplary history, an approach that would be meaningful or useful for those who rejected Providence.

Voltaire (1694-1778) had incomparable literary eminence and influence. His genius, witty and quick, commanded recognition almost as readily as it spurred the suspicions of authority and turned his victims into enemies. His father was a *bourgeois gentilhomme*, who accordingly arranged in 1704 to send the young François Arouet to the esteemed and fashionable Jesuit school, Louis-le-grand. There, as Voltaire wrote in 1746, "I was brought up for seven years by men who take immense and indefatigable pains to form the minds and the morals of youth."[1] The curriculum consisted of the classics (primarily Latin), French language and literature, some science, and religion. There was almost no modern history. For the study of religion, the curriculum prescribed an edition of the catechism of Peter Canisius, described by Theodore Besterman, Voltaire's learned and partisan biographer, as "essentially a practical guide for the man of the world. The subtleties as well as the worst excesses of doctrine are glossed over."[2] Louis-le-grand fostered Voltaire's dramatic and literary interests and possibly his hostility to religion — a hostility that his godfather, Abbé Chateauneuf, helped to inspire and advance. At any rate, upon leaving the college, he was vain and sensitive. Beyond that, and more important, he was self-assured: although he was never hale and hearty, his will could command the energy for his ambitions.

The Jesuits found him a bright but not a model pupil. One teacher called him a deist. While in school, he had met free-thinking hedonist wits, some of them clerics for whom blasphemy was a form of hedonism, who met in the one-time headquarters of the Knights Templars. After leaving school, he was their associate.

A family offer to purchase him a legal-judicial office, a mastership of requests, he spurned. As literature then could offer no livelihood, his father arranged that he should leave Paris and his undesirable companions for the Netherlands, where he joined the staff of the French ambassador. The paternal plan did not change the young scapegrace. Without fortune, Voltaire wooed and apparently conquered the daughter of an ambitious and resourceful mother. Even the course of fleeting fancy did not run smooth, and the incorrigible was recalled from exile.

The comedy is not finished. Enter father armed with a *lettre de cachet* against his son. This time there was the threat of exile to the West Indies, and the young man responded with dutiful blarney, including the promise to study law, which he pursued for his own short season. Paris and the law permitted association with his libertine friends who, enjoying the patronage of the prince regent for some years, achieved greater influence than might otherwise have been theirs.

Even in this company, wit outran youthful discretion, for Voltaire, who was to be for more than twenty years the lover of his own ugly, though sensual, niece, composed an epigram about the rumored incest between the regent and his own daughter. For this Voltaire was briefly exiled from Paris. Among those he visited in the country was his Templar associate Caumartin, marquis de Saint-Ange, whose stories about his own royal master Louis XIV and about Henry IV fascinated his young guest. Some of this material and the fruit of additional reading he put into an epic poem, the *Henriade* (1722), begun in the Bastille where he was briefly imprisoned (1717-1718) on the testimony of a police spy who reported words of Voltaire that compounded the earlier offense against the regent.

Verse dramas and the *Henriade*, which eventually brought him substantial income, early won him a literary reputation. In the midst of these triumphs, it was also his lot to experience the humiliation that a privileged society could inflict on a bourgeois. Gui August de Rohan-Cabot insulted Voltaire, who returned the insult. Rohan then had his servants thrash Voltaire, who attempted to compel Rohan to fight a duel. But the conflict of a Rohan and a bourgeois was unthinkable.[3] Cardinal de Rohan, therefore, had Voltaire placed once more in the Bastille (1726). The arbitrary Old Regime could also be easygoing, and the prisoner's offer to go to England instead was accepted.

In England Voltaire conceived the idea of composing a life of the Swedish king, Charles XII, his first major historical work. But Rohan's revenge cost the Old Regime dearly: Voltaire's observations in England (1726-1728) inspired the compilation (1729-1731) of *Les Lettres philosophiques* (1734). His description of English institutions and customs drew a contrast with the irrationality of French institutions. The severity of his satirical criticism was grounded in his use of England as a revolutionary model for France.

First of all, Voltaire noted, the English monarch rules according to law over free and equal subjects. It would be impossible for any church religion to be a model, but religious toleration, the issue of English religious divisions, was the grace that saved the land of Newton and Locke from the brutal inanity of persecution for the sake of doctrine. Happily, Englishmen were not recklessly deprived of the fruit of their labor, as Frenchmen in their servitude were. The English, therefore, honored man's true benefactors. They engaged in commerce without shame or restraint and on a higher level honored the work of scientists and philosophers. Voltaire's unrestrained contempt for Christianity compounded the effect of a final section of arguments against Pascal.

England served the *philosophe* well in every respect except the theater and poetry. Here English freedom conflicted with

Voltaire's passion for literary order. Shakespeare, he judged, was the ruin of English tragedy: others without his genius copied his art, which Voltaire likened more to nature than to a garden. For the English theater and poetry, Voltaire prescribed the geometrical spirit.[4]

The Parlement of Paris ordered that the *Lettres philosophiques* be burned by the hangman. As Voltaire generally feared the same fate for his later writings, he denied authorship of many of them. He often regarded being given credit for his work as a hostile act. Like some of the writers for the *Encyclopédie*, he would disavow his own strongly expressed views in favor of a limp statement of orthodox faith. In the fashion of his contemporaries, he often arranged for publication surreptitiously or under pseudonyms. When he did not enjoy the court's favor, he lived close to the French frontier so that he had ready exit from France. Attempts to find a protector in Frederick the Great of Prussia were in the long run unsuccessful. Voltaire had good reason to fear and hate persecutors and, valuing freedom and tolerance, he performed prodigies in their behalf. Nevertheless, he did not say that he would defend to the death the right of people to say that with which he disagreed — or, as one version has it, what he detested. It is even less likely that he would have acted on the statement. He hated the persecutors too much. He could find reasons to ignore or even favor persecution in the name of progress and enlightenment or in dealing with rivals.

After his triumphs in poetry and the theater, Voltaire, seeking a new field for conquest and glory, chose to write the history of a conqueror. His choice of a subject, Charles XII (1682-1718), is at first surprising but may be readily explained. The career of the Swedish warrior, a king wholly without weakness in royal-warrior virtues, promised the literary artist scenes of high drama: the young king's victories over an overwhelming coalition of Russia, Poland, and Denmark; his fortitude and refusal to surrender even when he sought refuge in Turkey, where he proved to be an unendurable guest and refugee; and his death on the battlefield.

The dramatist had as much to do with the history as did the *philosophe*. The latter had to recognize that the theater is a principal school of taste, good manners, and refinement. Barbarous and vulgar expressions such as Shakespeare used were offensive because, Voltaire argued, theater audiences were the first people in the land and for them common language had to be elevated. The theater must be a place of nobility: "It is the duty of a king and his court to give to the nation an example of noble behavior, and it is the function of the state to reflect that ideal."[5]

Voltaire told his tale and pointed his moral so vividly that Samuel Johnson drew on the *History of Charles XII* when he used some celebrated phrases in *The Vanity of Human Wishes.* Charles's name made the world grow pale. "Unconquered lord of pleasure and of pain," " 'Think nothing gain'd,' he cries, 'til nought remain.' " For the moral exemplary tradition Charles could be presented as the warrior *sans reproche* who carried his virtues to an excess that made them as dangerous as their opposite vices.[6] Voltaire's vision presented not dreams of glory but the cost of those dreams: "the moral tale of a warrior king whose very virtues made him incapable of being the wise leader of his nation."[7] Charles and his principal antagonist, Peter the Great, were, Voltaire judged, perhaps the two most remarkable monarchs in history.

The historian of Charles XII recognized the special problems of his project. All history, especially ancient, abounded in myths and fables. Modern history, he thought, could be more certain and more valuable, but there were a thousand chroniclers, gazeteers, and purveyors of random detail to two or three historians. He proposed to spare the reader needless information. The scoffer at all technical philosophy firmly settled for relevance, a word he did not at this stage define.

Voltaire based the *History* on serious, if limited, research. He read very widely, sought the recollections of many of the king's associates, and was persistent in correspondence to clarify events and motivation. Eventually he recognized that an effort to get all the details just right could lead only to despair. His sole function was to put true colors upon the designs others had furnished him.[8]

With ten printings in its first two years, the *History* made for a publisher's bonanza and has been such a literary success that Voltaire's interpretation has been widely held until our own day. Charles's recent biographer, R.M. Hatton, recognized that Voltaire's account, a triumph of art, was a principal obstacle to any attempt at presenting a reconsideration of Charles XII.

The *History* is still readable for four reasons. First, Voltaire sought and collected serious source material. Then there is the easy, fast-moving style, which, Condorcet said, was as rapidly mobile as the exploits of the history's hero.[9] There are, as well, the delightful anecdotes, some of which are untrue and others uncertain. Among them is the story of Charles's last battle and the "eccentric" French engineer, Captain Megret (Maigret), who had promised the king victory within eight hours. In an early exchange of fire, Charles XII was shot in the head (not hit by artillery as Voltaire wrote). Maigret's comment is worthy of a place in *Candide*: "Well, then, the matter's finished; let us go to dinner."[10] And finally there is Voltaire's interpretation of Charles XII, a satisfyingly aesthetic work framed for the moralizing service of history as philosophy teaching by example. In writing, Voltaire was judging as rigorously as the Abbé de Mably urged the historian to judge: "You must absolutely believe that he ought to exercise a kind of magistracy."[11]

Voltaire presented Peter the Great as the antithesis of the Swedish conqueror. We have these unqualified extremes: the latter left only ruins, which is not true, and the former was a creator in every field, which is about the most adulation Stalin ever received from his admirers. In revising the History of Charles XII, as he frequently did, Voltaire concentrated his additions on the wasteful conqueror. Earlier history, he explained, pandered to man's self-destructive inclinations; it was a work to satisfy curiosity and to amuse. Meanwhile, political attitudes had changed. Position and title claimed less attention, and readers were more interested in what a ruler had actually done.

Here Voltaire protested too much. He genuinely and with unforgivable lack of criticism admired Peter the Great and Catherine the Great as westernizers of Russia. His judgment was that Peter had undertaken a work of civilization that within fifty years secured Russian dominance of the Black Sea and the victories of disciplined Russian armies in Germany, made a polite society of a once unknown empire of two thousand leagues, and in his brilliant European court, where

Catherine later was the most zealous protector of letters, caused the arts to flourish in the midst of war. Peter, as author of that revolution, was probably the worthiest prince for posterity to recall and so for the historian to memorialize.[12]

Caution, if not fear and trembling, also inspired this panegyric of civilization — and the theme is worthy of another *Candide* or *Penguin Island*. Voltaire was seeking royal protection. The French court was hostile, and Frederick of Prussia was not dependable. To Mme. de Fontaine (February 16, 1762), he explained that one always had to have a queen behind one. One Russian queen yielded to his search. *The History of Russia under Peter the Great* (1760-1763) was written for Empress Elizabeth of Russia, who approved the first part before it was published. The commission for this work which he had sought in 1745 came only in 1757, after which the Russian chancellor, Shouvalov, sent him many documents, maps, and books. To Shouvalov he wrote that he was "your secretary at les Délices" (Voltaire's residence) and that he was "building for you the home for which you have furnished me with the materials."[13]

And yet the work did not hold Voltaire's interest. Dissatisfaction appears in a number of remarks about being well paid in pelts. Perhaps he found hagiography too constricting and the advance of civilization a strain to his reason. Nevertheless, such were his themes, the advance of reason and civilization with Peter as the very icon of the Enlightened Despot. Peter's Russia and later Catherine's Russia were images of Voltaire's heavenly, that is earthly, city, and yet he knew more about Peter than he wrote. To the duchess of Saxe-Gotha he confided, "If Tsar Peter were alive, I would flee 100 leagues in order not to be around that centaur, half man and half horse, who would destroy so many men for his pleasure, while he civilized others."[14]

He also loved Russia for its enemies — Turkey, mired in backwardness, and Poland, the apotheosis of feudalism and disorder. Against such enemies Russian conquests were a work of civilization. Voltaire here anticipated the crudest imperialism and renewed for the modern age the idea of a crusade not for doctrine but for ideas.[15]

Catherine, indeed, had won him by flattery and gifts, and her proclamations turned him into a propagandist. Even the

trowel of flattery required by imperial patronage hardly ac-
counted for Voltaire's subscribing himself as a lay missionary of
St. Catherine and the priest of her temple, or for his praise of
her conquest of Poland to impose religious toleration on it.
Later and privately, he confessed to Frederick the Great that
she had tricked all of them. Catherine herself was clear-
sighted, persistently avoiding a positive reply to his desire to
make a Russian pilgrimage: "For God's sake, advise the old oc-
togenarian to remain in Paris. Tell him that 'Cateau' [Voltaire's
pet name for her] is only good to see from a distance."[16]

Voltaire first alluded to his major work of history, *The Age
of Louis XIV* (1751), in 1732 while he was busy with the *Lettres
philosophiques*. The glorification of the age of Louis XIV
would continue his attack on Louis XV's France. By 1735 Voltaire announced that it was to be his life's work. Its originality
and significance appeared in the title, the history not of a king
but of the age bearing the king's name. Voltaire's innovation
may be emphasized if P. Daniel's *Histoire de France* (1703), a
conversation piece upon publication, is considered: "The
history of a kingdom or of a nation has for its object the prince
and the state." They form the center to which every detail is
related.[17] In his treatment of French history, Daniel was
respectful, as was his dedication to Louis XIV.

To those who criticized him for providing few portraits,
Voltaire replied with a simplicity that may induce apoplexy in
the analyst of method: presentation had to follow the facts, and
any other method was charlatanry. There next came the point
of contrast: "I have painted the age, and not the person of Louis
XIV, nor that of William III, nor the great Condé, nor Marl-
borough."[18] He wrote history as a *philosophe*, a social and
cultural history concerned to improve the condition of man
by preserving the memory of great human moments. He had
chosen Louis XIV because his reign has benefited not France
alone, but other men.[19] For the Enlightenment exemplary
tradition, the age of Louis XIV was the greatest of the four ages
that alone were useful for inspiration and imitation. The other
ages had great artists and writers, and like them, the French
age was an age of genius. Louis's glory was in patronizing and
sustaining genius and art, but the age's historical distinction
was that reason had been perfected. If Louis XIV was not a

philosopher king, his age made possible a kingdom happier in that it had many philosophers.

Richelieu prepared the way, but Louis himself reestablished the royal power, which meant that he imposed on the remains of feudal anarchy and constitutionalist pretenders the order necessary for a flourishing society. Forceful action indeed appears in the history but without emphasis, in order to avoid the dilemma that on other occasions prompted Voltaire to call history an imbecilic and immoral tale: human ambition, misused power and authority ending in the destruction of men and the works of the human spirit.

Later chapters dealt with the internal government of France, royal legislation, the mercantilist measures of Colbert, and that minister's many activities in a variety of fields, including canal-building and art, the street lighting of Paris, and the architecture of Versailles and Paris. Nevertheless, the history dealt at unexpected length with Louis's foreign policy, wars, and battles, even though the author had stated that such matters, which were the history of all times, were "the last part of my design."[20]

He sought details and the truth — not the truth which teaches nothing, but that which unfolds the genius of the master of the court and of the nation.[21] The Battle of Steenkirk he would consign to oblivion, and in its place he solicited anecdotes on Lully, Bossuet, Lebrun, and Descartes. A canal or a painting by Poussin, he wrote, was a thousand times more precious than all campaigns.

His criteria were utility and art, the useful and the agreeable. Consequently, his work would concentrate on great men, who have given pure and durable pleasure to men not yet born. Their achievements are what we call culture or civilization, the latter word not then invented. To capture the meaning of the former, Voltaire referred to the "history of the human spirit."[22]

The human spirit as a subject of history began to receive repeated mention in the early eighteenth century. Its importance as a historical subject on a level with war and religion reflected a changing intellectual outlook. Those who rejected earlier authorities as well as Providence thought that the direction and meaning of history had their source in the human

spirit. Fontenelle (1657-1757), whom Voltaire called the most
universal spirit of the age of Louis XIV, described the historian
as ordering and delicately interrelating history's immense heap
of facts to reveal the succession of events and ideas and "the
history of the human mind."[23] But Voltaire could not always
use the phrase without a cynical throwaway. When he wrote
to d'Oliver about the history of the human mind, he added,
"that is to say, of human stupidity."[24]

Voltaire's quick mind — or, at any rate, his mercurial pen —
sometimes expressed his wavering as to whether the history
could achieve the moral purpose of preserving the memory of
good and agreeable feats. Such a history, nevertheless, he had
committed himself to write. Its proper form, Voltaire recognized, could not be a narrative. To friends he described his
problem: he would be not the historian of Louis's age, "but its
painter," and "a painter looks at things differently from other
men and sees effects of light and shade which escape others."[25]

In calling himself the painter of an age, Voltaire recognized
that he needed a new form of historical organization. But his
words about a tableau did not solve the problem: he was a
writer, not a painter, and no amount of talk about tableaus
solved his problem. His work does not have the coherence of a
well-made painting. Nor did it occupy his time with the unrelenting demands of the work of a lifetime. After 1738 — that is,
after several years of devoted work — he gave it time left over
or snatched from other activities. When he became court historian, the luxury of royal favor made it impossible to continue
a work which, in origin, was to be another bomb against Old
Order France. Soon the going at court ceased to be good. By
the end of the decade, taking refuge in Berlin, he resumed
regular labor on a work that differed considerably from his
earlier plans.

Manifestoes are almost as hard to live up to as election plat-
forms have generally been: Voltaire did not solve the problem
of writing social history. He wrote an often vivid account of
Louis's reign, uncharacteristically devoted to policy and analysis. There is a sense of background and there are chapters that
present some account of the arts. Nevertheless, by 1750 Voltaire
was less concerned to celebrate his own guild of writers,
thinkers, and artists. Nor, had he wished to do so, could he deal

with the origins of great cultural achievement. The treatment was promising but brief, and suggested haste: "many years must elapse before the language and taste become purified," a "slow fecundity, followed by a long period of sterility."[26] His original plan was gradually subordinated to the crusade against the Catholic church, "l'infameux," to which his years from the late 1740s onward were devoted.

For nearly twenty years Voltaire had lived with Mme. du Chatelet as lover and intellectual companion. They lived and worked in her home at Cirey, from which he could easily escape to Lorraine. At Cirey they studied philosphy, science, and biblical literature, and he accumulated the learning he used so prodigally against the Catholic church and Christianity. The last chapter of *The Age of Louis XIV* dealt with the church, and the final pages with the church dispute about Chinese ceremonies. The language was mild, but the substance was bitter: the Jesuits were proselytizing the Chinese people and causing bloodshed among them. The fight against the church, carried on in Voltaire's plays and *Candide* as well as in his valiant defense of Calas and others, was the occasion for writing the *Essai sur les moeurs*, a historical essay begun for Mme. du Chatelet, who, as an eminent *philosophe*, considered history a nearly useless study.

The *Essai sur les moeurs* is a universal history of the human spirit, a history written *en philosophe*.[27] It has rarely been reprinted outside of editions of the author's complete works. As it was literally a compilation of several works, and not a work of art, most readers will use it for browsing rather than for sustained reading. Its historical significance lies in its being a humanist universal history designed to replace the Christian view of history, and its remaining significance lies in what it reveals of Voltaire's thought. These two points made the work very readable in the eighteenth century, which, apart from theology and French drama, had high standards of readability. Correspondents wrote Voltaire that they could not put it down, and Catherine the Great expressed her desire to read it again and again.

The work was a modern universal history, modern because men should know their own enlightened times about which, unlike ancient history and the age of fables, they can know something; it was a continuation and confutation of Bossuet's *Discourse on Universal History*, which, for all the bishop's erudition and eloquence, Voltaire condemned as mendacious and Judaeocentric; and it was a philosophic work, for in rejecting the Christian providential view, Voltaire presented what he called the philosophy of history, a history of man on his own. The last two points are interconnected. Voltaire denied the Christian teaching of a Fall, Promise, Redemption, and the church, which dominated universal Christian history. He sought inadequately, as he complained was inevitable, to cover all history; and his case was stronger in that no providential direction of Oriental history was worked out or discernible.

From the time of Charlemagne—in fact, from the fall of the Roman Empire—Europeans lived in unrelieved barbarism. During the thirteenth century in Italy, gentler, even refined, ways appeared amid ferocity and grossness. Luxury made possible this development of culture, and the period of sea explorations and discoveries augmented wealth. Portugal's Prince Henry the Navigator was a great man because the knowledge of the world he gained was prompted by a purely benevolent desire. For a time, there was the prospect that European wars of ambition would yield to the search for new lands, but the sequel instead resumed the idiot's tale.

The Italian Renaissance was exemplary for its rare geniuses who elevated an age marked by its quota of crimes and calamities. Some who had genius, like Pico della Mirandola, became the disciples and victims of ancient philosophers and ended up as masters of the lie, the manipulators of human stupidity.

For a time, the Hapsburgs threatened to dominate Europe, but they were checked by the balance of power that generally prevailed against such preponderance and had made of Europe a great republic of states. Occasionally Voltaire, unable to explain an event, defiantly emphasized the role of chance, meaninglessness that challenged the church but made him despair of history and the frequent disproportion between a slight cause and its prolonged effect. Thus, the source of all the wars of France and the house of Austria is to be found in the marriage of Maximilian I and Mary, heiress of Burgundy. The marriage itself was caused by the stubbornness of the burghers of Ghent, the cause, then, of all the subsequent calamities.

Modern Europe developed historical inquiry. Voltaire made this point not with reference to the seventeenth-century age of erudition but in a reference to Guiccardini and Machiavelli. They were men of a real Renaissance. In the ancient world, history had been developing into a useful source of knowledge when the triumph of Christianity so perverted it that until the time of the Florentine historians "we have not had a well-made history" (1:298).

The discovery period provided new tasks for historians in opening up contacts with China and India that required men to be informed about those civilizations. Contact with Africa, however, was not enlarging because it was merely contact with the worst of our past. The African intelligence was inferior to the European, for it was in the primitive and imbecile state concerned primarily with the immediate needs of the body. To the African applied a point Voltaire had made elsewhere: the growth of culture was slow and inexplicable because man can want only what he knows (2:15-16, 306).

Europe's sixteenth-century divisions were heightened by the Reformation, a rift caused by rival factions of clerical manipulators. Luther attacked indulgences, urged on by his Augustinian superiors, who were jealous because they had lost the indulgence-vending monopoly to the Dominicans (2:217). Later, Voltaire provided a surprising insight. In objecting to Catholic apologists who argued that Protestants offered people a light burden in place of the Roman one, he insisted that the Protestants opened the doors of convents in order to turn secular society into a convent (2:243).

Thereafter, Europe passed into the time of Enlightenment, although it was never without the crimes, ignorance, and lies that make up the march of the human spirit. In the same period, Europe faced the threat of the Turks, the counter-Enlightened people. Turkish power was based on the Janissaries, Christian slaves trained for Turkish service, who provided a bizarre example of the influence of education. Turkish government finance did not mount to the totals of the government resources of western states. Voltaire is mistaken in applying this point to the sixteenth-century. In later centuries, nevertheless, western states drew from richer economies. Turkey's masters, by their capricious confiscations, exemplified the way the world usually goes, since their public administration was a form of authorized brigandage (2:419).

Some exceptions might be cited in the modern world: small republican states where the rights of liberty and property were sacred or where government financial requirements were on a small scale. Elsewhere, order first required power, and sometimes an enlightened ruler developed policies to benefit his or her fortunate subjects. But, as Voltaire had written earlier, if one was to teach reason to one's fellow citizens and to avoid persecution, that person must be the strongest. To this there is a Voltairean "Catch 22," for "it happens almost always that the strongest redoubles the chains of ignorance instead of breaking them" (1:244).

The time of Enlightenment came when science, with a vanguard of Galileo and Newton, and the empiricism of Locke revealed the true system of the world and the means of understanding and controlling it. This breakthrough was sustained by encouraging the making of wealth and the blessing of work. To complete this development men had to liberate and use their good sense and had to cultivate refinement by means of the French language, the French theater, and the society of men and women such as the friends of Voltaire.

Voltaire's criticism of Bossuet for omitting China and India from a universal history is unanswerable, but his treatment of those civilizations was shaped to suit his polemical purpose. In a quarrel, Voltaire could be quite unscrupulous and betray his own humanitarianism. Bossuet, for example, composed his *Discourse* out of lessons for the dauphin. Thus, Bossuet praised the sage and religious Egyptian rulers for resisting the lust of conquest. Voltaire would have none of that. The Egyptians in their backwardness squandered their resources on pyramids and monuments instead of such useful projects as the Great Wall of China (1:78, 224).

Chinese chronology, Voltaire argued, was more ancient than biblical chronology and provided an alternative, even contradictory, system of dating. China was free of religious quarrels, Voltaire maintained. Its emperors had no controversies with the priesthood, and Confucius himself was not a prophet, but a sage magistrate.

The Indians were perhaps the most ancient of people, and their history was without bloodshed. "But Christian peoples have never observed their religion and the Indian castes have always practiced theirs." Theirs and "that of men of letters in China are the only ones in which men have never been barbarians." These sweeping remarks, which have the fabulous quality that Voltaire professed to abhor, completed their antithesis, with more validity, when Voltaire emphasized that the Indians and Chinese did not go out of their country for plunder unlike, among others, the Jews and Romans (1:58, 61, 235-36).

The Romans inspired Voltaire's larger vision, but they were also the victims of his historically constricting wit. They first appeared as persisting in warlike relations with the world. Roman patriotism was the virtue of a robber band concerned with booty and its division. As such, the Romans were not wholly despotic and, in time, became polished. They helped refine the barbarians they conquered and became legislators for the West — a major point not at all explained. Yielding often to a materialist view of history, Voltaire elsewhere suggested that because the Romans lived in the worst part of Italy, they first sought a livelihood in war and in more recent times used religion as a substitute for green pastures (1:180, 234).

Where Bossuet celebrated the survival of religion and the continuity of the church, Voltaire argued that there is one universal religion, similar in essentials and in moral teaching. The efforts of theologians, the church, and fantastics to go beyond this into naming the meaningless weakened the state and all order and drove men to atrocities. "Man everywhere adores the divinity and dishonors it" (1:41-42).

This Divinity did not intervene in the world and had no providential plan that man can read. In the 1750s and some other periods, Voltaire accepted a grim determinism, but this was not the foresight of a loving God. If he governed the world and history, if somehow all was part of a benevolent plan, then ultimately resignation to the will of God might be the Christian response.

When Bossuet argued for Providence and a meaning to history, he also recognized that the freethinkers who viewed history as meaningless had thereby a case for reckless hedonism. Voltaire, himself a hedonist, turned the argument against Bossuet. Man must do what he can, cultivate his garden, in order to lessen the misery of life. If there were earthquakes, then for God's and man's sake, one should not bow in submission to God for earthquake and all. Let man, instead, take into account that "our dwelling, the earth, has experienced in physical matters as many revolutions as rapacity and ambition have caused among its peoples" (2:792-93).

The apparently simple injunction about cultivating our garden turned out to be quite problematic for Voltaire. Historically the human spirit, he argued, was influenced by climate, government, and religion. Values and human nature itself varied with climate. Universally, however, man himself acted out of motives of self-love, a love that extended to the instrument (he revealingly did not use partner) of his pleasures and to the offspring, extensions of himself. In being selfish, he was also social, though one may find in India human excrement who lived without companions and in hardship to extort alms from passersby (1:25).

Man at first could know little, but his imaginings and fears outreached his mental grasp. There began then the great confidence game of men ready to accept fable and of the clergy and others who enjoyed fools gladly and profited from them. Enlightenment meant the liquidation of fable and, presumably, the curtailment of opportunities for cosmic tricksters.

Voltaire thought man might have had several distinct beginnings; this idea helped to explain the variations and inequalities of race and had the polemical advantage of rejecting the account in Genesis. At any rate, man's subsequent career was largely a mélange of fable and true accounts of brutality and crime. From such material, which is history, one could learn little; but the *philosophe* could learn to hate stupidities and crime and, by quarreling with history, refute it. He also could learn not to hate stupidities and beliefs just because they were strange. Finally, he would learn something more surprising: that virtue and civilization were the same everywhere. Virtue no more than civilization was particular and plural. In one of his most crude and vulgar judgments, Voltaire considered virtue to be abstract and universal. Thus, Pericles, Confucius, and Voltaire would find no difficulty in communication. There were, the *philosophe* allowed, infinite variations, but the base (*le fond*) was the same, and the variations — that is, history — were not important. This view limited the scope of his religious tolerance. Religions were basically the same and were intolerable when they insisted that they were not.

This belief in universal sameness is a major Voltairean conviction, and it is one of many that do not coexist in any state of logic. It served his campaign against the church, whose particular aspects he rejected as occasions for fratricide. Sometimes he emphasized uniformity in a way that cast doubt on his historical pessimism and his antipathy to Western religions: "Religion teaches the same morality to all people without any exception: Asiatic ceremonies are bizarre, the beliefs absurd, but the precepts are just." Against accounts that presented Oriental priests as preachers of iniquity, he wrote: "This is to calumniate human nature: it is not possible that there was ever a religious society instituted to invite a crime" (2:809). There was mockery here, but was not Voltaire, perhaps unwittingly, also mocking himself?

He had a twofold view of religion. The Enlightened man would take institutional religion lightly or fight it. But what about the mass of people who, he and almost all Enlightened writers agreed, need religion? Belief in no god at all was incompatible with wise government. Society needed belief in an ultimate judge of the unjust who managed to avoid the punishment of human justice. He insisted that this belief was necessary, but his own speculations wavered about its truth. There must, he thought, be a universal intelligence, and it was "impertinent" to believe that God is unjust.[28] To D'Alembert he wrote that the intelligence directing nature must be limited because there was so much imperfection and wretchedness in nature. The difficulty of Voltaire's thought on this matter may be illustrated by noting that the particular French language was a force for civilization but that any Western religious group, except possibly the Quakers, stood for folly and cruelty unless reduced to a cosmopolitan uniformity.

Very notable was Voltaire's limited and low view of human

nature. Many times he wrote that all was determined by the spirit of the age, and his recognition of the exclusive role of self-interest was the voice of the spirit of his age. For him there was no vision of man attempting to resolve great challenges. Instead, men were like the mice of a ship who could not hope to direct the captain, or they were like ants swarming in a drying mud heap. Poverty was the miserable lot of most men — no great concern for Voltaire — but luxury could lead men to aspirations of refinement. As evidence he cited the Arabs of South Yemen and Aden. Before the time of Mohammed these people had the blessings of plenty and of remoteness from other men. Because they were men, they held superstitious beliefs; but, as they were free of the bad example of other men and above every need and fear, their beliefs were "less absurd, baleful and barbarous than those of other nations" (1:54-55).

Colbert's efforts to order the monarchy's finances made possible the greatness of the age of Louis XIV. But even though Colbert created the necessary preconditions, Voltaire's great men were artists and scientists. Knowledge may become cumulative and know-how cannot be destroyed. When a nation knew the arts, its people, as long as they were not subjugated and transported by foreigners, could always emerge from their ruins to reestablish the society (*Essai*, 2:812). Nevertheless, in his own time, he found the state of his country's finance disquieting, and all the more did he rejoice when Turgot was placed in charge of French finances. Condorcet wrote: "Voltaire saw in the nomination of M. Turgot the dawn of the reign of that reason which had been so long mistrusted and persecuted."[29]

Two of Voltaire's remarks about creativity are puzzling: the first explains the poverty of Oriental art and taste by wrongly pointing to the slight position women had in Oriental society, but then one wonders how he would deal with Periclean Greece; the second point explains the presence of numerous artists in Italy and other Western countries on the ground that those countries, for all their disasters, were free of Turkish despotism and enjoyed the artistic patronage of the nobility, a class wholly unknown to Asia (1:252; 2:812).

Condorcet gave a *philosophe*'s praise to the *Essai:* it is "not the history of the centuries . . . but that which one would wish to retain from the reading of the history, that which one would love to recall of it."[30]

The complete history of mankind, then, was morally unexemplary and aesthetically boring. People were governed by custom and shaped by the spirit of the age. This human history presented such an unedifying record that the prospect of lasting reform or improvement was barely visible. Betterment — the sequel of refinement, reason, and wealth — was limited to the few. Despots might hasten improvement, but their power could be dangerous. The mass of people must always live on fables, which made them dangerous but restrained them from savagery.

Our own histories, Voltaire wrote, read like "the history of savage nations; we shudder for an instant, and then set out for the Opera."[31] It cannot be the best of all possible worlds. If things were perfect, Voltaire asked, what grounds were there for hope? But what hope did he have? He professed to blush for the heart of man and disputed the rigorous pessimism about human nature of Pascal, "that satirical believer." Pascal was the enemy of such hope as Voltaire held. He wrote in 1732 that Pascal taught humanity to hate itself whereas he would teach it to love itself.[32]

In his contradictions and his achievements, Voltaire was directed by the spirit of his time. For all his humanitarianism and for all his valiant defense of the persecuted, his *Essai* revealed mainly contempt for the mass of people and little imaginative concern for their cultures. It was a striking and ingenious inspiration to write the history of civilization, of the human spirit, for an age largely lacking in historical sense, that is, without sympathy for other ways and other times. For instruction as well as for antitheological polemics, he broadened the scope of history. The scope appalled and bored him. In seeing civilization as uniform and one, he obscured the vision that was his originality. Civilization was the very subject about which, as historian, he could not write adequately. His trio of forces (climate, government, and religion, to which he might have added custom and ideas) was not interrelated, that is, did not have a coherence comparable to that of his contemporary, Montesquieu.

In places Voltaire recognized that cultural developments

took long periods of time (1:201), but he had neither energy nor taste for patiently unfolding the temporal sequence of a culture. He read and discoursed intelligently and widely, wrote and rewrote quickly, but he was wholly free from the passions and loves of research and the painstaking industry of seventeenth- and nineteenth-century scholars.

There remained unresolved a question about history itself. Voltaire was not assured about the art he practiced. He could not write, as D'Alembert did, going beyond the rationalist contempt for history to the view that history consoled and encouraged the *philosophe*: "He pardons it for being uncertain in what it has to teach him, because such is the lot of human knowledge, and the obscurities of the physical universe console him for not being more clear in the moral universe."[33]

Voltaire sought something more substantial than D'Alembert's consolation. It is, therefore, all the more remarkable that he turned to history as a humanity so seriously, and it is disquieting to observe that Voltaire's own temperament and the spirit of the age condemned him to frustration. His critical powers tempted him to mistrust all sources: earlier ones were fabulous and later ones self-serving. Universal history and even ordinary history, nevertheless, required the historian to have standards of relevance and utility. Having rejected the traditional ones of theology, he found himself troubled by the uncertainty of other standards. In the problem of relevance or selection, he was experiencing a genuine ordeal of the historian. But for himself there was the compounded doubt that literature, for example his plays or *Candide*, would do the historian's teaching better.

At the end of his life, Voltaire wrote that history was only a gazette, the work of what D'Alembert called *"tristes compilateurs."* Style, the only merit of history, was the fruit of literature.[34] But then how far are we from Varillas, who altered facts with the defense: "That can be, but what of it? Is not the fact as I have recounted it better?" Or from Vertot, who, having read insufficiently about a famous siege, used his imagination for the scene: "I am annoyed by it, but my siege is done." Voltaire had insisted on facts and truth, but what did he mean by them?[35] Concern for facts can become pedantry and mindlessness, but unconcern means no history at all.

Voltaire's judgment may have been too strongly formulated, the fault of age or courtly flattery. But it does illuminate his ambiguity about history. All the more remarkable is the great labor Voltaire undertook when he sought to benefit men by undeceiving them (2:126), to destroy the Christian, providential view of history and to replace it with a conception of man on his own.

His labors, including his fight against religious persecution, made him the object of loyalty and admiration, sometimes quite uncritical, as befitted the man Flaubert judged to be a saint, obsessed with destroying the infamous thing. Condorcet, witness and hymnist to progress, wrote that the life of Voltaire was, in effect, "the history of the progress that the arts have owed to his genius."[36]

The critical spirit, which Voltaire sought to embody, compels qualified dissent. He wrote one work of historical art, *Charles XII*, which suffers from Voltaire's concern with moral example and narrative; his *Age of Louis XIV* is a pioneer social history, which finally explains too little and promises far more than the author provided; the *Essai sur les moeurs* is more important as a manifesto than as a cultural history. Indeed, the last may be called philosophy teaching not by example.

8. Edward Gibbon:
History as Art

The Decline and Fall of the Roman Empire is a supreme example of history as a work of art, a literary masterpiece.[1] That is a fact — or is it merely in some sense true or just temporarily true? Under examination facts may become a bog or even, like fog, give way meaninglessly before us.

That Gibbon's history is a masterpiece also raises questions. There is, first of all, some doubt about the lastingness of the masterpiece. Some modern readers respond with such yawning incomprehension to its well-wrought sentences and paragraphs that one may fear this classic, this thing of beauty, may not give joy for another century, let alone forever. Is Gibbon's history a temporary classic?

A second difficulty arises from a prevailing practice among modern historians. We have achieved something like the rapid pace of technological obsolescence in industry. Works of history are written with firm conviction, but alert historians soon revise them, revisit and condemn them, put them on reading lists, then omit them and consign them to oblivion. In these circumstances a historical classic appears to be, if not a contradiction, then a problematic mutant. Indeed, Hayden White, a serious and venturesome thinker about historians and history, has concluded that historical classics are works no longer read for historical purposes: the classics are works of little historical use that are read as literature.[2]

Gibbon himself knew that he had written a masterpiece. To use his own phrase, he was *the* historian of the Roman Empire and was pleased when others said so. As he contemplated the dwindling resources of approaching old age, he knew he had achieved his ambition and could hope for the likely immortality of his name and writings.

A great and learned work of history was the goal, the ambition, to which he gave the disciplined energies of his prime. In the service of this ambition he exploited what he precisely called the luck, the good fortune, of living through a sickly childhood, of surviving an uncaring mother and an insensitive and improvident father, of being born in Europe and in England during an age of enlightenment, of escaping an Oxford education by paternal order of exile and Protestant tutoring in Lausanne, of being able to live independently because his demands were modest, of possessing a cheerful temperament that meant he liked what he did.[3]

The eighteenth century in England had an emotional subculture in Methodism, but its dominant fashion was to distrust enthusiasm and to prize rules, restraint, moderation, and rationalism. These values of his culture Gibbon acquired by experience. He learned only too well that passion and enthusiasm can rob the individual of a comfortable life and society of civility. For the enjoyment of such security as men could attain in passing from life's uncertainty to death, he saw only the refuge of skepticism, to be steadfastly maintained though moderately expressed.[4] Rearing and experience attenuated the emotions in Gibbon. Apart from the care of an aunt, the young man did not experience family affection. Later in life he was content to share the home life of Lord and Lady Sheffield and, as it were, to adopt their daughters.

Gibbon's conversion to Catholicism, while he was (he should pardon the expression) a student at Oxford University, was a matter of conviction but very likely had an element of defiance of his father. His provoked father made it an emotionally searing experience by exiling the sixteen-year-old to Switzerland for five years, to be educated in Lausanne, then presumably a mightier Protestant fortress than Oxford. After more than a year's study under a Swiss clergyman, Edward accepted communion in a Protestant church at Lausanne, but the father achieved more than he had intended. The son's studies had ventured into skeptical Christianity and, as he wrote with precise irony, "I suspended my Religious enquiries, acquiescing with implicit belief in the tenets and mysteries which are adopted by

the general consent of Catholics and Protestants." This quotation from a memoir written late in life echoes the letter in
which he told Edward Senior of his return to Protestantism.[5]
The course of his studies also taught him the pleasure of
knowledge and systematic work. Gibbon highly praised his
Lausanne tutor for discerning how far he could be useful and
wisely leaving Edward to his own genius.

Gibbon had the stirrings of literary ambition, but study and
writing required means. For them Gibbon had to look to his
father and continue in a state of dependence. His father's power
of the purse thwarted young Gibbon's emotional and marital
aspirations. In Switzerland he fell in love with Suzanne Curchod, the bright and lively daughter of a Swiss minister. When
Edward returned to England in 1758, the "prejudice or prudence of an English parent" vetoed the marriage. "I sighed as
a lover, I obeyed as a son" is his account of what he also called
a painful struggle.[6]

Thereafter, he was the friend of several women but avoided
love and was in the main resolved against marriage as beyond
his means and possibly his endurance. One incident in 1774 appears, no more than that, to contradict that statement. The
wife of a friend and two female relatives tried to arrange a
match for him. The family of the lucky woman wrecked the
unproposed marriage by raising the question of Gibbon's
religious practice and belief, a subject on which he had deep
feelings. He allowed that they might properly ask whether he
was a gambler or a drunkard, but, if he visited them, he would
not be a party to family prayers "and Bishop Hooper's sermons.
I would not marry an Empress on these conditions. I abhor a
devotee, though a friend both to decency and toleration."[7]
More than a decade later, he and his Swiss friend and
housemate, Georges Deyverdun, agreed that in their ménage a
woman would be a grace and utility—but each thought that
the other should be the one to marry.

Gibbon's experience of dependence on his father confirmed
his skepticism and limited his emotional life. But he used these
experiences to the advantage of his ambition and in other activities acquired self-confidence. When the English government, fearing a French invasion during the Seven Years' War,
called out militia forces, Captain Edward Gibbon marched his

battalion through southern England for some twenty months. The experience of military life gave him a hernia, the practice of command, some knowledge of his countrymen, and experience of excessive drinking, which he recounted in the journal wherein he also described his serious and considerable reading. His supervision of a battalion helped him to understand the Roman legion. As he put it, "The Captain of the Hampshire Grenadiers (the reader may smile) has not been useless to the historian of the Roman empire."[8]

Before the war was ended by treaty, Gibbon set out on a grand tour of Paris, Lausanne, and the cities of Italy. The aristocratic and intellectual society of France received him in Paris. There he was at least a little known through his French *Essay on the Study of Literature* published in 1761, a rambling work — as it were, a collection of paragraphs that displayed his Enlightenment sensibilities and his love of learning. But for his "appearance, dress and equipage" the French, he reported, might have treated Gibbon, the gentleman and man of fashion, simply as a man of letters.[9]

From exciting and expensive Paris he went "home" to Lausanne for nearly a year of preparatory studies for the Italian tour. He was compiling materials for a book on the geography of Roman Italy. He reached Rome in October 1764, and it swirled him in beatitude. Christian communities and buildings provided a setting for pagan Rome, which captivated and presented the historian with a subject, its decline and fall.[10]

Several times, and with some differences, Gibbon referred to the inspiration of his history. Nevertheless he did not directly set to work. He cut short his Italian tour, but only because his father, like a monetarist politician, compelled him to do so by ending his supply of money. Two developments intruded before Gibbon rose to meet his inspired destiny.

In 1767-1768 the historian of the Roman Empire began writing in French a history of the Swiss republics and submitted the manuscript in progress to the philosopher-historian David Hume. The latter, admiring the effort, wondered why Gibbon brought coals to Newcastle by writing French instead of English. Doesn't everybody, so to speak, write French books? Isn't English the language of parts of two continents?[11] Gibbon recognized the point and by 1768 turned to a Roman history in the English language. Sometimes true love and destiny are revealed only through trial and error.

Sustained historical composition, however, did not begin until 1773, three years after the death of Edward's father. It was, Gibbon wrote, "an event which I sincerely deprecated," although it released him from "obscurity and indigence" and bestowed "the first of blessings, independence." At any rate, "the tears of a son are seldom lasting: I submitted to the order of Nature. . . . my father's death, not unhappy for himself, was the only event that could save me from an hopeless life of obscurity and indigence." Even independence, however, had its price tag, because his father had been bankrupt and by his projects for relief had worsened matters. Gibbon devoted nearly two years to ordering debts and assets to safeguard his own inheritance.[12] In doing so he discovered new energies and became a decisive and self-assured man of affairs. In 1774 he initiated arrangements to purchase a parliamentary seat in borough-rich Cornwall, a county abounding in what was eventually decried as corruption, which he called the unfailing mark of constitutional liberty. The Commons provided moments of excitement and, in sessions prolonged until dawn, more periods of tedium, especially for Gibbon, who in eight years never spoke. He was too shy, too fearful of ridicule and mistrustful of his own capacity to improvise.

Even with his parliamentary duties, Gibbon wrote so assiduously that the history (or its first volume as his plans expanded) was published to warm acclaim in July 1776. Some three years later Gibbon received a political plum, a lord commissionership of the Board of Trade. It was not a sinecure, but to discharge its untaxing duties brought Gibbon £800 a year. Because he understood the hyperbole of politics, he admired the wit, but not the accuracy, of the critic who ridiculed "the perpetual virtual adjournment and the unbroken sitting vacation of the board of trade." Occasionally Gibbon, then writing volumes 2 and 3 of the imperial decline, remarked on the coincidence that he was serving a government whose ministers struggled to halt colonial Americans from disrupting Britain's empire.[13]

The government's failure gave impetus to antipatronage reform in which the Board of Trade was abolished. By this time

Gibbon had published volumes 2 and 3 but before him was a long period of labor on the difficult remaining volumes. Politics, it was likely, would delay completion and offered little prospect of enlarging his income. He therefore yielded to disenchantment with Parliament and politics.

He told Lord Sheffield that he was more likely to finish the history in Lausanne than in London. In the Swiss city he could escape the distractions of London, command an agreeable social life, and live comfortably on his income. There, too, he would have the companionship of his only old friend, Georges Deyverdun. In Lausanne Gibbon could be the witty autocrat, smiling, even smirking, "rounding his periods." London society had little patience with a monologue, and only a monologue allowed him to formulate balanced sentences and, his usual gesture of emphasis, to rap his snuffbox.[14]

The move was made and, when Gibbon finished the history in 1787, he returned to England for eight months to correct the proofs, to visit the Holroyds at Sheffield Place, and to make the flattering rounds that his literary fame allowed.

Two years later Deyverdun died after a debilitating illness. Although Gibbon could not grudge him the relief of death, he long lamented the loneliness to which his friend had left him. Mortality, public and private, afflicted him. The fall of the French monarchy, a lightning fall compared to that of Rome, surprised him, and later revolutionary violence and war — touching him, menacing him even in Lausanne — shocked Gibbon. He described the French Revolution as madness, a reverse for the civilized life that the history had confidently celebrated.[15]

In 1793, on the death of Lady Sheffield, Gibbon, fat and ailing, traveled through warring Europe to comfort the bereaved husband. The journey was all the more difficult because his untended hernia had swollen remarkably. In society and to his valet, Gibbon pretended that it did not exist. After several operations he died in London at the beginning of 1794, a death caused by the swollen hernia, the operations, and cirrhosis of the liver, a consequence of addiction to Madeira wine.[16]

In *Decline and Fall*, the art is so well sustained that the "flexibility" of Gibbon's plan may not be recognized. He originally saw his theme as the fall of a city and empire and, as part of it, the decline of its public life and pagan culture. This story ended with the end of the eastern empire in 1453 and, in the West, the beginnings of modern Europe and the revival of ancient learning. That was his scope, but Gibbon thought it advisable to see how a first volume was received before undertaking volumes 2 and 3. The trial volume removed all possible doubts. After 1776 Gibbon and his public recognized that he was writing a masterpiece.[17]

Even so, as he wrote, at the outset everything—title, years of decline, the chapter divisions, and the order of narrative—was dark and doubtful. For the first volume he eventually settled upon the long decline of republican institutions, the ascendancy of imperial despotism, and the growth of the Christian Church in a condition first of toleration and then of imperial favor, the loss of pagan Rome's soul, and the triumph of dogmatic superstition, as Gibbon saw it. For his starting point he chose a peak of peace and prosperity, a height to make fall visible, the Age of the Antonines (A.D. 138-180). The reigns of Titus Antoninus Pius and Marcus Aurelius Antoninus "are possibly the only period of history in which the happiness of a great people was the sole object of government" (1, chap. 3, p. 68). But the eminence of a single ruler, however well intentioned, indicated that decay had already touched Roman institutions and virtues.

In truth, Rome fell because of its successes as a republic, because of "its immoderate greatness." The Republic with its mixed constitution, aristocratic senate, and army flourished in contention that made for seven centuries of conquests that transformed it. Its citizens came to learn "that the republic, sinking beneath the weight of its greatness and corruption, could not subsist without a master.[18]

By the time of the Antonines civic liberty survived only as appearance. Dictator Julius Caesar had leveled "every barrier of the Roman constitution," and under his nephew Augustus "Rome had become an absolute monarchy disguised by the forms of a Commonwealth." (1, chap. 3, p. 51). The capacity of the Senate to restrain the emperor was nullified by his power. Senators, fearful and otherwise self-interested, flattered and thereby misled the emperors. This corruption of the Senate destroyed its capacity for leadership and with it the civic virtue that only aristocracy makes possible.

Emperors grasping for unrestrained power trampled upon their subjects and, yielding to self-indulgence (a temptation of power difficult to withstand), destroyed themselves. The despotic Commodus, son of Marcus Aurelius, acquired the reputation of a monster, which is a reproach to the father-philosopher who named him for the succession. It is vainly argued in behalf of the philosophic emperor that he had arranged for men of learning and virtue to correct the son's vices and prepare him to be a worthy emperor, because, Gibbon added, in a melancholy observation on education, "the power of instruction is seldom of much efficacy, except in those happy dispositions where it is almost superfluous" (1, chap. 4, p. 74).

Rome's failure to regulate the imperial succession enabled the army to make emperors. The legions required successful candidates to reward the armies, and in Rome the Praetorian Guard exacted large donations for supporting or accepting an emperor, for acting as a mad electoral college. By the third century, force, not authority, reigned. There is also a worse side, even in this evil case: the wealth of the soldiers unfitted them for service, which is "best secured by an honourable poverty" (1, chap. 6, p. 119).

In the first half of the third century, Roman army fought Roman army, as the imperial title became the prize of a bloody lottery. Thereafter, a line of Illyrian soldier-emperors, devoted not to the city of Rome but to what they had known, the empire and Roman military culture, reduced the number of the conflicts. Of these Illyrians, Diocletian (A.D. 284-305) is memorable for consolidating the empire and brushing away the republican facade that was the legacy of Augustus. His achievement, like his virtue, was more utilitarian than splendid. Diocletian sought power to maintain the empire and to repair the weaknesses of Roman society that lessened his resources. He foreshadowed the Constantinian division of the empire, sharing authority not to limit power but to make it effective.

Gibbon's judgment on Diocletian goes in two directions: the emperor represented the claims of merit and of violence. The historian admired Diocletian's paganism, clemency, and success, and thought that he deserved "the reproach of establishing pernicious precedents, rather than of exercising actual oppression" (1, chap. 13, pp. 333-34). Here Gibbon could have concluded his story of Roman decline, but his interest in pagan and classical culture required an ending that was also a beginning, the reign of Constantine (A.D. 305-336). With him the Western Empire came to an end, the Eastern Empire began a life span of eleven hundred years, and pagan, classical culture was succeeded by the Christian Church. This beginning was the triumph of superstition, the end of civilization rather than a new one, because in Gibbon's mind there was only one civilization, not many.

Constantine's ruling passion, which was linked to his conversion, was boundless ambition, a judgment reminiscent of Tacitus on Tiberius. Such good as Constantine did in his early days may be explained by the limited power that compelled him to check, even to dissimulate, his ambition. When external restraints on him were removed, the Romans experienced the brutalities of a naked despotism. His costly victories as well as his failures contributed to the fall of Rome, the great change, the revolution that may be seen in the reign of Constantine. "The foundation of Constantinople, and the establishment of the Christian religion, were the immediate and memorable consequences of this revolution."[19]

Christianity played a role in Rome's fall as large as the Church's prominence in the empire. How was the Church's success to be explained? Gibbon prefaced his answer with the ironic statement that the historian, as he cannot be privy to divine intentions, must restrict himself to considering the human causes, the secondary causes, of the religion's triumph. Disavowing Providence as outside the historian's concern, Gibbon enumerated five secondary causes: the Christians' intolerant zeal, their belief in a future life, their belief in miracles, their pure morals, and the union and discipline of the Christian Church. These causes were so formidable that instead of seeing something miraculous in the growth of Christianity, Gibbon expressed surprise that the religion had not triumphed earlier. The story of Christian triumph was then cast in irony, as each of the secondary causes was presented as a source of the decline of Rome and civilized life (1, chap. 15, pp. 382-444).

Intolerant zeal was the prime source of decline. Religion —
that is, superstition — was necessary and dangerous. To the
mass of mankind, religions provided varying answers to questions that could not be answered by science, reason, or empirical inquiry. The answers were necessary because most people were incapable of skepticism and, with limited time and
faculties, all men sought to live less precariously than their condition allowed. The danger of so doing was compounded because faith then can be manipulated to serve the interests of
ambitious men. What Gibbon wrote of the Gnostics expressed
his fear of all religions: "they delivered themselves to the
guidance of a disordered imagination" (1, chap. 15, p. 394). Intolerance, then, as compulsive conformity to the disordered
fantasies of some interested and ambitious party, was a crime
against the human spirit (1, chap. 15, p. 432). Gibbon believed
that toleration should prevail in matters that reason could not
determine. People might sensibly settle for what custom
prescribed but should not impose one custom as authority. The
intolerant zeal of the Christians, corrupting all their other virtues, replaced a paganism in which one superstition did not
profess hostility to another and skeptical philosophers could
participate in the rituals of social and public life.

Belief in immortality diverted men from a concern with life
on earth, into resignation and passivity, while it supported the
pretensions of ambitious ecclesiastics. Belief in miracles yielded
to the very credulity that required restraint. The cult of the
miraculous fanned a brush fire against rationality. Even the
pure morals of the Christians warred with nature and perverted humanity. Christian meekness, Gibbon thought, fostered
pusillanimity, and to despise the world and the flesh was a defiance of nature that in retribution brought on corruption and
monsters of unreason. All four reasons served the fifth which
made them formidable: the united, disciplined, and authorita-
tive Church, to some the city of God but to Gibbon the anti-
city, the subverter of pagan Rome. (1, chap. 15, pp. 415-17,
421-24).

The second installment of Gibbon's history, volumes 2 and 3
(1781), continued "the laborious narrative" of the decline of the
Roman Empire from the reign of Constantine to the extinction
of the empire in the West. Before writing a conclusion, the
author in two chapters dealt with the origins of monasticism

and the conversion of the barbarians. To the late twentieth-century reader the topics might suggest an attempt to limn the beginnings of a new civilization. But for Gibbon there was only one civilization, that of the classical world. Thus, the two chapters recorded a relapse into barbarism or a continuation of it.

Gibbon concluded his third volume with about nine pages of general observations on the empire's decline in the West. The observations describe the civic and military virtue of republican Rome which decayed because of "its immoderate greatness," a process declared to be "natural and inevitable." In this view, even Christianity and monasticism are then reduced to lesser causes: "if superstition had not afforded a decent retreat, the same vices would have tempted the unworthy Romans to desert, from baser motives, the standard of the republic" To this Gibbon added the balancing note: Constantine's "victorious religion broke the violence of the fall, and mollified the ferocious temper of the conquerors" a note that he rarely sounded and did not develop.

The observations conclude with reassuring contrasts between the decline of Rome and the world position of eighteenth-century Europe. First of all, the Romans knew little about the temper and number of potential enemies, but Gibbon's Europe knew something of the whole world, and Germany and Russia were part of the eighteenth-century's world of civilization. Rome, too, was a "singular and perfect coalition," but the states of Europe were parts of a great republic, in which rivalries, the source of their progress, may issue in war, but where "the European forces are exercised by temperate and indecisive contests" (2, pp. 92, 93, 95). The barbarians would have to conquer the republics one by one, or, as was more likely, a confederation of members. Even then, the remains of civilized society could sail to the Americas, "already filled with her colonies and institutions" Third, gunpowder and the sciences serving war had nullified the barbarians' advantage that poverty and danger fortify their courage. The transformation of Russia demonstrated Europe's security against barbarians, "since, before they can conquer, they must cease to be barbarous." Finally, Gibbon offers "a more humble source of comfort and hope": the arts that foster civilization — cultivating grain, raising animals, working metal, and the rudiments of navigation — cannot be lost. These basic arts in their diffusion lead Gibbon to a great *non sequitur*, his hybris: "We may therefore acquiesce in the pleasing conclusion that every age of the world has increased and still increases the real wealth, the happiness, the knowledge, and perhaps the virtue, of the human race" (2, pp. 95, 96, 97, 98).

Such rare optimism never intruded into the pages devoted to the Eastern Roman Empire, the millennial continuation of the Roman Empire. Gibbon had misgivings about this subject; he feared that it would entertain neither his readers nor the author. At the end of volume 3 he reassured himself: "The majesty of Rome was faintly represented by the princes of Constantinople, the feeble and imaginary successors of Augustus. Yet they continued to reign. . . . and the history of the Greek emperors may still afford a long series of instructive lessons and interesting revolutions" (2, chap. 38, p. 90).

Volume 4 then was devoted mainly to Byzantine history from Zeno (474-491) to Heraclius (610-641). Gibbon was not entirely satisfied, and to deal with eight centuries more of Byzantine history as well as western Europe, the Church, Rome, and humanist learning, was an ungratifying and melancholy prospect. The eastern empire, he believed, provided a uniform and therefore uninstructive and unnecessary tale of vice, servility, despotism, and superstition. What except a kind of pornography is to be told about an empire that defies logic and biology by subsisting 1,058 years "in a state of premature and perpetual decay"? Gibbon once said that instead of emphasizing the fall of Rome it would be more proper to wonder at how long it survived. Byzantium's millennium he found too long, a time without a single discovery to promote human happiness or a single idea for speculation.[20]

Gibbon's failure to understand is monumentally expressed. The judgment of a historian of Byzantium, Steven Runciman, is that Gibbon's views delayed the development of Byzantine studies for a century. If they did, it was because these views coincided with the outlook of western Europeans that they are dynamic and that Orientals from Near to Far East are unchanging. By Enlightenment standards the eastern Greeks were servile, ineffectual, and superstitious. In sum, Gibbon found the prominence of religion, monasticism, and theology in the Byzantine Empire not only regrettable but offensive and disturbing.

In a remarkable feat of construction and compression, Gibbon nevertheless covered the reigns of sixty emperors over six centuries in his forty-eighth chapter. But the author had no sympathy for his subject: there is, at best, a moral passion wearily denouncing the same base spirit and rounds of violence varying only in degree of atrocity. As Gibbon proceeded through the six centuries, unable to find anything great in the subject and with his own moral judgment flagging, majesty of the narrative was lost, and an esthetic nemesis prevailed. The sentences, companies of clones, became wearisome. Perhaps in uneasiness he concluded the chapter with a discussion of the moral service history provides in enlarging the individual's experience and "the horizon of our intellectual view" (2, chap. 48, p. 577).

The next chapter is devoted to the iconoclastic controversy and the Holy Roman Empire until the fourteenth century. Thereafter, Gibbon proposed primarily topical divisions, among them Mohammedanism, the Bulgars, the Crusades, the Tartars, the restored eastern empire, the Turks and their conquest of Constantinople, the end of the Roman Empire in the East. "The schism of the Greeks will be connected with their last calamities, and the restoration of learning in the Western world. I shall return from the captivity of the new, to the ruins of ancient *Rome*" (2, chap. 48, p. 523).

Gibbon's account of the Islamic world is livelier because he was more interested in the religion of Allah and Mohammed than in Byzantine Greeks. In his childhood he had thought of the Orient as colorful, and he brought this love of *A Thousand and One Nights* to his adult concern with the influence of religion on a people and a state.

"Mohammed," he wrote, "with a sword in one hand and the Koran in the other, erected his throne on the ruins of Christianity and Rome."[21] This is well said, with the exceptions of the then unwritten Koran and of the word *throne*, which appears here because Gibbon enjoyed using words that present religions as worldly powers. Mohammed, enthusiast or fraud, was the benefactor of the Bedouin, idealized as independent and free, because he preached a simple religion that a deist philosopher could approve and a skeptical historian applying the test of human happiness could find useful. The prophet had the merit of preaching one god without, so the misrepresentation continued, complex doctrines, a priesthood, or moral prescriptions that defy nature and evoke monsters. Unlike Christianity, Islam favored a warrior's spirit and socially useful virtues. Its social utility helped to explain a rapid expansion that in the West reached into the center of France so that Gibbon could talk of the possibility of the Koran being preached to the circumcised clerks of Oxford. But the very extent of the initial Arab conquests, their immoderate greatness, put a term to further conquests.

Islamic Turkish conquerors took Jerusalem, a capture that eventually was the occasion for launching the First Crusade, a foreshadowing of later European expansion which, Gibbon thought, was a guarantee that his civilization woud endure. But the Crusades were enterprises of barbarous and superstitious people: the conquests could not be lasting, and the Latin conquerors of Constantinople, the fourth Crusaders, had destroyed the manuscripts of classical Greek works. Two and a half centuries later circumstances had greatly improved. When the Turks captured Constantinople, the Latin world, having been prepared, respectfully received the knowledge and treasures of the Greek exiles.

Rome and western Europe emerged from barbarism and superstition. The barbarian kingdoms and their descendants had been the realms of warlords, who during violent and dreary centuries established feudal institutions for which Gibbon had an enlightened bourgeois contempt. The barbarians nevertheless had a manly spirit of freedom whose promise set them off from the Byzantine Greeks. When freedom was made secure by laws and institution, it fostered curiosity, knowledge, and, for the fortunate, taste. Security was child and father of trade and the growth of towns. Taste and letters, first cultivated again in Italy, marked the reappearance of civilization. The barbarians, immersed in ignorance, spoke a rude, vulgar tongue. When among them appeared some students "of the more perfect idioms of Rome and Greece," they "were introduced to a new world of light and science; to the society of the free and polished nations of antiquity, and to a familiar converse with those immortal men who spoke the sublime language of eloquence and reason" In this dialogue of civilization there was first a necessary period of imitation, the century after Petrarch and Boccacio filled as it was "with a crowd of Latin imitators, who decently repose on our shelves." But with the imitators came the inspiration not only to emulate the classics, but to purity taste. Neither a people nor the artist may "hope to equal or surpass, till he had learned to imitate, the works of his predecessors."

The concluding chapter, turning to the remains of ancient Rome, began with Poggio Bracciolini's contemplation of its ruins from the Capitoline Hill, "formerly," as Poggio is quoted, "the head of the Roman Empire, the citadel of the earth, the terror of kings" (2, chap. 66, pp. 1303-4). But to Gibbon the ruins recalled the culture of classical Rome, which in the fifteenth century inspired the new era of civilization that Gibbon exemplified (2, chap. 66, pp. 1303-1304; chap. 71, p. 1438).

To Gibbon, the historian, the ruins of the classical pagan world with which he identified himself rose in a spiritual triumph over the monuments of Catholic Christianity. He made this identification explicit in a letter to Lord Sheffield. In it Gibbon expressed his admiration for Burke's *Reflections on the French Revolution* as "admirable medicine against the French disease. . . . I can forgive even his superstition. The primitive church, which I have treated with some freedom, was itself at that time an innovation, and I was attached to the old pagan establishment."[22]

The very last sentence of the history recalled that Gibbon conceived the idea of his work among the Capitol's ruins, but the preceding paragraph brought his themes together in a sentence of genius: "The map, the description, the monuments of ancient Rome have been elucidated by the diligence of the antiquarian and the student, and the footsteps of heroes, the relics not of superstition, but of empire, are devoutly visited by a new race of pilgrims from the remote and once savage countries of the North."

The Decline and Fall coheres in a remarkable unity of style, structure, subject, and outlook. The coherence is the masterpiece that won Gibbon the fame he sought. The style—and some readers equate style and masterpiece—was achieved by clear-sighted and efficient practice. Gibbon sought "a middle tone between a dull chronicle and a rhetorical declamation"; style was to be the clear mirror of his mind and the revealer of his meaning. He wrote the first chapter three times and the next two twice. (*Memoirs*, pp. 155-567). The chapter on Constantine also proved difficult. In the concluding volumes he allowed that he might have been too ready to be satisfied with the facility he had acquired.

He fashioned balanced sentences, excessively balanced because the other shoe is always dropped. These were structured into paragraphs composed in his head, and then written with little change. Speed reading of the history is a waste of time, and prolonged reading is difficult. The style never rushes the reader but encourages rereading and reflection. Because sentence and paragraph were tested by ear, the history is to be read aloud.[23]

The style, approaching declamation, identified the author as *the historian*, the impartial historian, a man of studied detachment. His detachment conveyed to the reader the sense of witnessing a world spectacle. It was the necessary mask of Gibbon, the censor of morals as well as the ironist, who mocked by pretending to take absurdities seriously, and by feigning ignorance or uncertainty. Irony was his principal and inevitable weapon against Christianity and the churches, inevitable because to deny the reality of the religion's spiritual claims required that the church be considered solely in terms of this world, swords, violence, lust for power and all. That Pascal, the protagonist of Christian belief, was Gibbon's annually read model enlarges the vein of irony.

The success of the history's first volume enhanced Gibbon's remarkable confidence in his readers. He knew them and knew how to reach them. This assurance took surprising form when Gibbon half-jokingly excused his delay in answering a friend's letter on the ground that he had been writing a page of his history. In writing the history, Gibbon told Lord Sheffield, he considered himself to be writing to his friend. To Lord Sheffield he later affirmed that he was likely to finish composing his

"Memoirs," although in fact he did not. "If I can please myself, I am confident of not displeasing." Early in the years of composition, Gibbon became so assured in his artistry that he found it pointless to consult others about his writing.[24]

The nature of his accomplishment is conveniently suggested in two epigrams of Dr. Johnson. The first was a judgment of Swift's "The Conduct of the Allies": "He had to count to ten, and he has counted it right." The second took care of Oliver Goldsmith: "Sir, he has the art of compiling, and of saying everything he has to say in a pleasing manner." These inadequate conceptions of the historian's task, counting, as it were, in an engaging way, become ludicrous when applied to Gibbon's history.[25]

Consider only the two principal steps, research and composition. Gibbon's researches were monumental in the manner of the late seventeenth century, the last phase of the Age of Erudition. He used its massive critical collections of sources. He loved the ancient classics and mastered the classical commentaries of two centuries as well as church history and other phases of historical literature. Sustained, self-imposed labor was his pleasure, an agreeable way of avoiding tedium and worse, and of making leisure welcome. The history as well as the critical footnotes communicated the pleasure that his studies afforded him. They must entertain and instruct him, and he must do likewise for his readers.

How do you compile such research? What does it mean to go from five to six or nine to ten? Gibbon had to select from the sources and commentary the materials that would provide an accurate and true account of the Roman Empire's history over thirteen centuries, not to mention an account of German barbarians, Arabs, Persians, and Mongols. The materials had then to be wrought into the narrative that he composed in his head. As an eighteenth-century historian, a historian-*philosophe*, he knew that his function was, on the one hand, to teach by providing instructive examples and the reflections appropriate for moral lessons, and, on the other, to give a narcissistic performance as a man of taste. The lessons should support tolerance and hatred of persecution, constitutional government and hatred of despotism, aristocracy and hatred of democracy, reason and enlightenment and hatred of superstition, prudence and hatred of folly, and good taste and aversion to the grotesque, the disproportioned, the unbalanced, and the inelegant.

Gibbon's entertaining and instructive narrative took form in a virtuoso display of his conscience and sensibilities as well as his erudition. His was the mind that made the selection, that found patterns in events others could not see, much as the gambler wagers on the regularities he sees or thinks he sees.[26] Style, then — no more a mere matter of the arrangement of words than Dr. Johnson's counter is a historian — is the image of the mind, expressing its vision. Gibbon's vision is a classical humanist view of the world, a view enriched by a love of learning and made lucid and sharp by the Enlightenment. He dwelt on the ruins of Rome and responded warmly to the pagan world with which he peopled it. The ruins were to him the witness of the fall of a pagan world, tolerant, Ciceronian, civilized; and that fall was an awesome revolution. But he could conclude with a reassuring post-decline, with the auspicious presence of himself and others amidst the ruins, personal witnesses to a victory over what he called superstition.

Gibbon's mind was shaped by many influences. These, being the elements of the outlook of a particular eighteenth-century man, are not always in harmony. Two examples may be cited. The first is Gibbon's account of human psychology, which is at odds with his occasional profession of belief in progress. His views, like his classical sources and Enlightenment models, are forceful and decidedly limited. Man is selfish and power-hungry. One man exploits another, and rationality is possible only for a small number, an elect as few as Calvin and the Jansenists would allow. These few have to be sustained by the labor of others. Heaven, or somebody, help the elite and other people when the populace gets out of hand.

But in professing faith in progress and the security of civilization, Gibbon yielded to late Enlightenment fashion and perhaps the logic of his psychology rather than the massive testimony of his scholarship. First of all, he believed that men never lost the major advances in economy, technology, and science and that, in spite of all the destruction in human history, each generation added to the sum of man's techniques and knowledge. Even more surprising is his belief that because the civilized world in his time consisted of many states, barbarian conquerors, even if they should defeat several of the states, could not conquer all of them. This is confirmed by another argument, that to make eighteenth-century weapons was beyond the capacity of barbarians. If the latter could make them, they would have become civilized. Although his thought and style incline him to such formulations as that men enjoyed and abused peace and wealth, he did not allow that men might enjoy and abuse technology, that his own civilization could regress into barbarism, and that morality had to be more than the inspiration of rational self-interest.

If the belief in progress subsists uneasily with Gibbon's dim view of human history, his unvarying hostility to religion also jars, because Gibbon's major convictions explain the pervasiveness of religion. The mass of mankind, he recognized, believed in religion because they could not live as skeptics. As a rule, religion made for social order among the multitude. The role he assigned to the humble Christian was to believe and submit. Nevertheless, Gibbon is unrelenting in his sneers, derision, irony, and innuendoes. Religion is the chief inspiration of his wit, and it becomes wearisome. Gibbon could have dismissed some ecclesiastical history as unworthy of his notice. Instead he was scrupulous, but every mention of religion troubled him and drove him to irony and mockery.

In his reaction to the French Revolution, Gibbon became more explicit about society's need of religion and superstition. He even played with the thought of writing a dialogue, including Lucian, Erasmus, and Voltaire, about "the danger of exposing an old superstition to the contempt of the blind and fanatic multitude."[27] In France, he was certain, something worse had taken the place of religion and superstition.

Gibbon's achievement as a historian is limited by his psychology and narrow sympathy. For an explanation of Rome's decline the history is peculiarly inadequate. Even more extraordinary is the view of civilization that enables him to describe the pre-Renaissance history of Western civilization as times of barbarism and superstition.

Do we, then, read it only as a work of art? Some people do, and many of them are professional historians. Others would say that in *The Decline and Fall* we get an incomparable eighteenth-century account of the past.[28] According to this judgment the history is read as a masterly expression of an eighteenth-century mind, as an account of its past that illuminates aspects of that past.

But we can read *Decline and Fall* for the history that it tells. This is to note that, like all general histories, Gibbon's work is incomplete and flawed. But religious critics of Gibbon make a mistake in searching for the historian's errors, because his details are generally accurate. The flaw is in the overall vision, grand and yet remarkably restricted. The history's reduction of the spiritual to power-seeking and self-interest sometimes amounts to a parody. Nevertheless, it is not simply wrong, because power and selfishness may intrude into our loftiest and basest endeavors. Gibbon's history raises in the sharpest way questions about the role Christianity, or any religion, can have in civilization without becoming hostage to worldly powers.

9. Ranke:

History as Worship

NOTORIOUSLY HISTORY HAS TWO principal meanings: the past itself and the historian's presentation of the results of his inquiry into it. When the latter meaning is examined, it is evident that, for all of his stance of common sense and matter-of-factness, the historian encounters his profession's form of the problem of knowledge. How and why does he select his sources? How valid or true is his account? What is the relationship between fact and generalization? Does his avowed or unconscious motivation affect the historian's search, selection, and presentation? Does his form of presentation affect his use of facts and his judgment?

Leopold von Ranke (1795-1886), modern founding father of critical history and patron saint of devourers of archives, raised these questions and responded to them. His masterly histories of Reformation Germany, Prussia, England, France, and the papacy were esteemed as the fruit and vindication of his method. In England and the United States, however, the method was identified with a few slogans and injunctions: history is primarily a study of politics and foreign policy; return to or search out the sources; evaluate them and prize, above all, the sources that present the testimony of participants and eyewitnesses; strive simply to tell things as they actually happened. So to reduce Ranke's position is intellectual primitivism, a primitivism that persisted because attempts to discuss the problem of historical knowledge were ignored or derided as futile.[1]

Ranke had developed his own views in the course of serious study of philosophy, theology, and classical languages and literature. From them he drew the conclusion that the historical study of the genesis of institutions and people yielded livelier and fuller knowledge than other studies. Some dilemmas and weaknesses of later historians may be clarified by recalling that Ranke's method and objectives were transformed so that they were looked on as a liberation from philosophy and the tiresome problem of knowledge, as a release to facts, objectivity, and science.

Ranke was perhaps too much at home in his time and place, and his life had no shattering experience: he was on the winning side in his own lifetime, or at any rate cheered its German winners. He was no Old Testament prophet denouncing his age in the name of God, and yet he did speak as one who saw the design of God. Lutheran pietist theology, German Idealist philosophy, classical studies, and German nationalism all enabled him to see what he declared his vision to be.

Religious influences surrounded the young Ranke in his Thuringian home and school. Leopold was the eldest of nine children born to a lawyer-father who had broken the Ranke line of Lutheran ministers and expected his oldest son to restore the succession. In his pietistic Lutheran society at home and in the Pforta school, a center equally strong in classical studies and Lutheran devotion, Leopold learned that the world was marked with characters and clues that pointed to God's design. This influence helped mold a youth predisposed to accept the things of Caesar and of man, and to explain them rather than radically to change them.

That temperament helps to explain the easiness of his decision to become a Prussian subject when his home area was annexed by Prussia after Napoleon's defeat. In 1814 he went to the University of Leipzig. Less than a year earlier Napoleon had there suffered a major defeat in the Battle of the Nations. During its troubles, 10 percent of Leipzig's civilian population had died. When Ranke arrived, the king of Saxony was a prisoner, Russian troops patrolled the city, and all its churches were used as hospitals or military storehouses.

The events of the time touched the young student, but his industry did not flag and he received his doctorate of philosophy in 1817. In these first university years Leopold discovered within himself what he wanted to be. (At any rate that statement approximates his way of speaking more than saying that he found himself.) It was a kind of conversion experience, beyond dogma, of a rich and vibrant wholeness that made it clear why what he called the rationalism and compromises of the absolute among the Leipzig theologians could not satisfy him. Nor could Lutheran orthodoxy, though he did not say so. Even when (1817), in Protestant fashion as it were, he turned from biographies of Luther to the sources of his life, Ranke was attracted by the Reformer's language and rejoiced in the absolute coherence of Luther's life, teaching, and experience — the prized coherence that in the historian's mind went beyond all allegiance to a sect or even a church.[2] To follow Luther, then, paradoxically meant that Ranke would not choose the ministry. He was, he found, born for learning, and that also meant teaching. In such a career Prussia offered many more opportunities than Saxony.

The transcendental Idealist philosopher, Johann Gottlieb Fichte (1762-1814), contributed to Ranke's vision of Luther and particularly to his decision that the scholar's vocation was for him. In *Addresses to the German Nation* (1808), Fichte urged Germans to be true to their spiritual core and therefore to resist French ideas as speciously universal, a struggle prefigured by Luther's quarrel with the papacy, also a regime with claims to universality. The philosopher's earlier writing, *On the Scholar's Mission* (more precisely "On the Scholar's Nature," 1806), clarified for Ranke his choice of a scholar's life. The man of learning, Fichte wrote, illuminated the divine ideas in the world. In willing to perform this function, his duty, the scholar obeys his true self, and his achievement may even be a fusion of his will and God's.

The influence of Fichte and other Idealist philosophers illuminates the point of Ranke's later remark that historical studies grew out of German opposition to the absolute rule of Napoleonic ideas.[3] Certainly Ranke's historical studies grew out of the concern he shared with the Idealists to understand the struggle against France and to clarify what Germany was, as well as the polity and culture that would properly emerge in an age of restoration.

Ranke's religious views readily accorded with the Idealist search to know the world by the divine ideas that are its ultimate reality. From this position he approached history as his principal study because his experience revealed that any abstract statement of an idea desiccates that creative presence of God in the world. These ideas, many rather than one, are so many emanations of God, and as each develops in time, the ideas may be glimpsed in history. The historian, then, may reach to the fullest meaning of life, and his study is a form of worship.

Ranke's conception of historical activity was shaped by classical philological criticism that taught him textual criticism and accustomed him to search for the pure source. An influential model was Barthold Georg Niebuhr (1776-1831), whose *Roman History*, Ranke said, convinced him that in his time a work of history need not be a soulless manual but could be a worthy literary endeavor. Another model and master was Thucydides, the subject of the work for which he received the doctorate. This Latin work on the political teaching of the Greek historian is not extant, but Ranke several times called Thucydides one of his models. Finally, Ranke recognized Walter Scott's *Quentin Durward* as a sort of negative inspiration. The aging historian recalled that upon reading Sir Walter's account he turned to historical sources such as the *Memoirs* of Philippe de Commines and found different characters and a different story. This experience, I believe, has been overemphasized because Ranke did not read the novel until well into 1823, and he had been engaged in writing a history as early as 1820 and referred to its subject (the German and Latin people) in 1822.[4]

Ranke began to carry out his ideas during his years as a teacher at the Fridericianum, a gymnasium in Frankfurt on the Oder, where he taught the ancient classics and history. Ranke's interest in the latter, something added to the traditional curriculum, was a reason for his appointment. In 1818, the year he began his work, he delivered a formal lecture at the gymnasium. The subject contrasted education in antiquity and in Germany. Teachers in Greece and Rome, he said, prepared students to educate themselves so that they could serve the public interest, the state. Then political life and education worked for the same end, a condition of spontaneous harmony. As that harmony did not prevail in contemporary Germany,

teaching had the larger task of self-education that would enable
the individual to understand his role and its attendant duties.
To work for harmony between public life and education was a
prime duty. The goal required an inner cultivation, the func-
tioning of a free and responsible individual. To recognize and
understand the contrast, historical studies must work with
traditional studies as principal means of self-education and
spiritual growth.[5]

As Ranke's teaching week was twenty hours, it is good that,
as his motto proclaimed, the young teacher found labor a
pleasure. At Frankfurt, then, he had something of an orgy
when he settled on a particular history. This may have taken
some time to define because he believed that the greatest
treasure of his study was world history, the organic whole
which gave full meaning to every particular. The young
historian's letters when invoking world history sometimes rush
to rhapsody. But the historian also recognized that before a
whole could be visible, he must work empirically by proceeding
to the mastery of fragments. If these were true, the historian
could hope to have a sense of God. There was, indeed, nothing
in the world that was wholly worldly and godless.[6] Human circumstances reveal the human condition, even though our
history may be regrettably dark and piecemeal. Yet, and it is
well to beware the German Romantic — and should I add the
historian? — when modest, for Ranke went on, we know much,
may recover more and grasp the whole.

The particulars Ranke chose for study were the beginnings of
the modern age, 1494-1535, a period in which Europe's universal powers, the papacy and the empire, declined. For this study
a library in Frankfurt provided a collection of memoirs and late
Renaissance historical works. Ranke composed *The Histories of
the Latin and Teutonic Nations* (1824) from these printed
sources. In choosing histories for the title, Ranke had judged
that his presentation of so much movement, rapid change, decline, and new birth as well as reformation lacked an ultimate
coherence. Because of this dissatisfaction he concluded the
histories with the year 1514: the political material for subsequent years, he explained, ran in too many directions. But
Ranke, aware that he had written a formidable study, hoped

that for all its inadequacies it would gain him an appointment
that would give him time and access to source materials.[7]

The Histories is memorable as a literate work of history, as
a first treatment of Ranke's principal subject — the great powers
of Europe — as a striking statement of historicism, and as a first
major statement and example of critical history. The pages
overcrowded with events justify Ranke's misgivings, but the
work is nevertheless a dramatic narrative written lucidly and
flexibly. The hypercritical poet Heinrich Heine outrageously
described Ranke's style as well-cooked mutton, but it is at the
opposite pole from the German style that vexes foreign
readers — a marathon of compound nouns and overwrought
verbs that in length aspire to the infinity of William Faulkner's
sentences.

The Histories recounted the making of the community of
Europe, the republic of great powers. The base was the Roman
Empire, which some Teutonic invaders and their successors
had sought to preserve. Their efforts — the project of King
Athaulf of the Visigoths to make a Gothic Roman Empire, the
Empire of Charlemagne, and the Germanic reception of
Roman law — prefigure modern Europe. But first came the age
dominated by the Catholic church with its impossible univer-
salism which the Holy Roman Empire presented in another
sphere. Ranke looked to actions for the evidence of community.
Such common and formative endeavors were the barbarian invasions, the Crusades, and European colonization of the world,
as it were, "three great respirations of this great confederation."
This view of Europe, a constricted Romanticism that excluded
Celts, Hungarians, and Slavs, was rooted in German nationalism and great-power piety.

The detailed diplomacy, his forte in research, of the Italian
Wars illustrates a general movement that includes the rise of the
Spanish monarchy, the end of Italian autonomy, French opposition to the Hapsburgs, and the condition of pre-reformation
Germany. France's contention with the empire and Spain limns
the future form of Europe, monarchical states in rivalry. The
theme, the end of universalism and subsequent European plurality, pointed to the subject of many of Ranke's histories: the suc-
cessive predominance of individual great powers.

The Histories is significant, that is, historically noteworthy, for its statement of what became historicism and for the critical analysis of sources that makes up the second volume. In the preface Ranke explicitly disavowed purposes that had characterized most earlier historical writing: to reinforce morality by memorializing good and bad actions and detailing their consequences, to provide the reader with material for his instruction in prudence, to apologize for a faith or institutional cause, and to entertain. In deceptively simple words he proposed to describe things as they really were. The historian, he enjoined, must present what really happened because the historian can only sense God in the actual world, including events that bear the presence and ideas of God. An inaccurate history, a history that is, therefore, a profanation of worship, will yield only false clues and forged hieroglyphics.

But, to complicate matters and to flee to idealist philosophy, even the true history and what is seen in it depends on something within ourselves: "Since everything comes from God, what matters is not the material of existence but the eye for the material," the talent, the empathy that somehow becomes part of the divine breath, a unity and an awareness.[8]

The all of which he presented a fragment is the revelation of God, and Ranke is consistent in that he did not write *The Histories* as the acts of God but wrote as one communicating a sense of the ideas of God and his moving presence. He saw the decline of the universal powers and the growth of new spiritual powers in the states and Protestant churches. Later works carry this further. In *The Histories* he stated the theme: "It is both the life and fortune of the German-Latin nations that they never became united." And, more forcefully, concerning the ambitious projects of Emperor Maximilian, which might have destroyed European liberty: "But God willed that this should not happen. . . . The development of the Latin and Teutonic nations that had just begun, would have been interrupted and hindered thereby."[9] In other remarks, some of which he omitted from a second edition prepared fifty years later, his views seem conventional and unreflective, for they imply that God willed everything. This may make for complacency, and the complacent Ranke is shown in a remark he wrote in the 1830s:

"Happy is it for man that pity stands ever by the dwelling of misfortune."[10]

The method by which he hoped to uncover what really happened is exemplified in an appendix, the second volume of *The Histories*, "On the Critique of Modern Historians." His method (Lord Acton called it a new method of employing authorities) is an extension of classical textual criticism to histories and memoirs written in the fifteenth and sixteenth centuries. A principal example of this critique is his assessment of the Florentine historian Guiccardini, whose *History of Italy* had long been used as a major source for Italian history. Ranke concluded that the Italian historian had used much information that he could not have known at first hand, that he had used other sources which were inaccurate and which he used inaccurately.

The critique of sources, which he made a feature of almost all his later works, required consideration of questions about the memorialist as an observer of the action he described. If he was not an observer, what was his likely source of information? Is the source distorted by partisanship? Is there evidence of factional traditions? How are differences in first-hand and other accounts to be reconciled — if they can be? With these and similar questions Ranke illustrates his own transcendental philosophy; for the method may be used mechanically, and even methodical industriousness may yield a barren harvest. To attain Ranke's level, one must add the discerning eye, reverence, empathy, and the artist's delight in communication and order.

The book was not a publishing sensation, but it won for its author an invitation to lecture on history at the University of Berlin (1825). The director of the education section in the Prussian Ministry of Public Worship hailed Ranke as the restorer of history. This praise expressed the official's criticism of what he regarded as a dangerous fashion: to write in support of liberal views of the state by exalting the history of the city-state republics of ancient Greece and Renaissance Italy. Ranke, so the official went on, recounted the development of the great European states in the spirit that characterized eighteenth-century balance-of-power politics, a spirit proper to past history as well as to present politics.[11]

In *The Histories* Ranke had queried printed sources. To its second edition (1874) he added that in 1824 he had become aware of the necessity of using manuscript sources. Fortunately, government archives were gradually to become accessible on such a scale that, the author added, *The Histories* was written on the threshold of a new age in history. In that age the professional historian had to criticize his sources methodically, and the sources had to include relevant manuscript material in accessible archives.

In Berlin he came across a collection of the Venetian Relations, reports of Venetian ambassadors to the rulers of their commercial republic. These late fifteenth- and sixteenth-century reports were unique in the West because the Venetians had pioneered the establishment of permanent resident ambassadors, who in their regular reports and their Relations every three years were charged with the task of describing the politics, economy, and trade prospects of the country to which they were accredited. The Relations were consigned to the archives of Venice, although many copies were in the private libraries of prominent Venetian families and a considerable part of Venice's archives had been moved to Vienna, after 1815 the master of the onetime imperial city of the Adriatic. The authors of these reports, the agents of Venice, in supplying political and commercial intelligence, generally cast a cold eye on human actions and motives, a disenchantment that Ranke enjoyed and that contributed to his admiration for the political acumen of the rulers of Venice and their agents. The Relations, he said, opened a new world to him, a world he extended by seeking other manuscript collections. He soon had an unusual opportunity. As Berlin was a research university and Ranke had the favor of the Prussian government, in 1827 he was enabled to set out on a tour of archives that lasted four years.

The first year was devoted to research in Vienna, where he had the friendly support of an advisor of Prince Metternich, the Catholic conservative writer Friedrich von Gentz. There he also met Serbian nationalists who supplied him with material for *The Serbian Revolution* (1829), an unusual item among Ranke's works in that it deals with Slavs and with contemporary events as well as their background.

In the fall of 1828 he went to Venice, Florence, and Rome. He was allowed limited access to the Vatican Library and freer access to many of the manuscript collections of Roman noble families. His letters express the joy he had in research and the belief that his historian's eye saw God's hand at work in the famous Italian cities that he visited; he made this reverent remark but gave no details of the vision.

When Ranke resumed lecturing in Berlin (1831), he continued the practice of using his home to receive the students of his seminar. The model for it as well as for his elaboration of historical method was the advanced course in classical philology established at Leipzig and some other universities. The members of Ranke's seminar usually met weekly and had to be chosen or approved by the director of the seminar, who presided at sessions where the philosophy of history and source problems were discussed until in later meetings each member submitted a research paper to the criticism of the members and the director. The seminar became an institution in the growth of graduate education that is a feature of the nineteenth-century university.

With the seminar Ranke's contribution to the university study of history, apart from his publications, is complete. It consists of four principal parts. The first is the emphasis on the use of manuscript sources. Among them the prominence of diplomatic reports was favorable to Ranke's belief that significant history consisted of action and reaction, and possibly strengthened that belief. The second part is the critical treatment of the sources, historical method. The third part was the seminar, sometimes called a historical laboratory, which encouraged many historians to write for other historians rather than for the general reader. The director of the seminar emphasized bibliographical thoroughness, criticism, precision, and penetration.

The search for sources, their critical assessment, training in criticism, and the provision of a critical milieu in the seminar all were necessary, because — and this is the fourth part — in the accurate representation of the past God's hand may be seen. History, therefore, was a self-justifying or God-justified study. It should not attempt to instruct in morals or prudence; as a kind of worship it was an end in itself.

These beliefs have a major role in inspiring the formidable
and vast nineteenth-century interest in history, an interest that
in some writers became historicism, a view that is diversely and
often obscurely defined. In effect, historicism is a belief that the
study of history is an end in itself, God or no God, that
historical tendencies must be accepted and not be subjected to
moral or instructive standards, and that the historical explanation of a thing is the only adequate account of it. In one of his
lectures (1832) Ranke declared that the proper introduction to
a subject is all that preceded it.[12] This could eventually mean
that, except when dealing with the first ages, a historian could
never get to his subject.

In religious veneration of history, Ranke, as Theodore von
Laue concluded, practically affirmed that "whatever is is right"
as well as the view that a state must develop in its own way,
even outside the demands of morality, but also that the holders
of power might be expected to wield it beneficently, that power
did not bring with it an almost irresistible temptation to corruption. Ranke saw no historical moral about corruption and
believed that reverential history such as his would educate the
human race.[13]

Because of these views, which help to explain his ready
deference to authority, Ranke was asked in 1831 to edit a journal that would present the policies of the Prussian government
and its institutions in a favorable light. The historian had been
disturbed by the French Revolution of 1830, which in affirming
popular sovereignty, he thought, provided the problems and
business of governments for decades. He accepted the editorial
mission because he thought Prussia to be a government of moderation midway between revolution and reaction. His editor-
ship, an opportunity, as he put it, to learn and understand contemporary politics, spanned the five-year life and the eight
issues of the *Historisch-Politische Zeitschrift*.[14]

He was his own principal contributor, and he found that
writing compelled him to definition and precision. The clarifi-
cation proved to be an application of historicism to politics, an
influence on his later historical writings, and his perception of
God's hand. To see God's hand is not theory in any usual sense
but is to present history as the way things are supposed to be.
Ranke's conservative view, which read God's hand marks, pro-

vided the basis for genuine politics. Liberalism he considered baleful, because it would impose similar and therefore alien institutions on states and thereby violate the processes of creation.

The great powers of the European system were ideas in the mind of God. As the highest form of community, of union for action, as an idea in the mind of God, the state must be true to itself. Prussia was exemplary. It had an unbroken history manifesting a spirit and idea free of distortion. It had not been convulsed and needed no constitution and no contract because it made adjustments, as they were necessary, without destroying its integrity, its coherence of king, bureaucracy, and army, all inviting the Prussians to participate in service to it. In the period of national awakening it had come to terms with the French Revolution by the abolition of serfdom and some restriction on class privilege; it had adapted itself precisely as far as its true development required.

The state, often not coterminous with the nation, is the product of history. It follows that the historian, after amassing the events and facts of a nation's history and grasping by intuition its idea and leading tendencies, gives the statesman an indication of the direction in which he must move.

God has evidently ordained that the states are in competition that may result in war, and this struggle keeps the states alert to their tendencies and expressive of their idea. If, then, power is decisive, the world is not therefore abandoned to brutishness, because moral strength is a part of power. This rivalry of state with state is beneficent and likely to be permanent because it makes for creativity and helps to preserve from death the system and institutions that serve the needs of mortals.[15]

Two final points require mention. The first is the historicist emphasis on the individual state and the necessity that it be free to follow the course dictated by its idea. The second is Ranke's belief that the competition of states requires unqualified support for military preparations and that the historian studies principally foreign policy. War, he believed, need not rupture the continuity of history: one part is joined to another, and its great changes usually come at a slow pace. The continuity includes struggle within the system of states that is marked by periods of the predominance of one or another of the contending powers.

While Ranke was clarifying his political and philosophical ideas, he composed *The History of the Popes* (vol. 1, 1834; vols. 2 and 3, 1836). The author took advantage of its many printings to enlarge its scope, which originally extended from the sixteenth century, through the post-Napoleonic Restoration, to years beyond the first Vatican Council (1870).

The popes, not the papacy, were his subject, for his philosophical position and genius in sketching personalities directed his writing. The occupants of the Papal See were presented as representatives of an idea within the competition of states and rulers of Europe, itself based on "that close union of Latin and Germanic elements." Initially, to tame the spirits of northern tribes, ecclesiastical supremacy was a historical necessity. As that supremacy ceased to be essential to the well-being of the growing kingdoms, new necessities supervened. "Universality retired and in its place appeared a new species of partition, founded on a higher principle." At the height of this universalism under Boniface VIII, nationalism, expressed in vernacular literature, and the states, which bear the idea that nationalism supported, began to restrain the universal papacy, to change the old relation of things. In the later Middle Ages it weakened, then to be challenged by the Reformation, which assured the political autonomy of states. Germany had "the undying merit of having restored Christianity to a purer form . . . of having rediscovered the true religion." The popes, with the help of pious Italians, new religious orders (particularly the Jesuits), the Inquisition, and moral reform, regenerated the Catholic church. This gave Ranke his main theme, which he exaggerated to heighten the drama: a new conflict between ecclesiastical supremacy on one side and political autonomy and reformed religion on the other. The regeneration reached a high point during the French Wars of Religion (1562-1598), when the issue extended to "the exclusion of a legitimate prince from the throne on considerations purely religious: the ecclesiastical impulse then pervading the world in all directions would thereby have achieved complete supremacy."[16]

The account of Henry IV of France (1589-1610) well reveals Ranke's concern with universal history and its movements. The movement here is from the papacy as universal idea to the European state system. The Protestant Henry accepted Catholicism as the only course that could assure him the throne. But the new convert and his Catholic supporters hoped to serve the interests of France. In this matter, then, Henry's espousal of the universal was in the interest of the new partitioned universal, the multiple European state system.

The movement persisted into the eighteenth and nineteenth centuries to conclude ironically with an unusual exaltation of the spiritual power. During the eighteenth century, dissidence among Catholics made formidable the critical opposition that the Catholic church had to face. Major events in this direction were the dissolution of the Jesuit order (1773) and the anti-clerical reforms of the Holy Roman Emperor Joseph II (1765-1790). Momentum accelerated with the French Revolution and Napoleon, "the autocrat of the revolution" who sought to compel and, as Ranke believed, compelled "the worthy old man," Pius VII, to subject himself to the French Empire.[17]

The post-Napoleonic Restoration gave the popes a new lease on febrile life, as later editions of *The History of the Popes* record, which culminated in the Vatican Council's proclamation (1870) of papal infallibility, utter spiritual supremacy, as Ranke thought, just when "French aggression" had provoked the Franco-Prussian War. The withdrawal of French troops enabled Italy to annex the remnant of the papal states and thereby conclude the age of papal temporal power. The war ended in victory for Prussia, a power that had among its origins hostility to the exclusive hegemony of the popes, a victory which "a convinced Protestant" would say was a "divine decision against the claim of the pope."[18]

This work has a powerful intellectual structure: detailed narrative and the biographical sketches relate to the general theme, which the author emphasizes at the beginning and end of each section of the history. Ranke took sides, but he declared his position and believed that his impartiality was assured because he was a German Protestant and thereby free of any inclination to defend the popes, whose very impotence removed from the Protestant the fear that might inspire attack.[19] Ranke's self-criticism and his determination to state contrary positions achieved a remarkable level of fairness. The biographical sketches of the popes are often brilliant. One defect is the limited number of Roman and papal sources he used. He concluded, as he did in most of his works, with a helpful and read-able evaluation of sources and excerpts from them.

From the popes and declining universalism, Ranke turned in 1836 to Germany in the age of the Reformation. It was a turn that compelled him to explore another road through the six-teenth century, the principal period of his earlier work. His new subject dealt with what he believed to be the formative powers of the modern age, reformed religion and the state.

In *German History in the Age of the Reformation* (6 vols., 1839-1847), Ranke used newly available manuscript sources, for example, the proceedings of the Imperial Reichstag from 1414 to 1613 in ninety-six volumes, and achieved an intellectual and esthetic triumph by persuasively uniting the narrative of particulars and the line of interpretation that revealed the universal significance of his subject.

There were two universal powers, the empire and the papacy. Although by divine arrangement, Ranke thought, they were destined to be supplanted by more comprehensive ideas, they were not to be despised as waste products of the historical process, a temptation that beset the followers of Hegel and Marx. In empire and papacy the contemplative historian might see God, because God is equally close to every age.

The two universal powers in the age of the Reformation did not act together. Emperor Charles V, conceiving his interests in family rather than national terms, could not rally the Ger-man forces; when he gained control of Italy, the popes, as tem-poral rulers there, turned against him. In the Reichstag the individual members sought constitutional reform which the emperor, thinking in universal terms, could not allow to be effected.

The supreme challenge came from Martin Luther and his teachings of justification by faith and of the Bible as the rule of faith.[20] Luther welled from and in turn shaped the German national consciousness. The challenge to Catholic hierarchy and to institutional universalism marked the most dangerous moment in German history because the religious change could have unsettled all things. Happily Luther, Ranke judged, was not one-sided as was the papacy and as were other early re-formers — the Anabaptists, even Zwingli. Luther's conservatism or his moderation saved him from the destructiveness of Münster and the Anabaptists. His achievements, therefore, were religious purification, a religious restoration rather than a revolt, and the autonomy of the temporal power.

German History in the Age of the Reformation ranks as a masterpiece, a triumph of intellectual and historical organization. It is spirited and dramatic, but it can hardly be described as a simple showing of what happened. Ranke's viewpoint, which organizes the story and points to its meaning, is pervasive and gains plausibility almost imperceptibly by accepting the issue of events as the design of God.

In later events that gravely troubled Ranke, France played a major role. To *French History, Especially in the Sixteenth and Seventeenth Centuries*, he devoted five volumes published between 1852 and 1861. In them he emphasized that France as a power came early to the modern scene, because France achieved a high degree of centralization under its monarchy. Like other states the French monarchy emerged from religious wars, or rather as the result of abandoning religious war. On this foundation was prepared the age of Louis XIV, the age of French predominance.

In resisting France, England and Prussia became great powers. Six volumes (1859-1868) make up Ranke's *History of England, Principally in the Seventeenth Century*, which provides a concluding review of English history to 1760. The special contribution of his study of English history is the presentation of foreign relations and the reciprocal influence of foreign and domestic politics in England.

English history, he wrote at the beginning of his work, had four principal conjunctions with world history. The first was English activity that formed part of the movement of world history from its Mediterranean center to the Atlantic Ocean and won for Britain an empire. This empire, an essential component of Britain, the great power, did not engage his sustained attention. The second is England's part in the Reformation. In England this purification of Christian revelation was less doctrinal than elsewhere, and characteristically the English monarchy and Reformation held on to many institutions of the Middle Ages, that is, the "old historical state of things."[21] Henry VIII, for example, attempted to do what Ranke judged to be impossible: to retain the doctrines and practices of the church system that he had attacked. As a consequence of this policy, the Catholic Mary became queen (1553-1558) in a reign that ended with "the national element, the creation of which had been the labor of centuries," imperiled. A new order of things was needed to save England from an unfruitful and reactionary future (1:221). Elizabeth provided that politic new order.

The old and the new clashed. In the seventeenth century this conflict made up England's constitutional struggle. Its resolution in the Glorious Revolution (1688) provides the third conjunction. This resolution, parliamentary sovereignty, gradual as was its unfolding, might have gone to the extreme of popular and absolutely overt parliamentary sovereignty. Instead, the monarchy remained. Even more important as a restraint was the continuing and saving power of the English aristocracy. In England, therefore, decisions were reached after competition and struggle. William of Orange was the ruler who for his own interest held together the divergent forces of England and, again for his interest, joined its power with the powers of Europe to resist the French effort to dominate Europe. This participation of England in Europe is the fourth conjunction.

Ranke's *English History* covers years intensively worked by historians for more than a century after the publication of his history, but it is still rewarding reading. The character sketches, the author's thoughtful reflections on the interweaving of foreign and domestic policy, and the lengthy examination of sources, some of which (for example, the correspondence of William of Orange, in Dutch) are reprinted, help account for its continuing readability and value.

The most recent of the great powers was Prussia, Ranke's adopted state. Apart from this bond, there was another tie: in 1841 his friend Frederick William IV made him Prussian historiographer. Two years later when Ranke, having traveled to Paris for research on the French Revolution, came across materials on Prussian history there, he postponed his French studies in favor of a Prussian history. To a brother he wrote that he had discovered rewarding material in the archives, and that he believed his good fortune to be the design of Providence.[22] He therefore turned to his own land, writing *Nine Books on Prussian History* (1847-1848), which twenty-five years later he expanded to *Twelve Books on Prussian History*.

Prussia, he believed, had made its first steps toward the status of great power out of necessity. With the Reformation it became a Christian state committed to particularity rather than universal dominion. Its later growth to a kingdom, in a major way based on a bureaucracy and an army, was the work of rulers, responding to their needs and thereby creating a new great power. Ranke justified Frederick the Great's seizure of Silesia on the ground that the Holy Roman Emperor Charles had not fulfilled the conditions on which the Prussian king had signed the Pragmatic Sanction that allowed a woman, Maria Theresa, to succeed to Hapsburg domains. In a later writing Ranke also justified the Partition of Poland.

Prussian strength meant that there was one independent German state. His opinion of the role of Prussia in German history may be epitomized in the words of Frederick the Great that he quoted: "My God, we are surrounded by cowardice and venality. Shall we alone be able to maintain the constitution of the Reich?"[23]

To the new Emperor William I he sent the congratulations of a historian who described himself as searching the consequences of great events and of the interconnectedness of things. The emperor had prayed that the will of God be done and it was done. The issue of events, moreover, reveals a striking contrast: in French revolutionary days all Europe had to mobilize its forces to cast down the powers of destruction; but in 1871 Prussia and the German states by themselves had performed a similar task.[24]

Ranke gave up his professorship in the University of Berlin in 1873. His position was offered to Jacob Burckhardt, who declined it, and then went to the strong nationalist, Heinrich von Treitschke. Bismarck claimed that Ranke and he were at one in politics; the claim is an unusual tribute to Ranke's eminence and, perhaps equally, to Ranke's discretion.

For the first years of his retirement Ranke devoted himself to rounding out his contributions to German history and to a share in editing his complete works (fifty-four volumes, 1873-1890). At eighty years of age and almost blind, he depended upon research and secretarial assistants. The old man's industry taxed their energies.

Germany's ascendancy, in his view, had clarified world history by eliminating the universalism of the French Revolution and restoring the republic of great powers. This development, just when his age and failing sight made archival search impossible, encouraged him to write a *Weltgeschichte* (unfinished in nine volumes, 1881-1889), a world history, the loftiest enterprise, "the last of life for which the first was made."

For a long time the volumes have been little read, a wholly understandable neglect. Although even in these last volumes the master's style did not fail him, concept and content are inadequate. First of all, he used *civilization* and *culture* as interchangeable words, and he thought that there is but one civilization, not many. The inability to recognize that there are many civilizations prevents Ranke from conceiving a true world history. Second, what Ranke saw as world history was in effect a line of development from ancient times to the Western nations that had formed the subject matter of his own historical works. His world history took a part for the whole. This is an error that he shared with the prevailing view of his age.

If with Ranke we recognize that each age, as immediate to God, is worthy of study and must first be described in its own terms, Ranke's own views require a similar effort. Like most articulate nineteenth-century Europeans, Americans, and some Asians, he believed that the Western way of life was superior to all others, that it was civilization. It had issued from the ancient world; but the Oriental nations, characterized by eternal changelessness (inactivity), do not help us to understand world history's internal movement. For the creators of world history we must look to universal empires and emperors — to the victories of Alexander, which advanced general civilization, but above all to the Romans, who made universal history possible.[25] The German Empire, created in his own time, had brought a stability to the rivalries of Western Europe, a "progressive community," a stability that he did not expect to be upset, although it could not be eternal.

Thus, Ranke's view of world history, for all his vast historical researches, is limited. But to have written about world history and to mean Western Europe was something in an age of nationalism. For his own endeavor, the approach he spelled out was to describe the leading tendencies of periods and to deal with each major nation when its history touched the general history and could be said to manifest leading tendencies.

This procedure is the one urged by Lord Acton on contributors to the *Cambridge Modern History*, which went beyond Ranke's view to a wider Europe.[26] In the twentieth century, Oswald Spengler described the main world cultures as organisms, each incomprehensible to the others, so that world history was without meaning, that is, unintelligible. Against Spengler, Arnold Toynbee puzzlingly professed empiricism when he saw civilizations as a response to challenge and then found his moral standards and judgments illustrated by the course of civilizations which also revealed the transcendence in which he believed.

The legacy of Ranke is a matter of controversy, and the conflict has been less fruitful than Ranke, who believed that conflict sustained life and perhaps progress, might have hoped. He has been blamed for what he wrote, for the misuse of what he wrote, and for what he did not write at all.

To him may be traced a principal contribution to the schism between historians who emphasized research and criticism and eventually addressed themselves to or wrote for fellow scholars and those concerned less to provide new knowledge than to present aspects of the human condition. Sometimes this schism is described as a division between critical historians and literary humanist popularizers, but this is at best inadequate. There are critical historians who are strikingly literate as humanists, and Ranke himself almost always wrote vivid and memorable history.

Ranke's profession of method and aims forms part of a Romantic, Idealist, and Christian way of thinking that was disregarded by many of his later disciples and unknown to many more. Among the Romantic Idealists, who influenced Ranke, philosophies of history were as common as was hostility to the philosophy of history among the English-speaking disciples of Ranke.

Historians who thought their discipline an end in itself, a science of the unique or simply a science, often seemed to mean that what they did was science. An essential part of this view was the influence of a crude positivism animated by a belief that the accumulation of facts, that is, positive knowledge, would eventually lead to the science of all, the architectonic science. Until that day historians could carry on with what they described as simple exposition and historical science. In doing so, they either made scholarship mindless or smuggled their own unexamined philosophy into their "scientific" writings.

The dispute over historical work as an end in itself, and over objectivity, has been long and rather unrewarding. As St. Thomas may not have been a Thomist, and could not have been a neo-Thomist, and as Marx is said to have denied that he was a Marxist, Ranke is not one with many who profess his name. Ranke's philosophy and his writings are testimony that he was not and could not have been objective. This recognition, nevertheless, does not logically lead to the conclusion that any viewpoint or historical activity is of equal worth, or that the historian should be a propagandist for revolution, social betterment, or corporate capitalism.

Ranke had an inadequate view of universal history and a limited conception of the scope of history. On occasion he dealt briefly with arts, letters, and the history of ideas, but he principally studied the great powers and their foreign policy: he was only too satisfied with the modern state. To explain his obsession we may refer to German divisions in an age of nationalism. But what can be said of the limited imagination of his followers in England and the United States who so restricted history? And yet, they and Ranke, who stressed our kinship with a past and future of conflict, were truer historians than some believers in progress who in effect thought we had passed out of the historical age, who as teachers skipped over wars and regarded scholars of wars as quasi-Fascist characters.

Far more serious is the consequence of adhering to his belief that the historian's function is not to judge but to present accurately what happened. Ranke sometimes was troubled by this waiver of the earlier moral function of the historian. When so troubled, he recalled that great crimes were somehow punished by the forces that made for order in the universe. Presumably, God took over the moral function.

In this matter Ranke was defended by Lord Acton, the very man who made the most trenchant criticism of Ranke's moral blandness. His stricture is that, as the Berlin historian failed to plumb the moral depths of mankind, "part of the story is left untold, and the world is much better and very much worse than he chooses to say." Nevertheless, Acton said, Ranke had done well in abstaining a little "from perpetual judging," in showing "a little reserve in uttering judgments," as though he were writing for grown-up men, and in abstaining "from the cheap moralities," "the short shrift."[27] The Acton who here so restrained judgment speaks in tribute to Ranke and not as the more familiar man, the historian-judge ready to cry "murder."

Ranke reflected on the consequences of his historicism. Intellectually and morally he is the superior of those who professed that they sought objectivity and had no further doubts. His own historicism had no place for prophetic criticism, which certainly creates grave difficulties for the historian in his search for the truth, the reality of events. In the great lines of history, Ranke eventually acquiesced, and there is a fearsome time-serving in his two notes about divine right and history: divine right is what has become historical and historical right is now divine right.[28]

On this historical blurring of judgments two points may be made. The first is to recall the religious inspiration of Ranke's historical studies—to read the divine hieroglyphs, to see the hand of God, to sense the divine presence in the world of man, in history. For Ranke this was the prime form of worship. But is not this worship a form of idolatry, the veneration, to use Arnold Toynbee's language, of one's own tribal idols—in this case, the state?

The second point is that Ranke's great qualities and his limitations appear to be all of a piece. Perhaps his limited view of history and what critics regarded as moral fudging or blandness alone made bearable to him the demands of what he considered essential, fairness to each of contending sides. This fairness, a quasi objectivity, required of the historian an emptying of himself, restraint, and self-scrutiny. Difficult as such efforts are—efforts that were sustained in writing some seventy volumes—they brought him through archives and the pioneering of documented history. Although fairness is difficult and final objectivity impossible, his works exemplify the criticism and self-scrutiny that make for fair and accurate history, the only possible goal of the historian. If the historian believes that he cannot approximate an accurate history, there is no point to his activity; other pursuits, such as writing poetry or novels, philosophizing, or propagandizing, would prove more honest and rewarding. But he must also recognize that his work and any work on a large subject may always be challenged by another effort on the same subject. The word *definitive* in historical writing has mainly a fugitive meaning.

10. Burckhardt:
History as a Humanity

JACOB BURCKHARDT SAW IN historical studies a principal source and refreshment of a true knowledge of man. As that knowledge had to take account of all human variety, the range of human capacities and limitations, it could not be abstract or simple. He looked to historical studies because he believed that the institutions and values of his European world threatened human values and were headed for disaster. As he understood them, historical studies might equip some people to survive the threatening catastrophe and provide a groundwork for later reconstruction. His hostile judgment extended to many historians among his contemporaries. They, too, abetted the work of destruction.

Burckhardt's writings are his considered response to the principal experiences of his life (1818-1897). In its decades he encountered most of the principal movements and forces of nineteenth-century life: religious liberalism, revolutionary democracy, industrial capitalism, nationalism, and socialism. He knew these movements in their European scope, but he reacted to them where they came home to him, in Switzerland. As Switzerland is *e pluribus unum*, a great deal more so than our own country, the point central to Burckhardt's biography is that he was born in Basel, a pleasant and venerable city-state. In that genuine community the Burckhardts for more than three hundred years had been burgomasters, clergymen, professors, doctors, and merchants, class people rather than mass people. Burckhardt's father was the minister of the red sandstone cathedral of Basel, near which Jacob spent his life.

This life had as much continuity with the past as he could

171

manage, but he did not follow the ways of his fathers. Burckhardt's presence in a changed Basel was a witness to disruption:
his vocation was a work of salvage in behalf of Basel, Europe,
and mankind.

Like the biblical prophets, although the decorous public
Burckhardt was not importunate as they were, he is described
as a pessimist. Under analysis the word suggests the problem
raised by the black joke: even though you know that you are a
paranoiac, that does not mean that they're not trying to get
you. There is surer ground in Burckhardt's account of himself
as a man of cheerful disposition with an uncommon awareness
of the frailty and uncertainty of earthly things.

Influenced by his father, Burckhardt began the study of
theology at the University of Basel. Now Switzerland was a
center of radical and skeptical Protestantism influenced by the
Enlightenment. Burckhardt came to believe that for him — a
member of a generation that faced the Higher Criticism of the
Bible — compromises, adaptations of orthodoxy to rationalism
and historical criticism, had to be decisively ended. To a friend
he described the influence of Professor De Wette, who interpreted Scripture as myth: "[His] system grows in stature every
day; one simply *has* to follow him, there is no alternative; but
every day a part of one's traditional doctrine melts away under
his hand. Today, finally, I realized that he regards the birth of
Christ simply as a myth — and that I do too. And I shuddered
as a number of reasons struck me why this almost *had* to be
so."[1]

In ceasing to believe in Christ's divinity and in Revelation,
Burckhardt concluded that he was not a Christian and that he
would therefore be an unworthy clergyman, an undependable
minister of the church in the testing time ahead. Throughout
his life Burckhardt rendered the same harsh judgment on
liberal theologians as summer believers who under stress yielded the spiritual substance of faith to compromise.

He is unlike some of the agnostics of his century, who,
though leaving faith behind and rejecting religious views,
strongly affirmed Christian ethics. Like Matthew Arnold he
recognized that the loss of faith had somehow to be made good,
that he had to rebuild the cosmos, the world of relationships

and points of reference with which he had entered into conscious and reflective living.[2] In this grubbing work of reconstruction he took history for his modest and humble guide to life (*historia vitae magistra*), a history in which skepticism had an indisputable place. How could it be otherwise, "in a world where beginnings and ends are all unknown, and the middle is constant flux, for the amelioration offered by religion is here beyond our scope."[3]

His problem of reconstruction acquired a new form as events in Switzerland, Berlin, and France made him realize that he was living in a revolutionary age, that the impetus of the revolution was likely to end in a despotism destructive of creativity, the spirit, and the finer culture of the past.

His first experience of the revolution came in his own city. The ruling patricians, who had an intense loyalty to their city-state, had demonstrated a capacity to consult with all social groups. In the 1830s they were challenged in the name of universal suffrage and the peasantry. This conflict produced a separation of the rural area from the city. Somehow the city struggled on and maintained its university, though the student body at one time dwindled to twenty-nine. It was during the troubled thirties that Burckhardt attended his city's university.[4]

For two years (1844-1846) Burckhardt served as an editor of the *Basler Zeitung*, a job that took the best hours of six working days a week.[5] It gave him an education in politics that he would gladly have done without. His days were concerned with the events preceding the Swiss Civil War, the brief Sonderbund conflict. A principal issue of that war was religion. Liberals in Switzerland, their radicalism intensified by a growing number of refugees, moved to seize monasteries, and several Catholic cantons decided to invite the Jesuits to return to Switzerland. Liberal groups then sent armed forces to overthrow the government of Lucerne, whose Diet had recalled the Jesuits. The forces were soundly beaten, and thereupon the Catholic cantons established the Sonderbund, a separate league that went against the Federal Pact of Switzerland. In 1846 the liberals seized control of Berne and Geneva. By late 1847 the brief civil war ended with the defeat of the greatly outnumbered Catholic cantons. The victors provided the cantons with what proved to be a workable federal government. This federal and liberal victory in Switzerland, as William Langer wrote, "had the effect of heartening the liberals everywhere."[6]

Burckhardt was not of their number. His experience in Basel had convinced him that democracy and popular sovereignty made for disorder, socialism, and despotism. He contrasted the freedoms that liberals and democrats professed with "slavery under the loud-mouthed masses called the People." In the name of the people any group of intriguers might claim to exercise executive power. In their name historic communities might have their legitimacy challenged and property seized. In their name historic institutions were destroyed to promote national states, states that would be centralized on the ruins of local liberties. In their name tyrannical restraints would be imposed on the spirit, and the pretext would be that "culture is the secret ally of capital." In their name moral restraints would be overridden and, if lack of restraint corrupts and diabolizes people of education, what brutalities might not be expected from the masses? Burckhardt was, therefore, the opponent of democracy, nationalism, and even liberal movements, because all of them stirred up mass movements in which the individual, having no power to control, would compromise himself.[7]

When in May 1846 he resigned his editorial job, he wrote to a friend that he was departing for "southern debauchery, in the form of art and antiquity, while in Poland everything is going to pieces and the messengers of the Socialist Day of Judgment are at the gates. Good heavens, I can't alter things, and before universal barbarism breaks in . . . I want to debauch myself with a real eyeful of aristocratic culture, so that, when the social revolution has exhausted itself for a moment, I shall be able to take an active part in the inevitable restoration."[8]

He was again in Rome, in the Forum, not far from the ruins to which Gibbon attached his inspiration, when news of the French Revolution of 1848 reached him at carnival time (March 4). The ruins and the Roman festival may have compounded the forebodings he expressed in a letter from Rome: "How provisional our whole life is!" For comfort he urged his friend to read the life of St. Severin, who had managed "to withstand the collapse of everything."[9]

To rebuild a cosmos, after he had ceased to be a Christian believer, and to prepare for reconstruction, Burckhardt had turned to the study of history in 1838. The University of Berlin, where Professor Leopold von Ranke taught, was the obvious place to study, especially for Burckhardt, who through his youthful years had joy and pride in German culture. But Berlin proved to be sandy and flat, and he found Berliners unattractive human beings.

As a student under Ranke he learned what kind of a historian he did not want to be — but initially Ranke's critical method and learning were overwhelming. The young Swiss loved history, but he felt that he had not known why until he heard Ranke. He admired the German's extraordinary industry and learning. As a young man, he told a former student, he had known sections of Ranke's *History of the Papacy* by heart.

Nevertheless, against this master of history Burckhardt eventually directed three formidable criticisms: he was a weak character, who was not prepared to criticize the powerful forthrightly and was overwilling to please those who could serve him; believing in the primacy of foreign policy, he wrote about the relations of state to state and thereby reduced the scope as well as the value of history, a limitation that Burckhardt illustrated by quoting the first sentence of one of Ranke's courses: "Gentlemen, great powers are ideas in the mind of God"; he was not objective, for his emphasis on presenting what happened without the intrusion of judgment or value was the mere profession of impartiality, because disavowal did not destroy the necessity of selection and judgment, and preoccupation with politics might result in the worst judgment prevailing by stealth.

In these criticisms stirs Burckhardt's desire for a history that would consider art and poetry, that would deal with the spirit of man. These were matters about which he was certain. He wrote and published poetry, and was a tireless sketcher of architecture; before the general use of photography, how could you lecture about art without sketches?

For these interests Burckhardt found a university guide, Franz Kugler, professor of the history of art. Kugler, a congenial spirit, befriended the young man, understood and encouraged his desire to study the arts as part of history, to look upon history, to contemplate it as the spirit looking at something outside itself, "as the highest form of contemplation." History, Burckhardt wrote early and late, must be approached "in a spirit of contemplation" in which the temporal and contingent yields meaning.[10]

He was a man thrifty of the spirit. The latter was not so abundant in the world that any person, nation, or age should try to live by itself alone. Past events, for good or ill — and the judgment should be made — should be considered. Some people could be wiser and richer because of the experience of others. This instructive form of history required totalities — wholes of action, politics, thought, art, the spirit. If his historical studies were to serve for survival and reconstruction, the subject matter had to be culture. He had worked his way to the form of cultural history.[11]

Early in 1848 Burckhardt outlined an idea for a library of cultural history, a series of readable, low-priced books on the major periods of European cultural development. The series did not come into being, but the two major historical works published in Burckhardt's lifetime were on topics proposed for his library of cultural history.[12]

His selection of the Age of Constantine (the work was published in 1852) was influenced by his own religious difficulties, by his belief after 1848 that Europe would produce an age of military consolidators, caesars, and by his love of Italy. In effect he had taken up Gibbon's subject, the decline of the Roman Empire, with a focus on the time of Constantine. Where Gibbon wrote for literary fame, to celebrate the tolerant paganism of antiquity, and to reveal in the story of Christianity the triumph of superstition and of the calculated exploitation of human credulity by power-seeking clerics and laymen, Burckhardt wrote with a broader and less polemical aim, to instruct and increase human understanding and sensitivity.[13] Like Gibbon, he made use of irony, but the irony was in his overall vision and was not an occasion for wit. Study and contemplation opened to Burckhardt the vision that he described: the pagan culture, high and low, of a senescent society that was to pass away intermingled with the makers of a new society and culture, the Church and the barbarians. The church had pene-

trated the classical pagan world, and in converting the barbarians it transmitted some of the classical culture, a diffusion
that lessened the destructiveness of the barbarian impact. For
their part, churchmen grasped all power and worldly pomp
that slipped away from the empire in its fall, and the Church
was saved from immersion in a doomed world only by its
ascetics who, having no worldly hope, had abandoned the
world they helped to save.

Where Burckhardt uses the word *doomed*, he means that the
society died, but his use of the word *senescent* is an analogy
based on an organism. This is not to say that old age and death
had inevitably awaited the culture from its beginning. Rather,
the various aspects of the society and culture had reached a
stage which in interaction and relatedness could be suggested
by the word *senescent*.

Central in the empire's decline was the position of the
emperor. To govern the lands from England to Arabia the
Senate was incompetent and finally irrelevant. There remained
the emperor, but in the absence of a regulated succession, the
imperial power was the object of rivalry and contention that in
the third century became anarchy. As the army made and un-
made emperors, the contention eventually was solely for military domination. When Alexander Severus (222-235) almost inexplicably promoted justice and moderation, he and his mother
were murdered by his own soldiers: he "strove in vain for respect in a century which recognized only fear." To the army,
nonetheless, the empire owed the more secure years of Diocletian (284-305) and Constantine. Improvement, which required
that the emperors look on their position not as a prize but as a
duty, began with the emperor Decius (249-251). The new direction was set by an agreement of the higher officers, "a kind
of Senate in arms." If the soldiers had been acting on their own,
they would have supported "some tall, handsome figure with
the talents of a petty officer." The complete military despotism
which was to prevail had been foreshadowed by Septimus
Severus (193-211), who is significantly described as un-Roman
and *modern*. Military rule, destructive of civic life and virtue,
had so advanced by the reign of Diocletian that the military
fashioned "the state mechanism after its own image; subordina-
tion is its very soul, and organization must be by ranks and

grades, with strict and visible means of gradation." Constantine completed the transformation.[14]

Burckhardt judged Diocletian to be a better man than Constantine, but he judged Constantine a great emperor. He won many victories, divided the empire, founded Constantinople, and favored the Church, which thereupon took a direction unsuited for the renewal of the empire. He also allowed no scruple — against murder of members of his own family, for example — to restrain his ambition. As a maker of Christian Europe (which he was, and it is part of his title to greatness), he barely knew what he was doing. His own confused, superficial religion exploited the surging worldliness of churchmen, but he in turn was victimized by the eulogies of Eusebius. By presenting Constantine as a cause rather than a man, as the model of a Christian ruler, Eusebius had made the deeds of the emperor seem all the more appalling to modern readers.[15]

Public culture declined apace with the empire's illness. The art of the past was literally pillaged in order to fashion the monuments of the Age of Constantine. Neither painting nor sculpture, becoming wholly subject to content (that is, to propaganda), could "fulfill its own internal laws." Decoration became an excess, an end in itself, as the taste for decoration prevailed over the requirements of structural parts. The reign of the vanity of the virtuoso finally meant not cleverness but triviality. The palaces and monuments produced restless and scattered effects as "the heaped-up individual forms pretend to significance in themselves." From the time of Diocletian onward, even the documents of the imperial bureau were involuted and bombastic, a fit style for the indignity of despotism and for the productions of a culture characterized by "labored and tortured form."[16]

Burckhardt concluded the section on the senescence of Roman culture with a question: "Cannot the true take the place of the beautiful, the useful of the agreeable?" The author left the question unanswered because there could be no solution involving such alternatives. "But," he added, "anyone who has encountered classical antiquity, if only in its twilight, feels that with beauty and freedom there departed also the genuine antique life . . . a once wonderful totality of being." The religion of this culture was superseded according to "a high historical necessity." The conflict of religions is no matter, as with Gibbon, of a tolerant and therefore bearable religion and a doctrinaire and power-hungry Church. It is not even remotely that revealing Victorian caricature of the poet Swinburne, a conflict of an austere and pallid Christianity with a life-rejoicing paganism. Burckhardt presented at length the anxieties, torments, and superstition of pagan men, futurologists—that is, omen readers—almost to a man. Christianity finally could meet the spiritual needs of ancient men, and that is what Burckhardt meant by "a high historical necessity." It also signifies the end of the ancient world and yet its preservation, "a new relationship with things of the senses and things beyond the senses, for love of God and neighbor and separation from things earthly to take the place of older views of the gods and the world."[17]

The disintegration of paganism was favorable to Christianity, and the individual symptoms of disintegration presaged it. Although the immortality of the soul was a major Christian belief, it was also a commonplace in many forms of late Roman religion, which, nevertheless, lacked the simplicity of the Christian teaching. Over three centuries the Church had also acquired a stable organization. When Constantine embraced this kingdom of God on earth for his worldly purposes, churchmen responded eagerly and then quarreled seismically over the nature of Christ. Meanwhile, charity and readiness for ministry impelled the Church to become formidable by assuming tasks once performed by the state. The church's immersion in secular affairs might have destroyed it along with the world it cultivated. It was saved from such self-destruction by the anchorites who, defying material wealth and power, "communicated to the clerical order of succeeding centuries the higher ascetic attitude toward life, or at least the claim to such an attitude." These recluses, Burckhardt believed, won freedom from the world for the spirit and for intellectual exchange, providing a heritage "of the supermundane which the medieval Church imparted to science."[18]

In the concluding section a few ironic sentences recount the activities of the philosophic schools of Athens, which in all but ancient fame became a backwater. Art and rhetoric had lost their substance, and teachers of philosophy had to subordinate the love of wisdom to hustling for students. They touted on the hills, in the ports, and on the sea. There were so many in rivalry that Athens-bound students had to face the hazards of being shanghaied by armed directors of admissions in the Piraeus and even off Cape Sunium. Socrates could not have gone home again.[19]

The century eagerly looked for a new home as the center of its aspirations. Where Gibbon in his conclusion saw in Rome's ruins secular visitors from the north venerating not the monuments of Christianity but the ruins of empire, Burckhardt ends on a similar note. The new city of the century's aspirations was Jerusalem and the Holy Land. Constantine was a man of his age in endowing Jerusalem and its vicinity with splendor. Burckhardt, making a strained and implausible connection with world history, then concluded that Constantine's lavish gifts attached the reverence of the Roman world and the Middle Ages to "these sites," and without him, "the land would not have been wrested back after half a millennium of bondage under Islam."[20]

The book was respected though it had but a modest success, two editions of limited run in Burckhardt's lifetime. The first English translation did not appear until 1949. Burckhardt once prayed that he be spared overvaluation, a prayer that was answered. But this undervaluing is a loss to all of us. The work is a model of superbly organized cultural history, elegant, provocative of thought in almost every paragraph, to be treasured for what it tells about the Age of Constantine and about humanity.

After seeing his book through the press, Burckhardt went to Italy for the fruitful year in which he culminated his preparation for the magisterial guidebook to the artistic monuments of Italy, *Der Cicerone*, that he published in 1855. The work, passing through many editions, was published in an English translation as late as the first decade of the twentieth century. His travels in Italy also advanced his next work. In Italy he had begun to consider writing on the age of Raphael, a work listed among the works of the planned library of cultural history, that eventually became *The Civilization of the Renaissance in Italy* (1860). He described the project as a history of the beautiful, an infirmity, a spirit that had taken possession of him and would tax all his powers for years.[21] He conducted his major researches, principally in printed histories and memoirs, in Zurich, which had a rich collection of Renaissance sources. There from 1855 to 1858, Burckhardt was professor of art at the Swiss Federal Polytechnic Institute.

His first major work had probed the transition from antiquity to the Middle Ages, and the work on the Renaissance also presented a transition: the emergence of the modern world from medieval culture. As he had said in the former work, the time had come for new views of man and his relationship to God, nature, the world, the state, other men, and the arts. The study, Burckhardt stated at the very beginning, would not cover architecture and the plastic arts, an omission he hoped to correct in a volume devoted to the arts. He failed to publish a second volume as equal companion to the first. Indeed, his original hope of fusing art history and general history was set back when he proposed to do two volumes; with many authors the promise of a second volume is an attempt to ward off self-reproach or the criticism of others. The essay ("ein Versuch" was the modest subtitle of the German original) deals with the new men and new views and values of the fourteenth and fifteenth centuries, when "most of the political powers actually in existence owed their origin to violent and illegitimate means."[22]

The Italian experience arose from an interaction with the first manifestations of the modern state, distinguished by the power of the political sovereign and by a drive for centralization. In this state, Burckhardt wrote, might be seen the modern political spirit of Europe yielding to its own impulses so that in its most fearful manifestations and unrestrained selfishness it derided every right and destroyed every bud and offshoot of a healthy culture. These ruinous cases, as well as more restrained examples, revealed a new reality in history, the state as the product of calculation, the state as a work of art.

These political observations have been almost as misunderstood as they are famous. "The state as a work of art" is a concept that Hegel had advanced, but Burckhardt rejected Hegel in most matters. He regarded the concept as dangerous and the practice that it justified as regrettable. To look on human institutions as plastic material for a despot, a political artist, is to make ruling an end in itself subject to no constitutional, customary, or moral limitation. This innovation was the reverse of the major current of medieval political theory, which saw the ruler as the trustee of a society already formed and composed of social orders, each of which had customary rights and recognized privileges.

The misunderstanding appears to be occasioned by critics who think that Burckhardt uses *modern* as a word of praise and approval. But in *The Age of Constantine the Great*, Burckhardt called the military despot, Septimus Severus, un-Roman and modern. Burckhardt's thesis about the Age of Constantine was that Christianity, for all of its dogma and intolerance, was morally superior to the decaying ancient world whose end, nonetheless, meant the passing of a glory from the earth. The Renaissance, as the birth of a new culture, also meant loss and gain, sometimes ironically inseparable: with the modern state came artistic developments and new ways of thinking, and in its wake threats of tyranny and moral dilemmas with which medieval men did not have to struggle. In Burckhardt's mind, then, *modern* is usually not a word of praise. His use of the word is revealed even in his selection of the despotic states of Italy as the more complete and clearly marked type of the modern state.

The political story begins with the remarkable absolutism that Frederick II established in southern Italy and Sicily. There Frederick's efficient tyranny foreshadowed the new political forms that emerged in the cities and principalities to replace the waning imperial and papal temporal powers after the empire's long struggle with the papacy. The mark of many of these states was illegitimacy, with city the rival of city, a rivalry paralleled by intense factional conflict within the city. The state was something to be made — often at the expense of other states. The means of such creation, war, also became a work of art, "an impartial delight in able generalship for its own sake," a "purely rational treatment of military affairs."[23]

The new political world required new men, individuals who did not identify themselves as members of an order or class, who could think, plan, and act for themselves in the light of the situation they faced. Successful aspirants to power had to be such people, and to their courts and councils they did not usually call bishops and feudal aristocrats, who would feel they had a right to such association. Instead, they might welcome the courtier described in Castiglione's work as the complete man who did not lack any conceivable excellence. The new individuals might be ruthless as the Sforzas were or, at the other end, creative spirits of serene vision and harmonious balance, such as Raphael, or the accomplished good company who formed Urbino's pleasant court society.

The treatment of "the revival of antiquity" is a clear departure from the view, conventional since the Renaissance itself, that it was a revival of letters. It was, Burckhardt argued, the result of the genius of the Italian people inspired by the revival of antiquity, although the latter in a measure "paralyzed native impulses," as is evident in the widespread literary use of Latin. The great Florentine historians wrote Italian because "they could only record in a living tongue the living results of their own immediate observations."[24]

To his fourth section Burckhardt gave a description borrowed from Jules Michelet, "the discovery of the world and of man." Here and perhaps in other sections Burckhardt is the victim of the law of exaggerating contrast to create a significant beginning. He concluded this part with a quotation about man from Pico della Mirandola which tells all: "thou bearest within thee the germs of a universal life."[25]

The author devoted his last section to "Morality and Religion." He confessed to being troubled by the brutality and evil he had to describe. Many, echoing his misgivings, have argued that England in the War of the Roses would have seemed a brutal league even to the Borgias. But this criticism does not adequately allow for the many political units in Italy engaged in ruthless rivalry. The country around Lake Como may inspire the northerner to cry out "O Paradiso," but its medieval and Renaissance history prompts the suggestion that its principal activity was local genocide.

Burckhardt found it significant that Renaissance Italians never undertook a Reformation on the Protestant model, that is, something based on more than hatred of papacy and clergy. Their individualism sought fame rather than immortality, fame little tempered by satire and wit, which should be the moral policeman of fame. Among them the strongest bulwark against evil was honor, an ambiguous concept. Honor as an uneasy combination of conscience and egoism, the latter "the root and fountain of evil," had the mixed effect its disparate elements suggest. Individualism in Italy came "through a historical necessity" and then pervaded the other nations of Europe as "the higher atmosphere that they breathe. In itself it is neither good nor bad, but necessary: within it there has grown up a modern standard of good and evil — a sense of moral responsibility — which is different from that of the Middle Ages."[26]

For all the faults that more than a century's criticism have found in Burckhardt's history, nothing comparable to it in scope, elegant organization, and reflective conciseness has since appeared. Within the criticism there has been a mistaken tendency to see in the work a glorification of individualism. Many groups combined in this misunderstanding: aesthetic individualists and those who admired an age in which art had an integral role, humanists who criticized modern uniformity, and proponents of aristocratic values against philistines, liberals, democrats, and capitalists.

In 1858 Burckhardt was invited to return to the University of Basel. The offer was supported by an appeal that his lectures were necessary to raise the spiritual and intellectual level of its citizens. Burckhardt took this appeal so seriously that he refused to allow travel, research, or lectures elsewhere to interfere with his duties at Basel. Invitations to other universities, including one to take Ranke's professorship in Berlin, were declined. His lectures at Basel were well prepared and well attended. From Burckhardt's tens of thousands of notes Werner Kaegi has presented an account of his reading, his thought, and his reactions to the last decades of the nineteenth century. And to the testimony of many of his students, that his enriching lectures were delivered with great care for tone and emphasis, it is now possible to add the very text of his lectures on the Age of Revolution. These, put together from student shorthand notes, reveal the lectures to have been vivid and direct narratives. Burckhardt prepared the lectures meticulously and delivered them as an artless work of art.[27]

Burckhardt taught history as a humanity, an art, and he so wrote it. In teaching, his hope was to have the student take a part of history and make it his own. This meant diversity, not consensus, and, one might add, mistakes. To Friedrich Nietzsche, who attended some of his lectures in the early 1870s, Burckhardt explained that he was not concerned to train disciples and scholars. Unlike many scientists, who teach general college courses as though they were preparing professional physicists and chemists, and historians who do the same for their subject, Burckhardt quite firmly devoted himself to general education. When his four-volume manuscript work on Greek cultural history was published posthumously and the famous scholar Wilamowitz reviewed it with the shattering German expression, "This work does not exist for science," the judgment was technically true but quite irrelevant.[28]

His views on history were presented several times in a course called "Introduction to History." The most available and provocative presentation was in a number of lectures, some university and some public, delivered in 1868-1869 and 1870-1871. these lectures on the study of history, on "Crises in History" and "The Present Crisis," "Great Men," and "Fortune and Misfortune in History," were collected and published posthumously in 1905 by Burckhardt's nephew, Jacob Oeri. The latter titled the volume *Reflections on World History.*

Burckhardt would have winced at the "World History," although "Reflections" would have pleased him, because he could find no guidance in a philosophy of history. Philosophy, he contended, subordinated events to principles and lost sight of "the material," "the visible nature," the diversity of time and of human experience. His emphasis on the historical caused Albert Salomon to write that Burckhardt viewed history as "a category of human existence," "an ontological category."[29] In history, philosophy is a form of egoism which allows for no true transcendence. Art reached beyond the sensual. For modern man, facing the cultural ordeal of things mastering him, there were also history and science; these "are alone capable of a detached, disinterested participation in the life of things." Theology could also give history a transcendent meaning, but Burckhardt had rejected Christian theology. Against the philosophers, the ideologists, and the theologians he affirmed his starting point: "the one point accessible to us, the one eternal center of all things — man suffering, striving, as he is and ever shall be."[30]

In his passage through time, man must seek the good and do so in freedom even despite the limitations of his particular culture. Man is not good but must seek the good. "Every people is incomplete and strives for completion, and the higher it stands, the more it strives." The recognition that "there is too little of high spiritual value scattered over the earth" to allow any individual, people, or age to settle for self-sufficiency compels us to draw from the continuum of past and present, the communion of humanity in history.[31]

In reflecting on history Burckhardt proposed that three key areas be studied — the state, religion, and culture — and particularly their interrelatedness. This study would have to be carried far enough to permit the student to watch men making decisions partly in freedom, partly out of necessity, partly in ignorance or passion, partly out of calculation, and almost never foreseeing the range of a decision's consequences.

He urged his audience to select an age or time that attracted them, that had significance for them. Interest was essential, but he advised against the study of very recent history as unlikely to provide a true sense of the historical and of humanity. The people of an age would inevitably study in another age what they thought to be important to themselves, but the age to be studied must first be reconstructed in its own terms. People were generally prompt to say that they found very modern history interesting. This, Burckhardt said, was true enough, because they were interested — that is, involved in it — and this participation greatly lessened the possibility of detachment. Wholeness is desirable for aesthetic contemplation, but it is beyond human capacity. To seek to grasp all history is to yield to illusion and to choose the misleading path of reductionism. World history presents an insurmountable range to those seeking the richest reward of historical study, to learn events in their sequence and interrelatedness and, in reflecting upon them, to approach wisdom.

History deepened the understanding by the coordination of observations. The wisdom it made possible was knowledge of oneself and of mankind, of what man could be in the worst and best cases. The knowledge of man's limits, needs, and possibilities could save culture and mankind from the specifically modern temptation to excess, to stretch beyond a human scale and in the failure produce a monster. The leveling spirit and the excesses of individualism made for a confusion of realms and led to bureaucratic arrogance in demands that the state "attempt to fulfill moral progress directly, for only society can and may do it." A threat of even greater proportions may be found among those who would indict the whole past: "The arrogant belief in the moral superiority of the present, however, has only fully developed of late years."[32]

The state, it is true, should provide a standard of justice, but Burckhardt detested the egoism of politics. In his eyes the state was almost a monster of corrupting power, for he believed, as Acton did, that power corrupts. To teach men to mistrust it and to help in restoring a healthy culture were his goals. His thinking, writing, and teaching served the same end. His life was a preaching by example. He had the detachment, even the determination, to resist his age, which Acton enjoined upon historians.

He resisted his age by analyzing its formative period and revealing the dangerous forces at play in it. His kinship was with the nineteenth-century prophetic historians, such as de Tocqueville and Acton. But for Burckhardt history was more fundamental than it was for them. He understood that the crisis of culture was a crisis of faith, lacking which men are unlikely to love, to surrender themselves, or to sacrifice. He himself could see no resources remaining in institutional religion. To this dilemma he could provide no solution, but he did what he could. He gave an example of love, and he argued persuasively that the historical sense, the cultivation of a sense of continuity that excluded facile talk of alienation, could serve as a constant reminder of what man is so that he could be armed against the egoist temptations rooted in the culture of his contemporaries.

11. Acton:

History and Conscience

JOHN DALBERG ACTON (1833-1902) was a serious child who aged in seriousness. As a sixteen-year old, he wrote upon meeting Ignaz von Döllinger, thereafter, his revered teacher; "He appears to have in some degree the imperfection of neglecting to complete what he has begun." Like teacher, like pupil, only more so; Acton's publications are posthumous non-books, assemblages of course lectures or articles, and a truly non-book, *The History of Freedom*, the never written project of a lifetime.

Fame, as any monastic writer or moral realist may argue, is, at best, a vanity, however golden, and Acton was a celebrated failure. But failure is not his whole account. He is celebrated as a man who devoted decades of his life to historical learning. For historians those were heady years, when rules of criticism had become method and the opening of archives inspired Acton and others with the hope that the study of history was approaching completion and science. This consummation, the profoundly earnest Acton believed, would serve the cause of liberty, morality and religion, for it would certainly reveal almost all eminent men as unworthy to hold extensive power. By unsparing judgment of the corruptions of the powerful, the historian would reassume a moral task and promote the cause of liberty, and divided power, as well as justify the way of God to man. As liberty prevailed, mankind would be seen to progress, an advance that Acton thought to be the only possible meaning of a beneficent Divine Providence in history. Contemporaries have described a transfigured Acton in conversation with ready and astonishing learning presenting this exalted vision of progress by freedom as uniquely memorable.

He stands out in his century because he linked the conventional view of historical writing as promoting morality by praising virtuous actions and criticizing evil ones with an enthusiasm for renewing history, as Leopold von Ranke had done, by using new sources of information, manuscript collections mainly in government archives. The linking is unusual because Ranke's influence had professionalized historians and persuaded them that their proper objective was not to judge actions but to depict events as they actually happened. Acton memorably dissented.

He was the only son of a gentry family in the English county of Shropshire that had connections with the Rhineland and Naples. The historian himself was born in Naples where his grandfather had served as prime minister to the king of the Two Sicilies.[1] His German mother, who preferred to write French, was the daughter and heiress of the duke of Dalberg, a south German luminary of the Holy Roman Empire and of its succesors, the Napoleonic Empire and the German Confederation. Widowed in 1837, she married in 1840 into the Whig aristocracy of England. Acton's stepfather, Lord Leveson, later Earl Granville, was a stalwart of the Whig and Liberal party and three times foreign secretary. The stepson himself married (1865) into the Bavarian Dalberg connection, the Countess Maria Arco-Valley. He had inherited the title of baronet upon the death of his father and became Lord Acton when his admiring correspondent, Prime Minister William E. Gladstone in 1869 arranged a peerage for him so that he could serve the Liberal party in the House of Lords. The last episode to be chronicled of Acton the courtier was his appointment in 1892 to be a lord-in-waiting upon Queen Victoria. His knowledge of German courts pleased the elderly queen who described him as "a charming person with such pleasant manners (rather foreign) very like his mother who was so agreeable and clever."[2]

His teachers were eminent priests. Briefly he had the instruction of Felix Dupanloup, confessor to his parents and future bishop of Orleans. At Oscott, near Birmingham, where he was a student for the years 1843 to 1848, the headmaster was Nicholas Wiseman, later cardinal archbishop of Westminister, whose vigorous romanticism made Acton and his fellows feel "that Oscott, next to Pekin, was the center of the world."[3]

Acton had prepared himself for a Cambridge college but as a Catholic was denied admission. Arrangements were made then for him to live (1850-1854) and study with Ignaz von Döllinger (1799-1890), a German priest and the most renowned Catholic church historian of the century. The young Englishman also attended lectures at the University of Munich and drew upon Döllinger's and the university's libraries and the Royal Library of Bavaria.

Association with Döllinger meant dinner conversations, tutorial sessions, walks, and visits to distinguished people, libraries and archives. As Acton kept few friends and experienced limited affection throughout his life, association with the priest-tutor stirred emotional tides in him perhaps proportionate to the intellectual influence of the tutor upon his pupil. The young man was capable of extraordinary industry and while reveling in learning brought many subjects before the tribunal of his lively conscience. He was assured and at ease with the most eminent people, moving as a matter of course in the highest circles — political, social, ecclesiastical and intellectual — wherever he lived. The point is equally true of his travels which in 1855 took him to the United States, in 1856 to Russia, and in 1857 to Italy.

In the rigorous standards of his research, Acton surpassed the master whom he followed in believing that the Reformation, the absolute states, and the French revolution were breaches in the history of the Church and in the continuity of European political life. The task of reconstruction — of re-establishing a Catholic Christian society — was, they believed, to be approached through the study of history, which should also guide theology and philosophy. Acton saw in the romantic vogue of history the effort of an age issuing from the Enlightenment to understand past ages. He approvingly quoted Leibniz: "History is the true demonstration of religion."[4]

From Döllinger, Acton learned to love history and perhaps to expect from it more than was possible: that the principal approach to theology should be historical and that historical research could lead to the emancipation of Catholics within the church and to the reconciliation of Catholic and Protestant. That, in turn, Döllinger hoped, might promote the national unification of Germany. In 1858 Acton saw an inquiry into the

experience of history as a source of light and after such diffidence stated perhaps too unreservedly: "our only sure guide is
the example of the Church herself."[5] No truth of history, disciple and master affirmed, contradict the Catholic faith. Subsequently, the Conservative Bavarian priest and the descendant
of English Tories recognized that, if truth were to prevail,
thinkers required freedom. This in turn meant that authority
should be wielded with restraint.

When Acton returned to England he looked for ways to raise
the intellectual level of English Catholics and of England itself.
He could be as rigorous and severe in tone and manner as his
enterprise was likely to rouse controversy. A "valid test of
sincerity," he repeatedly declared, is "whether a man begins by
appreciating and, even if it may be, fortifying and strengthen-
ing the adversary's position, supplying the gaps and correcting
the flaws of his argument before he declares it untenable."[6]

He essayed a work of reconstruction in the wake of the
French Revolution and beyond that, the Reformation. With
the former ensued the shipwreck of political arrangements and
Catholic adaptations to them. Where some churchmen sought
instead of reconstruction to preserve forms of absolutism, they
were serving the cause of modern error. In England, Acton
thought, Catholics had some advantages. They could, for example, appeal to elements of Catholic tradition preserved by
England's established Church and to genuine Catholic politics,
medieval constitutional traditions which the nonconformists
had helped to reinvigorate. For constructive work, then, Catholics had a higher course than that dictated by fear and desire
for security. They must claim and gain for themselves a place
in every movement studying God's works and advancing mankind. "They will remember that, while the office of ecclesiastical authority is to tolerate, to warn, and to guide, that of
religious intelligence and zeal is not to leave the great work of
intellectual civilization" to others but to give it to the children
of the church.[7] He looked to a free Catholic church in a free
state.

Acton recognized that if, as he had resolved, he were to write
a large historical work on a major theme, he would have to
devote years to research. He therefore chose another more immediate labor that in its day-by-day and year-by-year tasks

would serve as a balance for the major work. It was a youthful formulation, rational and breath-taking, to balance a major historical endeavor with a program to reform English Catholicism and England itself. One endeavor would support the other, as he hoped in 1858, when he became coeditor of *The Rambler* (1848-1862), a journal of learned commentary and opinion.

In defining his work Acton had opted for the Liberal Catholics against the Ultramontanes and, as succeeding years saw the victory of Pius IX and the Ultramontanes, his choice, in effect, decreed for himself a decade and more of controversy and frustration and a longer period of isolation.[8]

In 1864 Acton terminated the *Home and Foreign Review*, the quarterly successor to the monthly *Rambler*. He reached the decision after several critical attacks from English bishops, culminating in Cardinal Wiseman's warning to the Catholic clergy against the *Home and Foreign Review*'s irreverence and non-Catholic sentiments. Acton regretfully accepted the authority of episcopal criticism that restricted the journal's effectiveness. Although he deplored the practice of Rome and many bishops, who reduced the distinction between opinion and dogma "to the smallest possible limits," he submitted to authority which he believed to be legitimate but also in error. If he were to defy authority, he feared, the ensuing quarrel would only "deceive the world into a belief that religion cannot be harmonized with all that is right and true in the progress of the present age." He submitted because he did not wish to wound the church and because he firmly believed that the church would eventually adopt his position. As for the duty of obeying authority, it was no more "real than that of professing nothing beside or against his convictions." In a valedictory article he described the spirit of the *Home and Foreign Review* as "a partial and temporary embodiment of an imperishable idea — the faint reflection of a light which still lives and burns in the hearts of the silent thinkers of the Church."[9]

For six years after 1864, Acton nevertheless was not at all silent. He served as correspondent of *The Chronicle* (1867-1868) and contributed to the *North British Review* (1869-1871).[10] He initiated preparations for editing the correspondence of Cardinal Pole and a volume of essays by Catholic laymen and for writing a history of the popes.

Some months before Pius IX issued *Quanta Cura* and the *Syllabus of Errors* (December 1864), Acton undertook a research pilgrimage to the archives of Austria, Germany, Italy, France, and Belgium. He did so because the accessibility of archives meant that historians had new tasks. The preceding generation, he observed, had already destroyed the willingness to be content with compilers and those who merely threshed through the same material. Critical treatment limited to printed works and the manuscripts that happened to be in great libraries had now to give place to closer inquiry and methodical exploration. Failure to undergo the pains of such research is "to remain a victim to ill-informed and designing writers, and to authorities that have worked for ages to build up the vast tradition of conventional mendacity."[11]

The frustration of his Liberal Catholic endeavors strengthened his Liberal political convictions and, meanwhile, archival research provided material for his criticism of traditional history of church and state. As he saw modern history, one of its principal stories was the growth of state centralization and absolutism. The evil of these developments was revealed, he thought, in the debasement of moral standards that accompanied them. First came murder and then, to placate opinion, the lie.[12] He feared the proponents of papal infallibility because he thought them to be supporters of church centralization and papal absolutism, and saw in Ultramontane apologetics a defensiveness about the church—a *raison d'église* comparable to *raison d'état* (the moral debasement of politics) but worse, because it destroyed the possibility of reform. Papal infallibility, he often argued, was disproved by church history: the church had not held the belief, popes had taught error, and—an irrelevant point although it is revealing that he considered it a valid argument—some popes had acted immorally.

When the first Vatican Council met in 1869, Acton immediately prepared to impede the approval of papal infallibility. He was in Rome as an "unbidden guest" to organize opposition to the promulgation of infallibility. Although he was as tireless as he was learned, he saw the difficulties of his cause.

It depended on the bishops, and in the situation they faced the bishops were inadequate. After the council members opposed to infallibility had demonstrated that the council was not unanimous, he unsuccessfully urged the opposition to withdraw from the council. Additionally he hoped for the intervention of one or several governments, which happily proved to be a vain hope.

In July 1870, the council promulgated the doctrine of papal infallibility. In the aftermath doubts were expressed about the orthodoxy of those who had opposed its promulgation, and for some years Acton feared that he would be excommunicated. Döllinger, in fact, was excommunicated in 1871, but Acton, who had given Gladstone material for an account of the Vatican decrees in which the Liberal leader questioned the loyalty of Catholics to the civil authority, remained a Catholic. He refused to put an interpretation on the council's doctrine that the pope could not err when as vicar of Christ he addressed the whole church on matters of faith and morals. The strict interpretation of this doctrine, which in the main has prevailed, does not, as some Ultramontanes hoped, ascribe to the pope the extensive authority that inspired Acton's fears and his resolute opposition.[13]

The later 1870s and the 1880s intensified Acton's sense of isolation from contemporary life in the Church and even in society. This sense grew all the stronger because his wife preferred to live abroad, as their children's health and the family's economy made desirable. His belief in liberalism nevertheless grew in strength. Two expressions of this liberalism deserve mention. The first was his friendship with the Liberal leader William E. Gladstone, who, in Acton's eyes, exemplified the liberal ideal of a union of politics and morality. They maintained a long and high-minded correspondence, although Acton also came to hope, all in vain, that the elderly Gladstone would give him a diplomatic or political post. The second expression was Acton's undertaking to write the history of freedom. For this work he read voraciously. He had accumulated a library of sixty-thousand volumes in his English home at Aldenham, a library of perhaps four thousand volumes at Tegernsee in Bavaria, and a third collection on the Riviera. He was a tireless notetaker and on various subjects accumulated some fifty thousand individual notes, excerpts from books or some of his own thoughts, about one-eighth were for the history of freedom.

He wrote only two essays on the history of freedom, remarkable lectures delivered in 1877 to his neighbors and tenants at Bridgnorth in Shropshire. These lectures on freedom in antiquity and in Christianity were intended to awaken support for Gladstonian liberalism against Disraeli's assertive imperialism.[14] The general thesis was that in the ancient world freedom flourished but for brief spells. The precepts of ancient philosophers were better than the practice of the ancient world, which made for a universal degradation of freedom and human rights. The major deficiency was that the state of classical times was also a church and that the politics of men dictated morality. For freedom to prevail required a belief in a code of behavior such as the Stoic appeal to natural law, to a code not made by man. The teachings of Stoics worked against despotic rule and made a bridge between the ancient world and the political influence of Christianity, which, if it were to become the source of freedom, required three developments: the evolution of representative government, the ending of slavery, and the prizing of liberty of conscience.

Germanic barbarians destroyed the framework of ancient despotism. The political impact of Christianity, nevertheless, was remarkably slow. To ancient despotism succeeded a society threatened by anarchy, "a system very favorable to corporations, but offering no security to individuals." Not liberty but force was needed to "bring order out of chaotic ruin."[15] Then, the four centuries of conflict between ecclesiastical and feudal authorities made for the rise of civil liberty.

Acton gave a liberal formulation to Solon's achievement: he made "every citizen the guardian of his own interest." He did the same for Christ's teaching: "Although the doctrine of self-reliance and self-denial . . . was written as legibly in the New Testament as in the *Wealth of Nations*, it was not recognized until our age."[16] Christianity provides the essential limitations on the state: there exists a church and leaders that the state must respect, and there is a moral code and conscience.

The consequences of this outlook had been drawn by St. Thomas Aquinas, who argued that a king unfaithful to his duty had forfeited his claim to obedience, that government power should be limited by balanced institutions that allow for popular participation. This teaching, which Acton identified with the Whig theory of revolution, was long subordinated to the late medieval conflict of democracy and feudality, a conflict that in Machiavellianism gave new form to the denial of morality in politics, to the prizing of success and of the end over the means. Machiavelli's own teaching, which presumed that good faith need not be maintained with men because they would not have reciprocated — and it is a point in Acton's rigor toward Ultramontanes — could not have undergone "the test of Parliamentary government, for public discussion demands at least the profession of good faith."[17]

The centuries between the Reformation and the French Revolution brought forth mainly sorry political developments. Protestant and Catholic sought partisan advantage and maintained little faith with each other. The beneficiary was monarchical absolutism, modern despotism, the instruments of which French revolutionaries in their turn readily adopted.

Liberty in the modern age had been the achievement of the Whigs and of the Revolution of 1688 which, by curtailing the preponderance of France, delivered a substantial blow to continental despotism. But even English Whiggery so yielded its liberal impulses to self-interest that "Europe seemed incapable of becoming the home of free States. It was from America that the plain ideas that men ought to mind their own business, and that the nation is responsible to Heaven for the acts of the State . . . burst forth like a conqueror upon the world they were destined to transform under the title of the Rights of Man." Thus, liberty was a recent achievement and its story "the history of the thing that was not."[18]

Acton's failure to complete the history has been turned into a sentimental legend about the most celebrated book never written, or into a moral tale about the refusal of a scholar to accept human limitations in settling for a good rather than a perfect work. The problematic explanation of the failure is that over the years the industrious Acton could not bring himself to write the work. To the critics of his failure Acton made two replies: the first is that he sought historical knowledge of major and controverted questions as an end in itself and owed no responsibility of publication to any person; the second is "that I can only say things which people do not agree with, that I have neither disciple nor sympathizer, that this is no encouragement to production and confidence. . . ."[19]

This sense of isolation was partly self-inflicted, as may be seen in Acton's surprising and vehement criticism of the excommunicated Döllinger, who in 1879 had written some favorable comments in a brief notice of the recently deceased Bishop Dupanloup. Although the bishop had the reputation of a liberal and had worked with Acton at the Vatican Council, Acton ranked him among the debasers of truth, morality, and religion, among those evil forces who would defend the church by blurring moral issues. Acton wrote that when he found the protection of his teacher's name had been given to Dupanloup, a defender of the papacy, the *Syllabus*, the Jesuits, and the temporal government of Rome, the ground gave way under his feet: "I must never have known the principles that govern you." Of course, even John Henry Newman was "a brutal liar," and seeing such wickedness in the present, "I cannot doubt its existence in the past. And therefore I am very unwilling, in morals, and in discussing great men, to make allowance for their times. I allow for what they could not know. I do not allow for what they might have known."[20] In a revealing note, Acton described Döllinger's fault as "historical-mindedness," looking at events and men in their own terms.[21]

Acton, it should be clear, was a candid friend on principle. A person, he argued, was to be judged by his worst act and an institution by its lowest manifestation. To engage in historical study, then, was no lightsome occupation or casual preference. Changed circumstances had given the historian a new role as an agent in the moral advance of mankind. These changes were twofold: first, history had ceased to enjoy the imaginative freedom of literature and had become a science, "the science of progress," a matter of certainty, as it were, a "doctrine"; second, the sources of history had been made accessible so that all the disguised lies and inhumanity of public life could be found out and presented in all their reprehensibility. "The modern," he wrote more than once, "can usually be hanged out of his own mouth."[22]

The mission of history is to expose the false morality of

modern practical politics. As Machiavelli "reduced to a code
the wickedness of public men" — that is, the separation of ethics
and politics evident in the use of assassins not as a desperate ex-
pedient but as the usual practice of Venice's "decorous and
religious magistrates" — historians have the task of wresting
history from being a commentary on Machiavelli. Historical
writing itself reveals this moral deficiency. A higher form of
historical study is necessary in order to gainsay Ernest Renan's
view, quoted by Acton, that history presents the very contrary
of the reward of virtue.[23]

In higher historical studies Acton sought what did not pass
away, the abiding, the scarcely visible touch of the divine.
Although he thought human nature to be weak, he nonetheless
professed a belief in general progress as the necessary consequence of Divine Providence. This progress of mankind
depended upon understanding that God exists and that man
must seek proper relations with the Creator.[24]

The divine touch may be seen in the political limits on men.
As an example, Acton cited the French who, he thought, would
be able to build durably on the ruins of 1793 only by returning
to the principles they had then repudiated. If "states would
live, they must preserve their organic connection with their
origin and history." They must admit that they are not the
voluntary creations of men and must recognize "that men la-
bour in vain who would construct them [constitutions] without
acknowledging God as the artificer."[25]

History, then, was to serve God and man by holding on to
something permanent, outside the vicissitudes of time. Modern
philosophy, in the person of Hegel, confirmed men in accepting
their particular time, its judgments and prejudices. Hegel, by
identifying the dialectic of change with reason, influenced men
so that with their moral judgment blurred they failed to see
evil. Acton's case against purely historical judgments cited
Ranke. The German master presented things impartially as
they really are with the expectation that dumb facts would
speak for themselves. He thereby sanctified history instead of
freeing man from history. "Ranke never discovered the principle by which conduct may be judged, [he is] the exponent of
variable ethics and the Perverted Conscience." "Resist your
time — take a foothold outside it. See other times and ask your-

self whether the time of our ancestors is fit for us." "History governed when the knowledge of history did not exist. When the knowledge of history came, the power of history departed."[26]

History, then, in providing a choice of ancestors (though most of them are bad), is a study to save the future from the past. The moral magistracy of the historian is necessary because his primary sphere is public life. In this sphere, Acton thought, the New Testament, although distinguished for its ethical teaching, not for metaphysics, gave the European world little light. If regrettably there was no adequate code for public life, the historian should be all the more emphatic about murder, lies, and oppression, matters that might receive lively response from the consciences of many people.

Reform required freedom. For progress in knowledge, spirituality, moral behavior, and ethics, freedom was a prerequisite. Mankind could advance only by recognizing and profiting from error as well as moral misbehavior. The oppression and censorship imposed by modern states and the papacy in the sixteenth century and afterwards destroyed the possibility of progress by miring people in error. Such actions by statesmen are at least crimes, and such actions by churchmen are sins shrieking to heaven through the centuries. Unless they are called by their proper name, the world is surrendered to Machiavelli and the Inquisitors.

Power corrupts the holder of power, and the self-interest of others facing power corrupts them. The historian and, for that matter, every honest man must shout "murderer" and "liar" against the agents of a conspiracy and in behalf of its victims. The conspiracy was "to uphold the hierarchy. So that respect for the hierarchy could accord with respect for the law of God, so that men might believe the Pope, it was resolved to make them believe that vice is virtue and falsehood truth."[27]

Acton understood that he was giving the historian a warrior role, and he blamed historians who cultivated serenity and had no battle scars. He called the Anglican Bishop Mandell Creighton, because of his moderation in criticism, an English gentleman. Creighton, in effect, admitted that he was. Acton believed that Ranke had chosen the easy course in urging the historian to refrain from judgment. The restraint permitted him to choose the interesting. "He is the staff officer who leaves all the rough work to the regimental officers. He appears always in pumps and kid gloves."[28]

In criticizing, the historian must use an absolute code. Killing is to be called murder; no lofty aim or intention to do good can extenuate king and especially pope and saint, who may be parties to killing. If the views of their age accept or approve such an action, its standards are evil and can afford no palliation. To this statement Acton surprisingly added that to learn to think historically was of vital importance. To think historically made for certainty, and in thinking historically people would concur with him, a sentence I paraphrase not in irony but in wonder. To think historically meant engaging in research, in observation of the Actonian injunction to mistrust received opinions. In this matter Acton intended no comfort to academics; he regarded universities as subtreasuries of received opinion. In one striking sentence he presented this point as a theory of education: it is acceptable to take information from others, but ideas must be worked out independently, because it is dangerous to take ideas from other people. Ideas, "like experience, must be your own."[29]

But Lord Acton was a man of his own time in his liberalism and in his belief in progress, tempered though it was. He himself emphasized the distinctively personal element in his liberalism: "I carried further than others the Doctrinaire belief in mere Liberalism, identifying it altogether with morality, and holding the ethical standard and purpose to be supreme and sovereign."[30]

His distrust of people as power wielders was consistent. No class, he insisted, was worthy to govern. Power, the corrupter, must be tamed by dividing and restricting it — that is, by constitutions, tradition, federalism, and aristocracy. Nationalism poses an especial danger, because it is likely to magnify state power. It threatened to provide the modern state with a dangerous power comparable to that ancient religion gave the state of antiquity. When coupled with democracy, nationalism may make plausible the insidious claim that a government is the people.

For all his admiration for William E. Gladstone, he certainly could not identify himself with any government. Ironically, the most acceptable recognition that he received, a university post, came not from Gladstone but from Lord Rosebery's government (1894-1895). In 1895 Acton's appointment to the Regius Professorship of Modern History in Cambridge University challenged him to congenial tasks and a public life that he found rewarding until his death in 1902.

In these last years he provided a final synthesis of his views in four labors, of which the first is his "Inaugural Lecture on the Study of History" (1895). To it he added notes from his abundant store, which as well as his books, he shared generously with students at Cambridge. But it is a fair maxim of historical composition that to write too close to notes makes writing rigid, and excessive use of notes may blur meaning, as Acton here did. For the occasion of the lecture he presented his views fully but with some moderation of pitch.

The thesis he presented was that the modern age, the aftermath of the fifteenth century, marked a break in continuity with the Middle Ages. The study of history had contributed to the breach, but it also could contribute to understanding what had happened and, thereby, to the progress by which men may carry out the Creator's providential design for mankind. "Whatever a man's notions of these later centuries are, such, in the main, the man himself will be. Under the name of history, they cover the articles of his philosophy, his religious, and his political creed."[31] History, he believed, permitted a proper understanding of the modern age's movement toward freedom. The exchange of the control of will over will for the rule of reason over reason was made so that men should be *free to do their duty*, so that every man should be "unhindered by man in the fulfillment of duty to God." This "essence of the Rights of Man" was "the indestructible soul of Revolution."[32]

Liberty meant that there would be error as well as that error would be protected. Because men were sinful, excess of rigor in judgment was the better bet. In the name of liberty men had made revolutions to annul human history, which Acton here described in Voltairean terms as the reign of force, lies, and crime. The rival Conservative and Liberal interpretations of the French Revolution as continuity and breach add to our understanding of human life. Austerely critical and impartial history, Acton hoped, would pass beyond that polarized division and achieve a scientific conclusion commanding acceptance. That conclusion would include moral judgments.

His audience and students of history were urged to go beyond the historians of earlier times to achieve a history "more rigidly impersonal, disinterested and just than they" had been, to fashion historical work that looked "with remorse upon the past, and to the future with assured hope of better things."[33]

Lectures on Modern History, the second fruit of these last years, was phrased in terse, thought-provoking sentences. It concentrated on the play of conscience in a Europe characterized by trade and expansion, the slave trade, the Renaissance, the Reformation, and absolutism. Acton prepared his conclusion with an account of the grounding of liberty in England's Revolution of 1688. The principle of the victorious Whigs, the social contract, it was almost needless for Acton to add, had spiritless and unworthy champions.

In the reign of George III, when it appeared that the English Revolution was exhausted, the American colonies made "a more glorious Revolution, infinitely more definite and clearcut, with a stronger grasp of principle . . . [which] began to influence England and Europe."[34]

Acton's *Lectures on the French Revolution*, his third Cambridge achievement, has the admirable qualities of the *Lectures on Modern History*: sustained narrative, learning that quickly reveals the subject's importance, and an economical style that flashes into epigrams. Two features of his account may be mentioned: first, he found noteworthy the abuses and bankruptcy of the Old Order and saw legitimacy in some of the revolution's aspirations. Second, he argued that the French Revolutionaries used the same means as the rulers of the Old Order, ranging from centralization to murder and fraud justified by *raison d'état*.

The hanging judge condemned equally murders perpetrated by despots, kings, and by revolutionaries who killed in the people's name. When Lally Tollendal denounced the killings at the fall of the Bastille, Barnave rhetorically asked whether the blood shed was so pure. Acton then recalled other statesmen who sought to exculpate the Bastille slaughter, but to his mind the historians who did so were worse than "these anointed culprits. The strong man with the dagger is followed by the weaker man with the sponge. First, the criminal who slays; then the sophist who defends the slayer."[35]

"The Declaration of the Rights of Man and the Citizen" is summed up in as concise and striking a manner as the historical thinker can achieve. The Declaration's fatal flaw is the passion for equality without a similar love of liberty or an awareness of the hazards that may menace it.

The final achievement of Acton's Cambridge years was to plan and organize the *Cambridge Modern History*, the ancestor of a new modern history and of the Cambridge ancient and medieval histories, and, among others, the histories of Africa and Islam. Each volume is the cooperative effort of many experts. The cooperative project, a division of labor according to expertise, is an obvious arrangement for covering a large subject. Acton conceived the work as general history which was also to be concerned with ideas and to feature or introduce an area's or a country's history at the time when it played a significant role in an important aspect of general history.

To contributors, the editor made a characteristic point. He expected them to achieve an impartiality and certainty that would render the individual unidentifiable. In the history, he insisted, the account of the Battle of Waterloo must satisfy French, German, Dutch, and English scholars. Nobody should be able to "tell, without examining the list of authors, where the Bishop of Oxford laid down the pen, and whether Fairbairn or Gasquet, Liebermann or Harrison took it up."[36] This emphasis upon depersonalized historical writing, and the success of his insistence, made *The Cambridge Modern History* needlessly tedious reading; and it is incongruous in a scholar who frequently noted that he stood for a minority view, almost a personal view, that the historian must make moral judgment possible.

It is also characteristic of Acton that he thought complete history to be certain. Indeed, Acton's belief in certainty in a century of historical erudition reveals three areas of difficulties. The first is his affirmation that history is or was about to be a science, with science's certainty. If he had spoken of certainty about many facts and the rejection of some versions of the past, there could be no dispute. His research, for example, had established some conclusions about the St. Bartholomew Massacre, but questions remain and will remain. That he was not more diffident is surprising, because he dealt with the historiography of controversial issues and might have been expected to know that a future time provides a new ending to a past event or, at any rate, gives a new perspective that may raise new questions.

His certainty about historical knowledge was strengthened by a second conviction: that the sources of history, the great state collections and the papers of prominent men, had been located and that most of them had been made accessible. Even though he referred primarily to the history of the sixteenth, seventeenth, and probably the eighteenth centuries, his view was gravely limited. When he stated that certainty had been achieved or was upon us, his judgment assumed that the areas of history are more limited than the scope of history as revealed by the practice of his contemporaries and successors.[37]

Finally, Acton's insistence on moral judgment was polemical and arbitrary, which is also to say that it was lacking both in humility and historical sense. He would have no part of that affront to all concerned with moral responsibility, the view that to understand all is to pardon all. But his moral judgment lacked historical sense: what he called murder and fraud simply could not be considered in relation to the views of the perpetrator's century and intent. It must be allowed to Acton that consideration of the relationship of a principle to individual circumstances — that is, the casuistry that moral judgment requires — permits only too readily the Philadelphia lawyer and the egoist indulging in selective indignation to flourish. Acton made his judgments and populated history with bad men; as Bishop Mandell Creighton put it, "his view would reduce history to a dreary record of crimes."[38] But even the Inquisitor must not be lynched. When this is said against Acton, it must be recognized that in the 1860s he had been scandalized by the canonization of an Inquisitor.

He held somewhat contradictory views about the study and function of history. There is something implacable and obsessive about his insistence on moral judgment and about his amazing belief that history was soon to be fully worked out and presumably agreed upon. He observed that over the years life brings out disagreements and partings in all friendships. This is not necessarily true, but he had a capacity in his harsh language and in confrontations with others cast as agents of evil and enemies to make the observation come true for him.

As a young man Acton recognized that his position took in both liberalism and Catholicism. That the times, especially in the church, were inopportune for the reconciliation of the two, gave him, he might have thought, a worthy challenge. The struggle was all the more difficult because some of the conflict took place within his own soul. He was not a casualty of the struggle, but he was hurt.

The ground on which he chose to fight was historical writing, which he conceived to have an ultimate function. The exercise of moral judgment would serve the cause of reform and progress. But the moral function, as he saw it, required him to restrict historical-mindedness.

He had the utopian hope that historical criticism of sinful mankind could nullify history as the story of violence and deceit and bring about a moral age, a Gladstonian dawn. The hope as well as the belief in certainty confirmed him in his temperamental harshness and extremism. Acton would go from history into a new age. The transition, the progress evident in man's observation of the divine moral code and in cooperation with God's design, would vindicate Providence. But this position cannot deal adequately with two interrelated difficulties. The first is to explain how people of any time, of any now, can become the new people of the future's new order. The second is to admit his own fellowship with past humanity, and to recognize that men of the past have not been as debased as Acton implied. Statesmen, ordinary people, bishops, even Ultramontanes, may often have been people of middling goodness. The religious person would insist that the past was not without grace and not outside the view of God's Providence, which, however, it is arrogant to claim to know. Acton achieved his moral condemnation of the past by selection, by insisting that a man's worst act is the man.

Historians must describe the past in its own terms, and serious historians cannot escape detailing and explaining the difference between the moral views of their subjects and themselves. But they are not hanging judges, although they may become false or even real prophets — and some histories of the Cold War have embodied Actonian willfulness and selectivity. Acton was a Liberal prophet and, like the biblical prophets, a harsh judge. He resisted monumentally, excessively, the historian's temptation to blur moral judgment and to minimize the responsibility of the individual.

Although his writings are few, his lectures, many of his pages, and, indeed, entire essays, make for reading at once profitable, stimulating, and uplifting. If his liberalism rested on excessively confident hopes for the future, his mistrust of power and the powerful is well-grounded. His confidence inspired him to live up, though not invariably, to the austere requirement that everyone's position, especially an opponent's view, should be stated as formidably as possible. In his own age — and today — the importance of his life and work is that in reasserting, however exaggeratedly, the duty of the historian to be a moral judge, he testified against the temptations to worship history and to use historical sympathy to expunge all evil men from history as though man made history but not its crimes. He is therefore a model whose high purpose, industry, and acuity are to be imitated and whose harshness and baseless certainty may remind us of our limitations.

Notes

2. Herodotus

1. Page references (following the colon) are to the translation by Aubrey de Selincourt: *Herodotus the Histories*, rev. ed. by A. R. Burn (Harmondsworth, 1972). My quotations are from the same source. I have followed the chronology of Kurt von Fritz, *Die griechische Geschichtsschreibung* (Berlin, 1967), vols. 1 and 2. See especially the texts on pp. 121-24, 126-27 and the notes thereto.

2. Herodotus 4.95: 302. De Selincourt's translation is rather free in this passage about a Thracian slave who had lived in Samos under Pythagoras and so had acquired "an insight into Ionian ideas and a more civilized way of living than was to be found in Thrace."

3. Lionel Pearson, *Early Ionian Historians* (Oxford, 1939), p. 3; Dionysius of Halicarnassus, "On Thucydides," in *Critical Essays*, trans. Stephen Usher, vol. 1, Loeb Library ed. (Cambridge, Mass., 1975), pp. 473-75.

4. Felix Jacoby, *Die Fragmente der griechischen Historiens*, pt. 1 (1957; rpt. ed., Leyden, 1968), pp. 7-8.

5. This thesis is argued on the numerous pages of von Fritz, *Die griechische Geschichtsschreibung*.

6. The reality that Herodotus reports distortedly is presented in detail by Alan B. Lloyd in his sympathetic commentary, "Herodotus, Book II, Commentary 1-98," in *Études préliminaires aux religions orientales dans l'empire romain*, ed. M. J. Vermaseren, vol. 43 (Leyden, 1976), see esp. pp. 146-71.

7. Edda Bresciani, "Egypt and the Persian Empire," in *The Greeks and the Persians from the Sixth to the Fourth Centuries*, ed. Hermann Bengston (New York, 1968), p. 334. At Memphis was found a sarcophagus and hieroglyphic epitaph of Apis provided by Cambyses, whose figure is presented in pharaonic dress adoring Apis. William Culican, *The Medes and Persians* (New York, 1965), p. 60.

8. In the translated quotation I omitted "and the religion he was brought up in," which is the translator's amplification.

3. Thucydides

1. References to *The History of the Peloponnesian War* will be presented in the text. The page numbers are from the Penguin edition of the translation by Rex Warner, with notes and introduction by M. I. Finley (1972). Quotations are from that translation. Occasionally I refer to the Loeb Library translation in 4 vols. by Charles Foster Smith (Cambridge [Mass.], 1935-45). Reading the *History* may be made more profitable and absorbing by consulting: A. W. Gomme, *A Historical Commentary on Thucydides*, 5 vols. (London, 1945-81), vols. 4-5 by A. Andrewes, K. J. Dover; and J. H. Finley, Jr., *Thucydides* (Cambridge, Mass., 1942), a work to which I cannot begin to specify my debt.

2. 1.16:45. This passage referred to tyrannies, but many of the major speeches make this point about oligarchies as contrasted with Athenian democracy.

3. Victor Ehrenberg, *From Solon to Socrates: Greek History and Civilization during the Sixth and Fifth Centuries B. C.* (London, 1968), pp. 257-58, 237-41; Russell Meiggs, *The Athenian Empire* (Oxford, 1972), pp. 202-4, 430-31.

4. Gomme, *Commentary*, 2:709.

5. The use of Hippocratic methods by Thucydides was well argued by Charles N. Cochrane, *Thucydides and the Science of History* (New York, 1965). Eric Voegelin in *The World of the Polis* (Baton Rouge, 1957), pp. 356-57, put the point effectively: "Thucydides has his place . . . as the first craftsman who tried to transform the empirical knowledge of politics into a science, using the science of medicine as his model for this purpose."

6. 4.1-23:265-78. The Athenians cut off some Spartan hoplites on the island. To circumvent that, other Spartans in full armor went into the water, fighting and trying to take their captured ships from the Athenians. Thucydides spelled out the battle's reversal of the combatants' usual roles: "For the Spartans, in their desperate excitement, were actually fighting a sea battle on land, and the victorious Athenians, in their anxiety to take the fullest possible advantage of their success, were fighting an infantry battle from their ships" (p. 273).

In discussing armistice terms, the Spartans urged that the Athenians perpetuate their good fortune by making peace and conciliating their enemy before fortune turned against them. The latter, however, proposed to win "still more" (4.21:277).

7. The seventeenth-century philosopher Thomas Hobbes, who translated Thucydides, criticized Dionysius, who had cited Cratippus concerning the lack of variety in Thucydides. The latter, according to

Dionysius, erred in choosing his subject. The Peloponnesian War as the beginning of Greek decline was a painful subject and not to be memorialized. Such an opinion, Hobbes wrote, was contrary to all common sense: For it makes "the scope of history, not profit by writing truth," but the pleasure of the hearer, as if it were a song. The argument of history would, therefore, exclude the miseries of his country and regard only its "glorious and splendid actions." Ronald Syme, "Thucydides," *Proceedings of the British Academy*, vol. 48 (1962): 43.

8. *Epistle to a Godson* (London, 1972-73), p. 25.

4. Tacitus

1. Almost all my quotations from Tacitus are from the Church and Brodribb translation edited by Moses Hadas for Modern Library College Editions. Here and there paraphrases from all but the *Annals* may echo the volumes in the Loeb Library. Very infrequently I use my own translation or paraphrase from C. D. Fisher's edition of the *Annals* in Oxford Classical texts. Sir Ronald Syme, *Tacitus*, 2 vols. (Oxford, 1958), is an exhaustive work, sufficiently opinionated for its controverted subject. Gaston Boissier, *Tacite* (Paris, 1903), remains useful. The *Cambridge Ancient Histories*, vols. 10-11, and Harold Mattingly's *Roman Imperial Civilization* (New York, 1957) are helpful; and Chester G. Starr, *Civilization and the Caesars* (New York, 1965), is stimulating. Michael Grant, *The Ancient Historians* (New York, 1970), is serviceable. Other useful works are Ronald Martin, *Tacitus* (Berkeley, 1981); the varied essays in T. A. Dorsey, ed., *Tacitus* (London, 1969); G. E. F. Chilver, *A Historical Commentary on Tacitus' Histories I and II* (Oxford, 1979), esp. pp. 22-30; and F. R. D. Goodyear, ed., *The Annals of Tacitus, Books 1-6*, vol. 1 (Cambridge, 1972):25-46.

2. I accept the arguments of Sir Ronald Syme (*Tacitus* 2:670-73) for Tacitus' authorship of the *Dialogue*, which accorded with the biography of Tacitus and presented thoughts that pervade his works.

3. Ibid., 1:205.

5. Bede

1. References to *The Ecclesiastical History* are, unless otherwise indicated, to book and chapter in Leo Sherley-Price's translation in the Penguin Classics edition (Harmondsworth, 1955).

2. Henry Mayr-Harting, *The Coming of Christianity to England*

(London, 1972), pp. 103-13; C. W. Jones, "Bede as Early Medieval Historian," *Medievalia et Humanistica* 4 (1948): 26-36; Denys Hay, *Annalists and Historians: Western Historiography from the Eighth to the Eighteenth Centuries* (London, 1977), p. 27, 39-43; W. Levison, "Bede as Historian," in *Bede's Life, Times and Writings*, ed. A. H. Thompson (Oxford, 1935).

3. 1.32. Pope Gregory used the word *terrendo*, which means "terrifying." Sherley-Price in the Penguin edition used the misleadingly gentle "warning."

4. Charles Plummer edited the Latin text of Bede's *History* (Oxford, 1896, 1946), Notes, p. 4. In the margin of the text Plummer listed the sources of each of Bede's borrowings.

5. Edwin's successors, Osric and Eanfred, returned to paganism. Bede noted that recorders of events were agreed upon expunging the memory of these kings and the Celtic tyrant Caedwalla, who destroyed them, and assigning the year 733 to their God-fearing successor, Oswald. Bede did not expunge (3.1).

6. The material just discussed is from book 2. Book 1 concluded the story of the advent of the missionaries with another expression of Saxon pride. The same King Aethelfrith defeated King Aidan of the Celts of Scotland at Degsastan (603). Thereafter, the monk noted, no king of those people dared to come in battle against the Anglo-Saxons.

7. The quotation is from the English-Latin edition prepared by Colgrave and Mynors (Oxford, 1969), 4.24:415-19. Here and elsewhere Sherley-Price has taken liberties with Bede's text.

8. The account of Ecgfrith provides evidence of Bede's impartiality because the historian's monastery was on land that came from the king.

9. David Knowles, *Saints and Scholars* (Cambridge, 1962), p. 17.

6. William Camden

1. For the life of Camden see the *Dictionary of National Biography* and the Latin life of Camden by Thomas Smith (London, 1691), with Camden's letters, in Latin and English, and letters to him in Latin, English, and French. Camden is placed within the historiographical achievement of his age by F. J. Levy, *Tudor Historical Thought* (San Marino, 1967), and F. Smith Fussner, *The Historical Revolution: English Historical Writing and Thought, 1580-1640* (New York, 1962). Each, with some exaggeration I believe, emphasizes the influence of the Tacitean tradition on Camden, but they do not provide convincing material. Unless otherwise stated, references to *Britannia*

in text and footnotes are to Richard Gough's four-volume translation (London, 1807); the citations will be Gough, volume number and page. References to the *Annals*, cited as *Annals* and page number, are to *The History of the Most Renowned and Victorious Princess Elizabeth, Late Queen of England*, 4th ed. (London, 1688).

2. *Britannia* (London, 1600), "Ad Lectorem."

3. *Calendar of State Papers, Domestic, 1591-1594*, ed. M. A. E. Green (London, 1867), p. 479.

4. G. Goodman, *The Court of James I*, ed. J. S. Brewer (London, 1829), 1:126.

5. *Britannia* (London, 1586), "Dedication to Burghley," p. A2.

6. *Remains Concerning Britain* (London, 1637), p. 9.

7. Henry Peacham, *The Compleat Gentleman* (London, 1627), p. 51.

8. William Camden, *The History of the Most Renowned and Victorious Princess Elizabeth*, Classics of British Historical Literature (Chicago, 1970). Wallace T. MacCaffrey is the editor and author of the useful introductory essay on pp. xi-xxxix. He described the choice of annals as "somewhat unimaginative" (p. xxix). In the same essay he provided ample material about the delicacy of Camden's situation and the limitations he had to observe (pp. xxxvi-xxxvii). MacCaffrey's selection reproduces (without correction) the 1688 edition of a translation published in 1675. For example, "The Author to the Reader," p. 7, presents a caricature of Camden's good temper—a profession that he respects all foreigners. This should read "as foreigners are accustomed to do." By limiting himself to the 1688 translation the editor was unable to take advantage of hundreds of mainly minor corrections and revisions made by the author and incorporated in Thomas Hearne's edition of the *Annals*, 3 vols. (Oxford, 1717).

9. Almost all of the account of Camden's profession, objections, and method is based on Camden's introductory "The Author to the Reader," eight unnumbered pages at the beginning of *The History*.

10. The seventeenth-century translator rendered this "as good as many," which was accurate but is now ambiguous as a translation of "instar multorum."

11. Latin, p. 291, stronger than English (1688), p. 227. The Latin on p. 291 warrants using "minion" for the English version "servant" (p. 227).

7. Voltaire

1. Letter 3044 in Theodore Besterman, *Voltaire* (London, 1969), p. 43. There is a good account of Voltaire on history and civilization

in Karl J. Weintraub, *Visions of Culture* (Chicago, 1966), pp. 19-74. The critical scholar and the admirer of Voltaire struggle in Peter Gay, *Voltaire's Politics* (Princeton, 1959).

2. *Voltaire*, p. 35.

3. Voltaire did not have clean hands in this matter. In 1719 he had accorded the same treatment, duel refusal and the hire of thrashers, to an actor, Poisson. In his later career, Voltaire protested against the social prejudices experienced by stage people.

4. *Lettres philosophiques*, ed. F. A. Taylor, Blackwell's French Texts (Oxford, 1976), Lettre XVIII, pp. 68-72. On p. 93 Voltaire suggested that the Académie Française edit the great works of the age of Louis XIV. This meant correcting the faults of language which Voltaire found numerous in Corneille and Molière and abundant in La Fontaine.

5. Besterman, *Voltaire*, p. 149; Voltaire, "The World as It Is," in *Candide, Zadig and Other Stories*, trans. Donald Frame (New York, 1961), pp. 198-99.

6. Voltaire, *Oeuvres historiques*, ed. R. Pomeau (Paris, 1957), p. 272.

7. This terse paraphrase is by Ragnhild M. Hatton in *Charles XII of Sweden* (London, 1968), p. xiv.

8. *Oeuvres historiques*, pp. 303-4.

9. *Oeuvres*, ed. Condorcet O'Connor and M. F. Arago (Paris, 1847-49), 4:47. Style and vision are the grounds on which Voltaire criticized André Michel Ramsay's *Histoire du vicomte de Turenne* (1735). The author, Voltaire agreed, copied material from de Retz, a vivacious scoundrel, and phrases of Fenelon, "but he has not made his hero interesting. He calls him great but he has not rendered him such; he praises him in rhetoric." Voltaire's letter is quoted by Marie Rose de Labriolle (ed.), "Le Pour et Contre et son temps" by l'abbe Prevost in *Studies on Voltaire and the Eighteenth Century*, vol. 35 (Geneva, 1965); 439.

10. *Oeuvres historiques*, p. 271.

11. *Two Dialogues Concerning the Manner of Writing History* (London, 1783), p. 31.

12. "Histoire de l'empire de Russie sous Pierre le Grand" and "Preface" (1759) in *Oeuvres historiques*, pp. 339, 1687. Peter is a hero of civilization and Enlightenment, even though the work is finally presented as a study not of Peter but of the Russian Empire under him.

13. Ibid., p. 599.

14. Letter, March 25, 1760, quoted in Albert Lortholary, *Le Mirage russe en France au XVIIIᵉ siècle* (Paris, 1951), p. 65.

15. Lortholary, *Le Mirage russe*, p. 134, characterized Voltaire's

writings on Peter and for Catherine as an assurance, hallowed by the mantle of the *philosophes*, that the empress "could with a secure conscience draw the sword for ideas." Violence, thereby, was made an instrument of civilization. This point is evident in the emetic letters of Voltaire to Catherine in A. Lentin, *Voltaire and Catherine the Great: Selected Correspondence* (Cambridge, 1974), esp. p. 44.

16. Lentin, p. 31.

17. (Paris, 1722), p. lv.

18. *Oeuvres historiques*, p. 1255.

19. Ibid., p. 607.

20. Letter 876, 24 August 1735, in *Correspondence*, ed. Theodore Besterman (Geneva, 1964), 4:114. There is a good account of the history in J. H. Brumfitt, *Voltaire: Historian* (London, 1958), esp. pp. 48-61. The standard edition of *Le Siècle de Louis XIV* is by Emile Bourgeois (Paris, 1906). I have used Pomeau's edition in *Oeuvres historiques*. Brumfitt translated Voltaire's *Philosophy of History* for *Studies on Voltaire and the Eighteenth Century*, ed. Theodore Besterman (Geneva, 1963). The work is the first part of the *Essai*. Voltaire might have made mordant comments on later philosophies of history.

21. *Oeuvres historiques*, p. 1274. Voltaire professed that his age required authors to set order into our ideas and ridiculed "pedants" who, without thinking themselves and lacking taste, recorded in lengthy detail "what was thought." "Lettre à M. de Cideville" and "Le Temple du goût" (1732) in *Oeuvres complètes de Voltaire*, ed. Louis Moland (Paris, 1877-1885), 8:552-57.

22. These two paragraphs follow closely two of Voltaire's letters (1735): one, already cited, to Olivet and another to his friend Nicolas Claude Thieriot. *Correspondence*, nos. 876 and 864, 4:114, 94.

23. Fontenelle, "L'Eloge de Leibnitz" in M. F. Thuret, *Oeuvres de Locke et Leibnitz* (Paris, 1839), p. 480.

24. *Correspondence*, 4:89.

25. Ibid., no. 860, June 1735, 4:89; no. 864, c. 15 July 1735, 4:94; no. 876, 24 August 1735, 4:114.

26. Ibid., p. 369.

27. Voltaire, *Essai sur les moeurs et l'esprit des nations*, ed. R. Pomeau (Paris, 1963). All references will be in the text and to this edition.

28. *Correspondence*, no. 15931, 78:26-27.

29. *Oeuvres*, 4:149.

30. Ibid., p. 96.

31. Besterman, *Voltaire*, p. 583.

32. Voltaire, "Poem to a Lady" (1732) quoted in ibid., p. 541.

33. D'Alembert, "Reflexions sur l'histoire et sur les différents

manières de l'écrire," in *Oeuvres philosophiques, historiques et litteraires* (Paris, 1805), 4:188.

34. Besterman, *Correspondence,* letter of 1778 to Frederick the Great, no. 19818, 98:9.

35. D'Alembert, "Reflexions," 4:193.

36. *Oeuvres,* 4:1.

8. Edward Gibbon

1. References to *The Decline and Fall* are to the Modern Library Giant edition in two volumes (New York [1932]), which will be cited as *D. and F.* Chapter numbers will also be given. Gibbon's letters have been edited by R. E. Prothero in two volumes, *Private Letters of Edward Gibbon,* 2d ed. (London, 1897), and by J. E. Norton in three volumes, *The Letters of Edward Gibbon* (London, 1956).

2. White has expressed his view in a number of articles and in *Metahistory: The Historical Imagination in Nineteenth-Century Europe* (Baltimore, 1973).

3. Georges Bonnard, ed., *Edward Gibbon: Memoirs of My Life* (New York, 1966), pp. 189, 186, 28; cited hereafter as *Memoirs.* Bonnard's is the best edition of a work often described as *The Autobiography.* After completing *The Decline and Fall,* Gibbon wrote six memoirs of his life, which John Murray edited in 1896. Lord Sheffield, Gibbon's executor, taking some liberties with Gibbon's text, published the sketches as one work (1796), *The Autobiography.*

4. In Paris he disapproved of the "intolerant zeal" of the followers of Helvetius and Holbach, who "laughed at the scepticism of Hume, and preached the tenets of Atheism with the bigotry of dogmatists." *Memoirs,* p. 127.

5. Ibid., p. 74.

6. Ibid., pp. 74, 84-86, 85, n. 7.

7. Prothero, *Private Letters of Edward Gibbon,* 2d ed. (London, 1897), 1:247.

8. *Memoirs,* p. 117. Gibbon enjoyed studying and sometimes reproached himself for periods of failure to read while he served in the militia. The times of industry are, nevertheless, impressive. They are recorded in D. M. Low, ed., *Gibbon's Journal to January 28th, 1763* (New York, 1929).

9. *Memoirs,* p. 126. Gibbon recorded his French visit in a journal, wherein he insisted that he wished the French to see him as a man of letters and a "man of condition. . . . I do not wish that the writer make

the Gentleman wholly disappear" (Georges Bonnard "Le Séjour de Gibbon à Paris du 28ᵉ Jan. au 9ᵉ Mai 1763," in G. R. de Beer and Georges Bonnard, *Miscellanea Gibboniana* (Lausanne, 1952), p. 109.

10. *Memoirs*, pp. 134-36. Gibbon claimed that "the place and moment" of the conception of *The Decline and Fall* had been recorded in his journal. The surviving journal has no entry for the time and place he cited. But the journal discussed his diligent readings and recounted the arrogance of Gibbon, the English tourist in Italian churches, particularly in Genoa. Georges Bonnard, *Le Journal de Gibbon à Lausanne* (Lausanne, 1945), and *Gibbon's Journey from Geneva to Rome: His Journal from 20 April to 2 October 1764* (New York, 1961), p. 85. Lord Sheffield published Gibbon's manuscript on Italian topography in *Miscellaneous Works* (London, 1796), 4:157-328.

Bonnard has demythologized Gibbon's account of Capitoline inspiration and emphasized the development and definition of Gibbon's historical awareness during studies in Lausanne. See "L'Importance du deuxième séjour de Gibbon à Lausanne dans la formation de l'historien," in *Mélanges d'histoire et de litterature offerts à Monsieur Charles Gilliard* (Lausanne, 1944), pp. 400-420.

11. Gibbon, *Miscellaneous Works*, 1:204-5.

12. *Memoirs*, pp. 150-54.

13. Ibid., p. 161. On p. 317 Bonnard quoted a poem attributed to Fox, alleging that King George, fearful that Gibbon might write the story of Britain's imperial disgrace, used the office to try to purchase Gibbon's silence. In Rome "his writings declare / A degeneracy there, / Which his conduct exhibits at home."

14. The younger George Colman quoted in Boswell, *Life of Samuel Johnson* (Oxford, 1971), 3:54, n. 2 Importance in society, Gibbon pronounced for himself, was relative: "in London I was lost in the crowd; I ranked with the first families of Lausanne." While some look on conversation "as a theatre or a school," the historian after a morning of work wished "to unbend rather than to exercise my mind." As to missing the great men of London, "I am too modest or too proud to rate my own value by that of my associates" (*Memoirs*, pp. 177-78).

Gibbon's conversations, Sir James Bland wrote, allowed no one a chance of reply. It was not, he thought, "what Dr. Johnson would have called *talk*." The Abbé Raynal was loud in conversation, but the sovereign state of Edward Gibbon revealed something of himself in the complaint about Raynal that you would imagine that "he alone was the Monarch and legislator of the World" (Prothero, *Private Letters*, 1:28, n. 1; 2:483).

15. Against the revolutionaries Gibbon urged maintaining "things as they are," because to admit the smallest change is to be lost to the "total subversion of all rank, order and government," to a "popular monster, which after devouring everything else, must finally devour itself" (ibid., 2:298, 309).

16. Gavin de Beer, *Gibbon and His World* (London, 1968).

17. *Memoirs*, pp. 155, 157-58, 164.

18. Gibbon, *Essai sur l'étude de la littérature* (London, 1761), p. 217, English translation (London, 1764), p. 156; *D. and F.*, "General Observations on the Fall of the Roman Empire in the West," after chap. 38, 2:92.

19. *D. and F.*, 1, chap. 14, pp. 345, 346, 382. "Like the modesty affected by Augustus, the state maintained by Diocletian was a theatrical representation; but it must be confessed that, of the two comedies, the former was of a much more liberal and manly character than the latter. It was the aim of the one to disguise, and the object of the other to display, the unbounded power which the emperors possessed over the Roman world" (chap. 13, p. 332). Diocletian was free of vanity, but Constantine was corrupted by the imperial power.

20. Ibid., 1 chap. 32, pp. 1150-51; 2, chap. 48, pp. 520-21; 2, chap. 53, p. 877. Gibbon worked his magic on J. B. Bury, who knew Byzantine history and prepared the standard edition of *The Decline and Fall of the Roman Empire*. All of Gibbon's faults, Bury judged, had not invalidated his section on Byzantium. "The arrogant autocracy with its servile subjects which Gibbon attributed to Byzantium never in fact existed," is the view of Steven Runciman, a British Byzantine scholar, in "Gibbon and Byzantium," *Daedalus, Proceedings of the American Academy of Arts and Sciences*, vol. 105, no. 3 (Summer 1976), p. 109. The judgment about Gibbon's effect on Byzantine studies is on the same page. Some of Gibbon's lapses may be explained by his lack of a good guide to Byzantine history, but he read very widely and the major defect is lack of empathy. His account was shaped by Western, Enlightenment, and classicist prejudices. The prominence of the church in Byzantine history repelled him. Finally, the design of his history was based on his view that the West revived. For contrast, the uncreativity of the East had to be emphasized. Nor did he have any taste for Byzantine art; even St. Mark's Square in Venice he found decorated "with the worst architecture I ever yet saw" (Norton, *Letters*, 1:193).

21. *D. and F.*, 2, chap. 50, p. 634. Gibbon's account of Islam is as much eighteenth-century Europe as it is Islam. For example, Islam did have a clergy and it was torn by divisions that Gibbon simply ignored. See G. E. von Grunebaum, "Islam: The Problem of Changing

Perspective," in *The Transformation of the Roman World: Gibbon's Problem after Two Centuries*, ed. Lynn White, Contributions of the UCLA Center for Medieval and Renaissance Studies (Berkeley, 1966), pp. 147-78; and Bernard Lewis, "Gibbon on Mohammed," *Daedalus*, Summer 1976, pp. 89-101.

22. Prothero, *Private Letters*, 2:234-37. The date is 1791.

23. *Memoirs*, p. 159.

24. Prothero, *Private Letters*, 1:213; 2:280; *Memoirs*, p. 156.

25. James Boswell, *The Life of Samuel Johnson* (Oxford, 1971), 2:65, 236.

26. Gibbon, *An Essay on the Study of Literature*, translation (London, 1764), 48:98-99.

27. *Memoirs*, p. 195.

28. Critics as different as Lytton Strachey in *Portraits in Miniature* (New York, 1931) and Christopher Dawson in a British Academy Lecture (1934) agree on this point. Dawson's lecture was reprinted in John J. Mulloy, ed., *The Dynamics of World History* (New York, 1956), pp. 319-45. It is the best short essay on Gibbon.

9. Ranke

1. For this article I have used the collected works (54 vols.) of Ranke and the more recently published collections of his letters, notebooks, and early writings. I acknowledge a particular debt to the essay "Der junge Ranke" in *Leopold von Ranke: Aus Werk und Nachlass*, ed. Walther Peter Fuchs (Munich, 1973), 3:13-45 (the essay deserves translation). Ranke's teaching, his courses and his seminar are treated in Gunter Berg, *Leopold von Ranke als akademischer Lehrer* (Göttingen, 1968). Theodore von Laue's study, *Leopold von Ranke: The Formative Years* (Princeton, 1950), remains valuable. Leonard Krieger in *Ranke: The Meaning of History* (Chicago, 1977), a remarkable and painstaking analysis of the historian's themes and outlook, a rare book indeed, shares too many of his pains with the reader. There is useful material, including an introductory essay in Georg G. Iggers and Konrad von Moltke, eds., *The Theory and Practice of History: Leopold von Ranke* (Indianapolis, 1973). Georg G. Iggers has also written an important work, *The German Conception of History* (Middletown, 1968), in which see especially pp. 63-89. Peter Gay, *Style in History* (New York, 1974), has a sympathetic treatment of Ranke. There is a provocative chapter, "Ranke: Historical Realism as Comedy," in *Metahistory* (Baltimore, 1973), by Hayden White. The pamphlet *Ranke* by H. Liebeschutz, Historical Association

Publications, G 26 (London, 1954), is admirably brief. A University of Chicago Ph.D. thesis, "Ranke: The Development of the Historian's Craft" (1975), by Constance Nichols Gengenbach, is mainly devoted to Ranke's *German History in the Age of the Reformation*. I am also indebted to the works of Carl Hinrichs, Ludwig Dehio, Herbert Butterfield, Friedrich Meinecke, and Friedrich Engel-Janosi.

2. Ranke's writing on Luther (1817), a fragment, is in *Leopold von Ranke: Aus Werk und Nachlass*, vol. 3, "Frühe Schriften," ed. Walther Peter Fuchs and Theodor Schieder (Munich, 1973), pp. 329-467.

3. Ranke, *Sämmtliche Werke* (Leipzig, 1890), 53-54:47.

4. Ranke, *Neue Briefe*, ed. Bernhard Hoeft and Hans Herzfeld (Hamburg, 1949), p. 37.

5. *Aus Werk und Nachlass*, 3:484-97; see also pp. 609-27; and Berg, *Ranke als akademischer Lehrer*, pp. 17-19.

6. *Sämmtliche Werke*, 53-54:96.

7. Ibid., pp. 121-24.

8. Ranke in letters quoted in Krieger, *Ranke*, pp. 10-11.

9. *History [sic] of the Latin and Teutonic Nations*, trans. G. R. Dennis (London, 1909), pp. 75, 227-28.

10. *History of the Popes*, trans. Mrs. Foster and revised by G. R. Dennis (London, 1908), 1:139.

11. The official was Karl von Kamptz. His opinion may be found in Ernst Schulin, "Rankes erstes Buch," *Historische Zeitschrift* 253 (1966):586.

12. Berg, *Ranke als akademischer Lehrer*, pp. 12, 55; and for everything past as an introduction to a subject, p. 114.

13. Von Laue, *Ranke*, chaps. 3-6, pp. 55-138, esp. pp. 80-81, 100. Ranke provoked Lord Acton, the English Liberal and Catholic historian, to lifelong internal debate over moral judgment. He wrote appreciatively of Ranke's good-naturedness, his fairness, and his restraint from hasty or popular moral judgments. Nevertheless, the Ranke who would not say directly that the Inquisition was wrong troubled Acton, who thought that judging a past age in its own terms debased moral currency. Ranke rejoiced in the manuscript materials for history, but Acton thought that historians' use of private letters, after about the 1860s, would put great men to a deeper probe of character that none could survive with undamaged reputation (Herbert Butterfield, *Man on His Past* [Cambridge, 1955], pp. 83-85, 92-95).

14. Letter to Heinrich Ranke, 21 November 1831, in *Sämmtliche Werke*, 53-54:258. The next four paragraphs are based on von Laue and two of Ranke's articles of this period which he printed in English.

15. Von Laue, *Ranke*, pp. 83, 86, 99, 100, 115. This is a constant

theme in Ranke's writings. In *The Histories of the Latin and Teutonic Nations* (London, 1909), he wrote that those nations were fortunate in not having been united. This is the source of their life; it also helps to explain the artistic achievements of Florence and the Italian Renaissance: "It grew mainly from the antagonism of parties . . . from the vigilance of human forces engaged in conflict" (pp. 75, 321). People must be true to themselves, and the motive for imitation is weakness. In the European system there is a dialectic, a tension which inhibits universal dominance that might end conflict: no such dominance "can be thought of that would not necessarily be one-sided and limiting compared to the ideal and its highest demands." *German History in the Age of the Reformation*, cited by Gengenbach, "Ranke: The Development of the Historian's Craft," p. 100. Finally, "age follows age so that what is not possible in any single age happens in the whole course of ages and the entire fullness of the human race's spiritual life, inspired by God, can be revealed in the succession of the centuries" (*Deutsche Geschichte im Zeitalter der Reformation*, Rankes Meisterwerke, [Munich, 1914], 4:3).

16. *The History of the Popes During the Last Four Centuries* 1:26-27, 101, 448. The Protestant League of Schmalkald brought together provinces often separated. The impetus for it came from below and by an inner necessity. So it was that the League made for the unity of development of the German spirit (Rankes Meisterwerke) *Deutsche Geschichte im Zeitalter der Reformation*, 4:106-7.

17. *History of the Popes*, 2:512.

18. Ibid., p. 570.

19. Ibid., 1:xii-xiii.

20. After describing Luther's troubled search for divine assurance, Ranke added: "But the eternal laws of the universe seem to require that so deep and earnest a longing of the soul after God should at length be appeased with the fullness of conviction" (*Germany in the Age of the Reformation*, trans. Sarah Austin, 2 vols. [New York, 1966], 1:145). This reprint of the 1905 translation contains the first six books of Ranke's reformation history.

21. *History of England* (Oxford, 1875), 1:vi.

22. *Neue Briefe*, p. 327. Krieger commented: "Now it would seem clear, *a priori*, that a historian who discovers more suitable materials for a Prussian than for a French history in French national archives must be working from a definite perspective" (Ranke: *The Meaning of History*, p. 192).

23. Quoted in G. P. Gooch, *Studies in German History* (London, 1948), pp. 251-52; pp. 210-66 provide an admiring account of all of Ranke's writings on German history.

24. *Neue Briefe*, p. 548.

25. *Weltgeschichte*, vol. 1, pt. i, p. viii; vol. 2, p. 217.

26. Lord Acton, "German Schools of Historiography," in *Historical Essays and Studies* (London, 1907), p. 353.

27. These are from Acton's manuscript notes, quoted in Butterfield, *Man on His past*, pp. 92-93.

28. *Aus Werk und Nachlass*, vol. 1, "Tagebücher," ed. Walther Fuchs (Munich, 1964), p. 256.

10. Burckhardt

1. *The Letters of Jacob Burckhardt*, ed. and trans. Alexander Dru (London, 1955), p. 36.

2. Ibid., p. 48; Lionel Trilling, *Matthew Arnold* (New York, 1955).

3. Burckhardt, *Force and Freedom*, ed. and trans. James Hastings Nichols (New York, 1955), p. 78. This is a translation of *Weltgeschichtliche Betrachtungen*.

4. Werner Kaegi, *Jacob Burckhardt: Eine Biographie* (Basel, 1947-1977), vol. 1, chaps. 7-8.

5. Ibid., 2:377-458.

6. *Political and Social Upheaval, 1832-1852* (New York, 1969), p. 136.

7. *Letters*, p. 93; Kaegi, *Burckhardt*, 2:564-82; Karl J. Weintraub, *Visions of Culture* (Chicago, 1966), pp. 117-18.

8. *Letters*, p. 97.

9. Max Burckhardt, ed., *Jacob Burckhardt: Briefe* (Basel, 1955), 3:103.

10. *Force and Freedom*, p. 76; Weintraub, *Visions*, pp. 118-19.

11. Weintraub, *Visions*, chap. 3, pp. 115-60, including a valuable two-page appendix, presents a good account of Burckhardt's conception of cultural history.

12. M. Burckhardt, *Briefe*, 3:92-97.

13. Kaegi, *Jacob Burckhardt*, 3:320-321.

14. *The Age of Constantine the Great*, trans. Moses Hadas (New York, 1956), pp. 5, 12, 17, 18, 19, 48.

15. Ibid., pp. 205, 249-50, 261ff., 281-95, 321.

16. Ibid., pp. 224, 216, 229, 230.

17. Ibid., pp. 232, 111.

18. Ibid., pp. 202, 203, 313, 312. Burckhardt, entirely at odds with Gibbon (who emphasized self-interest as a motive and often appealed to deluded or even gulled self-interest), contrasted the imperial egoist and his calculations to increase his power, "an essentially frivolous

authority," with "the great and selfless devotion of many who gave away all their possessions" to serve God. This was a merger of charity and asceticism that Burckhardt admired because he looked to the transcendence of self.

19. Ibid., p. 359.

20. Ibid., p. 363.

21. Irene Gordon, ed. *The Civilization of the Renaissance in Italy* (New York, 1960), p. xiv.

22. Ibid., p. 148. In reserving the arts and architecture, Burckhardt fell short of his idea of cultural history, but he wrote a large part of the second volume. The manuscript was not published because too many sentences ended with question marks, an experience of the "sorrows that do not make men young." Burckhardt's comment is cited by Irene Gordon in a footnote on pp. 40-41.

23. Ibid., pp. 40-41, 102-3. In these Italian states, Burckhardt wrote, "for the first time we detect the modern political spirit of Europe, surrendered freely to its own instincts, often displaying the worst features of an unbridled egotism, outraging every right and killing every germ of a healthier culture." The principal feature was the adaptation of means to ends when the latter were not restricted. On modernity in Burckhardt see E. M. Janssen, *Jacob Burckhardt und die Renaissance: Jacob Burckhardt Studien*, pt. 1 (Assen, 1970), pp. 79-83.

24. *Civilization of the Renaissance*, pp. 162, 188-89.

25. Ibid., p. 257.

26. Ibid., pp. 304, 315, 319-22.

27. Kaegi, *Burckhardt*, vols. 5 and 6. Ernst Ziegler, *Jacob Burckhardts Vorlesung über die Geschichte des Revolutionszeitalter* (Basel, 1974).

28. Nichols, "Introduction," *Force and Freedom*, pp. 48-49.

29. "Crisis, History and the Image of Man," in *Review of Politics* 2 (1940):418.

30. *Force and Freedom*, pp. 91, 73.

31. Ibid., pp. 80, 92.

32. Ibid., p. 105. Useful accounts of Burckhardt's Renaissance work are in W. K. Ferguson, *The Renaissance in Historical Thought* (Boston, 1948), chap. 10; Denys Hay, "Burckhardt's Renaissance: 1860-1960," *History Today* 10 (1960):14-23; Hans Baron, "Burckhardt's *Civilization of the Renaissance*, a Century after Its Publication," *Renaissance Studies* 13 (1960):207-22. At the copyediting stage I read Hugh Trevor-Roper, "The Historical Spirit" in *The Times Literary Supplement*, Oct. 8, 1982. This valuable essay is a review of

an edition of the several sets of notes Burckhardt drafted for the work posthumously published as *Weltgeschichtliche Betrachtungen.*

11. Acton

1. Gertrude Himmelfarb, *Lord Acton: A Study in Conscience and Politics* (New York, 1952); David Mathew, *Acton: The Formative Years* (London, 1946) and *Lord Acton and His Times* (London, 1968). The latter, particularly good for aristocratic connections, and atmosphere, is readable and helpful but leaves much unriddled and some phases unilluminated. Recent and useful is Robert L. Schuettinger, *Lord Acton: Historian of Liberty* (Lasalle, 1976).

2. G. E. Buckle, ed., *Letters of Queen Victoria*, 3d ser. (London, 1926), 2:188.

3. Wilfrid Ward, *Life and Times of Cardinal Wiseman* (London, 1897), 1:349.

4. Lord Acton, *Lectures on Modern History*, ed. John Neville Figgis and Reginald Vere Laurence (London, 1956), p. 12. For Döllinger's influence on Acton, see Stephen J. Tonsor, "Lord Acton on Döllinger's Historical Theology," *Journal of the History of Ideas* 20 (1959):329-52, and "Ignaz von Doellinger: Lord Acton's Mentor," *Anglican Theological Review* 41 (1959):211-15.

5. *History of Freedom and Other Essays*, ed. John Neville Figgis and Reginald Vere Laurence (London, 1907), p. 194.

6. *Selections from the Correspondence of the First Lord Acton*, ed. John Neville Figgis and Reginald Vere Laurence (London, 1917), p. 214.

7. *History of Freedom*, pp. 459-60.

8. Josef L. Altholz, *The Liberal Catholic Movement in England: The Rambler and Its Contributors, 1848-1864* (London, 1962), and *The Correspondence of Lord Acton and Richard Simpson*, ed. Josef L. Altholz and Damian McElrath, 3 vols. (Cambridge, 1971-1975).

9. *History of Freedom*, pp. 482-84, 489, 491.

10. Guy Ryan, "The Acton Circle 1864-1871: The *Chronicle* and the *North British Review*" (Ph.D. thesis, University of Notre Dame, 1969).

11. Acton, "Notes on Archival Researches, 1864-1868," ed. James Clarence Holland, in Damian McElrath, *Lord Acton: The Decisive Decade, 1864-1874: Essays and Documents, Bibliothèque de la Revue d'Histoire Ecclésiastique*, fasc. 51 (1970), pp. 139-40.

12. *History of Freedom*, p. 148.

13. During the main part of the council, Acton wrote long letters

almost daily to provide Döllinger with information for the German's journalistic polemic against the supporters of infallibility. The Englishman even hoped that Prime Minister Gladstone would intervene in the council. The British representative in Rome, Odo Russell, and the foreign secretary, Lord Clarendon, disapproved of any intervention as counterproductive. Russell also criticized the council opposition who thought that the promulgation was inopportune because "I cannot help thinking that a clearly defined position between the papacy and the Civilized world will prove more beneficial to Humanity in the end than the half-measures of the opportunists who wish to preserve the benefit of the Doubt." Russell's words are quoted in pt. 3 of McElrath, *The Decisive Decade*, p. 158, from Noel Blakiston, *The Roman Question: Extracts from the Despatches of Odo Russell from Rome, 1858-1870* (London, 1962), p. 397. See Victor Conzemius, "Lord Acton and the First Vatican Council," *Journal of Ecclesiastical History*, 20 (1969):267-95.

14. *History of Freedom*, pp. 1-60. The choice of subject was in itself political. It permitted a Whiggish emphasis and a use of Liberal words and concepts that evoked the spirit of Gladstone, not Disraeli. See chapter 10, "Acton's History of Liberty," pp. 153-72, of George Watson, *Politics and Literature in Modern Britain* (Totowa, N.J. 1977), esp. p. 157.

15. *History of Freedom*, pp. 32, 33.

16. Ibid., pp. 13, 28.

17. Ibid., pp. 36-37, 41.

18. Ibid., pp. 55, 57.

19. "That any man should spend years in acquiring many thousands of documents at his own expense, for nobody's use but his own, and with no better purpose than to form a defined and certain judgment on the problems of controverted history that bear on the living world, was a form of mental infirmity not dreamed of in his pedestrian philosophy" (McElrath, *The Decisive Decade*, p. 135). The second point is from a letter not completely reproduced in Herbert Paul's edition of *Lord Acton's Letters to Mary Gladstone*, 2d ed. (London, 1913), and presented in Owen Chadwick's admirable "Creighton Lecture in History, 1975," *Acton and Gladstone* (London, 1976), p. 23.

20. *Döllingers Briefwechsel mit Lord Acton*, ed. Victor Conzemius, 3 vols. (Munich, 1963-1971), 3:262, 285.

21. Acton's notes quoted by Lionel Kochan in *Acton on History* (London, 1954), pp. 78-79, 164.

22. Ibid., p. 157, n. 65.

23. Ibid., pp. 108-9; *History of Freedom*, pp. 213, 225.

24. Cambridge University Library, Add. Mss. 5011, fol. 21.

25. *History of Freedom*, pp. 238-39, 243.

26. Kochan, *Acton on History*, p. 67; Cambridge University Library, Add. Mss. 5011, fols. 314, 108, 238.

27. Conzemius, *Briefwechsel*, 3:284.

28. *English Historical Review* 2 (1887); Louise Creighton, *The Life and Letters of Mandell Creighton* (London, 1913), 1:376. The description of Ranke is from a manuscript printed in Herbert Butterfield, *Man on His Past* (Cambridge, 1955), p. 222.

29. Cambridge University Library, Add. Mss. 5011, fols. 22, 25, 56.

30. *Selections from the Correspondence*, p. 54.

31. *Lectures on Modern history*, p. 28.

32. Ibid., pp. 10-11.

33. Ibid., p. 28.

34. Ibid., pp. 51, 232.

35. Lectures on the French Revolution (London, 1910), p. 92.

36. "Letter to Contributors to the Cambridge Modern History," in William H. McNeill, *Lord Acton: Essays in the Liberal Interpretation of History* (Chicago, 1967), p. 399.

37. Acton in his report (1896) on the *Cambridge Modern History* to the Cambridge University Press wrote of an imminent "ultimate" history, "now that all information is within reach and every problem has become capable of solution." The quotation was omitted when the letter was originally printed. David Thomson, *The Aims of History* (London, 1969), p. 39.

38. Creighton, *Life and Letters*, 1:376.

Index

Acton, Lord, 155, 167, 168-169, 187, 218 n. 13, 222-223 n. 13, ch. 11, *passim.*
"The Acts of the Apostles," 73
Addresses to the German Nation (Fichte), 150
Aeschylus, 21
Aethelbert, King of Kent, 78
The Age of Constantine the Great (Burckhardt), 176-180
The Age of Louis XIV (Voltaire), 114-116, 127
Agricola, 51, 54-55
Agricola (Tacitus), 54-55
Agrippina, 64, 65
Aidan, 82, 83
Alcibiades, 39, 42, 43, 44, 46
Aldenham, 194
Alexander Severus, 177
Alfred, King, 74
American Revolution, 196, 202
Annals, 75, 76
Annals (Camden), 89
Annals (Tacitus), 56, 60-65
Aquinas, St. Thomas, 168, 195
Arco-Valley, Countess Maria, 189
Aristagoras, 19, 20
Aristocracy, 28, 30, 51, 66, 67, 68, 134, 135
Aristotle, 47
Army (Roman), 177-178
Arnold, Matthew, 172
Asceticism, 179
Athens, 7, 28, 29, 33, 179
Auden, W. H., 49
Augustine of Canterbury, 77, 78, 79

Augustine, St., Bishop of Hippo, 72, 73, 74
Augustus, 57, 60, 61

Basle, 171, 172, 173
Basle, University of, 172, 173, 184
Basler Zeitung, 173
Bastille, 109
Bede, ch. 5 *passim*
Benedict Biscop, 74
Berlin, University of, 155, 156, 157, 165, 175, 184
Besterman, Theodore, 107
Bismarck, Otto von, 165
Board of Trade, 132
Bossuet, 118, 120, 121, 122
Britannia (Camden), 90, 92-95
Brut, 93
Buddha, 49
Burckhardt, 165, 221 n. 22 and n. 23, ch. 10, *passim*
Burghley, Lord (William Cecil), 93, 95, 96, 97, 98, 99, 100, 104

Caedmon, 85
Caligula, 63, 64
Cambridge Modern History, 167, 203
Cambridge University, 20
Cambyses, 12, 13
Camden, William, ch. 6 *passim*
Campion, Edmund, 103
Candide (Voltaire), 117, 126
Canterbury, 78

225

Castiglione, 183
Catherine the Great, 112-113, 114, 117, 213 n. 15
Catholic Church, 72, 73, 98-99, 102, 103, 117, 129, 137, 142, 191, 205
Cecil, Robert, 95, 104
Cecil, Wm., *see* Burghley
Chadd, 84-85
Charles XII, 110
Chatelet, Mme du, 117
Cheops, 15
China, 118, 119, 120-121
Christ, 49, 73, 179
Christianity, 72, 73, 78-79, 136, 138, 147, 182, 195
Christ's Hospital, 90
Chronicles, 88
Cicero, 6
The City of God (Augustine), 73-74
The Civilization of the Renaissance in Italy (Burckhardt), 180-184
Clarenceux-King of Arms, 91
Claudius, 64
Cleon, 36, 37, 38
Colet, Dean, 90
College of Heralds, 104
Colman, 83, 85
Commodus, 135
Condorcet, 124-125, 127
Confederacy of Delos, 28
Constantine, Emperor, 73, 135, 176, 177, 178, 179, 180
Corcyra, 32, 37, 38
Cornwall, 94, 132
Cotton, Sir Robert, 91
Creighton, Bishop Mandell, 199, 204
Croesus, 11, 12
Cromwell, Oliver, 3
Crusades, 141
Curchod, Suzanne, 130
Cyrus, 12

D'Alembert, 126
Daniel, P., 114
Darius, 18, 19, 20, 21

Decelaea, 44
The Decline and Fall of the Roman Empire (Gibbon), 128, 132-133, 134-144, 145-147
Delian Confederacy, 7
Delphi, 12
Democracy, 20, 26, 28, 29, 30, 34-35, 37, 174, 200
Der Cicerone (Burckhardt), 180
Despotism, 136, 178, 181, 182, 196
Deyverdun, Georges, 130, 133
Dialogue on Oratory (Tacitus), 52-53
Diocletian, 135, 177, 178
Dionysius of Halicarnassus, 9
Discourse on Universal History (Bossuet), 118, 120
Disraeli, Benjamin, 195
Döllinger, Ignaz von, 188, 190, 191, 194, 197
Dupanloup, Bishop Felix, 189, 197

Easter, 75, 82, 83
Eastern Roman Empire, 139-140
Ecclesiastical History (Eusebius), 73
The Ecclesiastical History of the English People (Bede), ch. 5 *passim*
Edwin, King, 80, 81
Egypt, 10, 12-17
Elizabeth I, Queen, 89, 91, 95, 96, 99, 100, 101, 102, 103
Enlightenment, 106-107
Essai sur les moeurs, (Voltaire), 117-125, 127
Essay on the Study of Literature (Gibbon), 131
Essex, Earl of, 96, 100
Eusebius, 73, 178

Fichte, Johann Gottlieb, 150
Flaubert, 127
Fontenelle, 116
France, 100, 101
Frederick II, 182

Freedom, 141, 194, 195, 196, 199, 201
French History, Especially in the Sixteenth and Seventeenth Centuries (Ranke), 163
French Revolution, 133, 150, 190, 191, 201, 202-203: (1830), 158; (1848), 174

Galba, 58
Gandhi, 49
German History in the Age of the Reformation (Ranke), 162-163
Gibbon, Edward, 71, 176, 179, 180, 215 n. 10 and n. 14, 216 n. 20, 216-217 n. 21, and ch. 8 *passim*
Gildas, 94
Gladstone, William E., 189, 194, 195, 200, 201
Glorious Revolution (1688), 164
Gnostics, 137
Goldsmith, Oliver, 144
Graeco-Persian Wars, 6
Granville, Earl, 189
Gregory I, Pope, 76, 77-78, 79-80
Guiccardini, Francesco, 119-155

Halicarnassus, 7
Hayward, John, 96
Hecataeus, 9
Hegel, G. W. F., 181, 198
Heine, Heinrich, 153
Henry IV, 101, 160
Heralds, college of, 91
Herodotus, 4, 87, ch. 2 *passim*
Hippocratic medicine, 46, 208 n. 5
Higher criticism of Bible, 172
Hilda, 83, 85
Historicism, 153, 154, 157, 158, 159, 169
The Historie of Philip de Commines, 96
Histories (Tacitus) 56, 57-60, 70
The Histories of the Latin and Teutonic Nations (Ranke), 152-156

Historisch-Politische Zeitschrift, 158
History, accuracy, 169-170; annals, 96, 97; antiquarianism, 92; art, 48, 49, 133, 155; certainty, 2, 203, 204, 205, 206; change, 51; character, 62, 63; Christianity, 72, 73, 74, 118; civilization, 125, 136, 138, 166; continuity, 25, 159, 186, 187, 210; critical, 153, 154, 155, 157, 169; culture, 175, 176; despotism, 69, 125; detachment, 143, 185, 186, 187; drama, 110; economic interpretation, 31; empire, 50, 56; *en philosophe*, 114, 122-123, 144; enquiry, 8, 24; entertainment, 25, 29; exemplary, 96, 107, 111, 114, 118, 125, 127; geography, 14, 89; God, 151, 152, 154, 157, 159, 162, 163, 168; of history, 1, 2, 4, 6; hope, 125; humanity, 48, 126, 175, 178, 184-187; human nature, 124; human spirit, 115-116; impartiality, 61, 66, 161, 175, 202, 203; incompleteness of our knowledge of, 2, 4, 5; irony, 143; knowledge, 148; lessons of, 4; liberty, 188; lies, 193; meaning, 107; meaningless, 115, 118; memory, 3, 8, 25, 92, 93, 96; method, 97-98, 148, 157; morality, 2, 50, 51, 55, 57, 68, 69, 70, 71, 87, 96, 105, 111, 140, 143, 144, 146, 154, 166, 188-189, 193, 197, 199, 200, 204, 205, 206; myth, 8, 9; narrative, 86-87, 116; objectivity, 168; Oxford professorship of, 104; painting, 114, 116; the past, 3; patriotism, 89, 92, 93; philosophy of, 25-26, 30-32, 35-36, 37, 40, 46, 47, 68, 118, 138, 145, 146, 147, 148-149, 167, 185; pity, 57; positivism, 168; power, 25, 31, 32, 33, 35, 49, 63, 68, 158, 159, 186, 187,

199; professional, 167; progress, 138, 145, 146, 188, 197, 198, 199, 201, 205; Providence, 73, 77, 87, 106, 107, 118, 122, 127, 136, 188, 198, 205; prudence, 2, 96, 154; psychology, 31, 145; rational order, 66; recreation of the past, 3, 4; reckoning of time, 75-76; relativism, 2; religion, 86, 190; research, 2, 144; revisionism, 9; scepticism, 172; science, 29, 47, 48, 197, 203, 204; secondary causes, 136; social, 116; solipsism, 2; sources, 4, 31, 66-67, 76, 87, 97, 126, 152, 155, 156, 157, 162, 164, 193, 197, 204; speeches, 31, 39, 40, 48, 49, 67; spirit, 176, 186; style, 126, 143, 145; superiority of the present, 185; taste, 144; theology of, 72, 73, 74; tolerance, 3; tragedy, 96; truth, 2, 3, 6, 87, 115, 126, 169-170; uniformity, 122-123, 125; vision, 65, 66, 67, 68, 69, 145, 149, 153, 154; war, 30-31, 32, 36, 159; world, 118, 119, 120, 121, 126, 152, 160, 166; worship, 151, 152, 154, 157, 158, 169
History of Charles XII (Voltaire), 111-113, 127
History of England, Principally in the Seventeenth Century (Ranke), 163-164
History of Freedom (Acton), 195-197
History of the Popes (Ranke), 160-162, 175
History of Russia under Peter the Great (Voltaire), 113
Hobbes, Thomas, 32, 36, 208-209 n. 7
Home and Foreign Review, 192
Honorius, Pope, 80, 81
Hooker, Thomas, 91
Howard, Philip, Earl of Arundel, 103
Hume, David, 131

Hybris, 11, 22, 23, 24, 25, 28, 44, 139

Idealist Philosophy, 150
Immortality, 179
Individualism, 183, 184, 187
Iona, 83
Ionians, 7, 19, 20
Ireland, 105
Islam, 140-141

James I (of England), 95, 96, 103, 104
Jarrow, 74, 83
Jerome, St., 87
Jerusalem, 180
Jesuits, 103, 107, 108, 117
Johnson, Dr. Samuel, 144
Josephus, 24
Julian Calendar, 75

Kaegi, Werner, 184
Kant, Immanuel, 107
Knowles, Dom David, 87
Kugler, Franz, 175-176

Lacedaemonians, see Spartans
Langer, William L. (quoted), 174
Lausanne, 129, 131, 133
Lectures on the French Revolution (Acton), 202
Lectures on Modern History (Acton) 202
Leibniz, 190
Leicester, Earl of (Robert Dudley), 99, 100
Leipzig, University of, 149, 150, 151
Les Lettres Philosophiques (Voltaire), 109, 110
Liberal Catholics, 192
Liberalism, 159, 174, 194, 200
Liberals, 172, 205, 206
Liberty, 203
Lindisfarne, 83

Livy, 50
Logographoi, 9
Louis XIV, 108, 114-115
Luther, Martin, 119, 150, 162
Lutheranism, 149, 150

Machiavelli, 119, 196, 198
Marathon, 21
Marx, Karl, 168
Mary, Queen of Scots, 101, 102, 104
Masses, 174
Melos, and the Melian Dialogue, 39-41
"Memoirs" (Gibbon), 144
Michelet, Jules, 183
Miltiades, 21, 30
Modernity, 177, 182, 221 n. 23
Mohammed, 140-141
Mountjoy, Lord, 105
Mytilene, 36

Napoleon, 161
Nationalism, 160, 174, 200
Nero, 57, 64, 65
Newman, John Cardinal, 197
Nicias, 38, 41, 43, 44, 45, 49
Niebuhr, Barthold Georg, 151
Nietzsche, Friedrich, 185
Nile River, 14
Nine Books on Prussian History (Ranke), 164-165
Norfolk, Duke of, 102
Northumbria, 74, 79, 80, 82

Oligarchy, 25, 28, 30, 37, 49
On the Origins, Geography, Institutions and Tribes of the Germans (Tacitus), 55-56
On the Scholar's Mission (Fichte), 150
Oratory (Roman), 52-53
Orosius, 74
Ortelius, Abraham, 93
Oswald, 82
Otho, 58, 59
Oxford University, 89, 90, 129

Papal infallibility, 193, 194
Parliament, 132
Pascal, 125
Paulinus, 80, 81
Peace of Nicias (421 B.C.), 38
Pericles, 10, 28, 29, 30, 32, 33, 34, 35, 47
Persian empire, 7, 10, 12
Peter the Great, 112, 113
Phalanx, 8
Philosophes, 107
Philosophical Dictionary (Voltaire), 71
Pius IX, 192, 193
Plague, 33, 34, 35, 36, 84, 90
Plataea, 33-34
Pliny the Younger, 52
Plutarch, 24
Poland, 113, 114
Politiques, 101
Polycrates, 16-18
Poppaea, 65
Principate, 53, 57, 60-61, 70
Protestantism, 130
Providence, 26

Raison d'eglise, 193, 199
Raison d'etat, 39, 193, 202
The Rambler, 192
Ranke, Leopold von, 104, 148, 175, 198, 199-200, 218 n. 13, and ch. 9 *passim*
Raphael, 183
Reflections on the French Revolution (Burke), 142
Reflections on World History (Burckhardt), 185-187
Reformation, 119, 162, 163, 165, 183, 190, 191
Renaissance, 89, 141, 142, 181, 184
Renaissance, Christian, 89
Renaissance, English, 89
Renan, Ernest, 198
Rights of man, 196
Rome, ch. 4 *passim*, 73, 74, and ch. 8 *passim*
Rosebery, Lord, 201
Runciman, Steven, 139
Russia, 138

St. Paul's Cathedral, 90
Salamis, 23
Sallust, 51
Salomon, Albert, 185
Samos, 7, 16-18
Science, history of, 1
Scotland, 96, 103, 104
Scott, Sir Walter, 151
Scythians, 18-19
Seapower, 28
Sejanus, 63
Seminar, historical, 157
Senate (Rome), 61, 62, 64, 70,
    134-135, 177
Septimus Severus, 177, 182
The Serbian Revolution (Ranke),
    156
Seven Books Against the Pagans
    (Orosus), 74
Severin, St., 174
Sheffield, Lord, 129, 133, 142, 143
Sicily, 41-46
Society of Antiquaries, 91
Solon, 11
Sonderbund, 173
Spain, 100, 101
Sparta, 29, 32
Spartans, 17, 22, 23, 34, 37, 40
Spengler, Oswald, 167
Spenser, Edmund, 95
State, absolute, 190, 191, 196, 199
State, modern, 104-105, 168, 181
Stoics, 195
Suetonius, 65
Swinburne, Algernon Charles, 179
Syme, Sir Ronald, 59
Syracuse, 39, 41, 42, 43, 46

Tacitus, 72, 96, 136, 210 n. 1, ch.
    4 passim
Thebes, 33-34
Themistocles, 23
Theodore of Tarsus and Canter-
    bury, 84, 85
Thrace, 29

Thucydides, 4, 6, 8, 10, 20, 25,
    151, ch. 3 passim
Thurii, 7
Tiberius, 61-63, 69
Time, 66, 72
Toleration, 109, 110
Toynbee, Arnold, 167, 169
Treitschke, Heinrich von, 165
Turks, Ottoman, 119-120
Twelve Books on Prussian History
    (Ranke), 164-165

Ultramontanes, 192, 196
Universities, 200

Vatican Council I, 161, 193, 222-
    223 n. 13
Venetian Relations, 156
Vespasian, 56-57, 59, 60, 68, 69
Victoria, Queen, 189
Voegelin, Eric, 32
Voltaire, 71, 201, ch. 7 passim

Wearmouth, 74
Weltgeschichte (Ranke), 166
Westminster School, 90
Whigs, 196, 202
Whitby, Synod of, 83, 84
White, Hayden, 128
Wight, Isle of, 86
Wilamowitz [-Möllendorf], U. von,
    185
Wilfrid, 83
William I, Emperor, 165
William of Tyre, 77
Wiseman, Cardinal Nicholas, 189,
    192

Xerxes, 21, 22, 23

Zurich, 181